School Leadership and Complexity Theory

Interest in complexity theory, a relative of chaos theory, has become well established in the business and scientific communities in recent years. Complexity theory argues that systems are dynamically evolving interactions of many parts which cannot be predicted easily. In this book, Keith Morrison introduces complexity theory to the world of education, drawing out its implications for school leadership.

This book suggests that schools are complex, nonlinear and unpredictable systems, and that this impacts significantly on leadership, relationships and communication within them. As schools race to keep up with change and innovation, this book suggests that it is possible to find order without control and to lead without coercion. Key areas are:

- Schools and self-organization.
- Leadership for self-organization.
- Supporting emergence through the learning organization.
- Schools and their environments.
- Communication.
- Fitness landscapes.

This book will be of interest to headteachers and middle managers, and those on higher level courses in educational leadership and management.

Keith Morrison worked in primary and secondary schools for many years before moving into teacher education, where he works in the fields of management, curriculum, sociology, research methods, policy, and evaluation. He is the author of eight books, including *A Guide to Teaching Practice* (fourth edition) with L. Cohen and L. Manion, *Research Methods in Education* (fifth edition) with L. Cohen and L. Manion, both published by Routledge, and *Management Theories for Educational Change*. He was Senior Lecturer in Education at the University of Durham, UK before taking up his present post as Professor of Education at the Inter-University Institute of Macau, China.

School Leadership and Complexity Theory

Keith Morrison

London and New York

First published 2002
by RoutledgeFalmer
11 New Fetter Lane, London EC4P 4EE

Simultaneously published in the USA and Canada
by RoutledgeFalmer
29 West 35th Street, New York, NY 10001

RoutledgeFalmer is an imprint of the Taylor & Francis Group

© 2002 Keith Morrison

Typeset in Times by GreenGate Publishing Services, Tonbridge, Kent

Printed and bound in Great Britain by Biddles Ltd, Guildford and
King's Lynn

British Library Cataloguing in Publication Data
A catalogue record for this book is available from the British Library

Library of Congress Cataloging in Publication Data
A catalog record for this book has been requested

ISBN 0-415-27783-3 (hbk)
ISBN 0-415-27784-1 (pbk)

July 17, 2002

For Phukuntsi Abbey Kgaile, a shining, complex leader

Contents

List of tables   viii
List of figures   ix
Acknowledgements   xi
Introduction   1

PART I
The theory of complexity   3

1   Complexity theory   5

PART II
The practice of complexity in schools   33

2   Schools and self-organization for complexity   35

3   Leadership for self-organization and emergence   56

4   Supporting emergence through the learning organization   91

5   Schools and their environments   114

6   Communication   138

7   Fitness landscapes   164

8   Retrospect and prospect   188

Notes   192
Bibliography   195
Index   213

Tables

1.1	Conventional wisdom and complexity theory	9
1.2	Modernistic and complex organizations	16
2.1	Formal, informal, temporary and permanent groups	43
2.2	Leaders' tasks in stages of team development	45
2.3	Leaders' problem solving in team development	46
2.4	Teamwork problems and leaders' solutions	52
3.1	Leadership style and organizational climate	79
3.2	Leadership style and emotional intelligence	81
3.3	Typologies and components of organizational climate	84
3.4	Organizational climates for complexity theory	86
4.1	Leaders' competencies in Senge's five disciplines	100
4.2	Ten major features of successful organizational learning	105
4.3	Self-assessment scale for types of learning in a school as a learning organization	106
4.4	Stages of organizational learning	110
4.5	Levels of contents of organizational learning	111
5.1	Macro-environmental contexts of education	119
5.2	Opportunities for information exchange	125
5.3	Components of a needs analysis	128
6.1	Characteristics of the ideal speech situation	140
6.2	Fitness for purpose in communication	146
7.1	Stages in the construction of a fitness landscape	177

Figures

1.1	Components of complexity theory	8
1.2	The rise of emergence in complexity theory	10
1.3	A sequence of emergence	23
1.4	A self-assessment questionnaire to judge the school's fitness for complexity	32
2.1	Moving from a pyramidal to a web structure	39
2.2	Incentives and rewards for motivating people	48
2.3	Rewards at different stages of team development	49
4.1	The virtuous cycle of learning	103
5.1	Schools affecting and being affected by their environments	120
5.2	Schools sensing and responding to their environments	121
6.1	The chain of communication	144
6.2	The Y-shaped model of communication	144
6.3	The star model of communication	145
6.4	The circle of communication	145
6.5	The all-channel model of communication	146
6.6	Understanding the communication process	149
6.7	Adult to adult communication in Transactional Analysis	156
6.8	Parent and child communication in Transactional Analysis	156
6.9	Adult and child crossed wires in Transactional Analysis	157
6.10	Parent and adult crossed wires in Transactional Analysis	158
6.11	Leadership styles and communication	159
6.12	An inclusive model of communication	160
7.1	Components of a fitness landscape	166
7.2	A three-species fitness landscape	167
7.3	A rugged and rolling fitness landscape	172
7.4	Widely dispersed peaks in a fitness landscape	173
7.5	Dangerously sharp peaks in a fitness landscape	174
7.6	Rounded peaks in a fitness landscape	175
7.7	A very rugged fitness landscape	175
7.8	Intermediate peaks on a very rugged fitness landscape	176

7.9   The fitness landscape of a fit school   179
7.10   Fitness landscape for the mathematics and geography
       departments   180
7.11   The fitness landscape of components of organizational
       health   180
7.12   The fitness landscape of the use of IT in a school   181
7.13   The fitness landscape of a failing school   182
7.14   The fitness landscape of student achievement in
       mathematics and science   183
7.15   The fitness landscape of teacher expectation and teacher
       morale   183

Acknowledgements

This book is dedicated to Phukuntsi Abbey Kgaile, whom I have been privileged to know for several years. He came to the United Kingdom from South Africa, as a Ruth First Scholar, and he imbued everyone that he met with his sense of life and commitment to his emerging country and the freedom which it had grasped through so much pain. He is a true inspiration; I have no words to express my admiration for his ongoing leadership.

I am also grateful to the following: (i) my son Thomas for the diagrams of fitness landscapes which appear in Chapter 7; (ii) Roger Kirk, with whom I had the pleasure to work in the UK, some of the results of which can be found in Chapters 4 and 6; (iii) Mike Conn, headteacher of Bexhill High School, East Sussex, United Kingdom; (iv) Mike Wallace and Frank Pocklington, for Wallace, M. and Pocklington, F. (1998) *Managing complex change: large scale reorganisation of schools*. Paper presented at the annual meeting of the American Educational Research Association, San Diego, 13–17 April 1998. I thank Kurt April, of the Graduate School of Business, University of Capetown, who has given me very much support throughout the writing of this book.

Acknowledgements are given to the following for permission to reproduce material in this volume: (i) Blackwell Publishers Ltd., for material from Brown, R. (2000) *Group Processes* (2nd edn); (ii) Business Week for material from Kelly, S. and Allison, M. (1999) *The Complexity Advantage*; (iii) Butterworth-Heinemann, for material from *The Intelligence Advantage* by McMaster, M., p. 215; (iv) Doubleday, a division of Random House, for material from Senge, P. (1990) *The Fifth Discipline*; (v) Emerald (MCB University Press), for materials from: Cacioppe, R. (1999) 'Using team – individual reward and recognition strategies to drive organizational success', *Leadership and Organization Development Journal*, 20(6): 322–31; Popper, M. and Lipshitz, R. (2000) 'Installing mechanisms and instilling values: the role of leaders of organizational learning', *The Learning Organization*, 7(93): 135–44; Van den Brent, J., Paauwe, J. and Williams, R. (1999) 'Organizational learning: an exploration of organizational memory and its role in organizational change processes', *Journal of Organizational Change Management*, 12(5): 377–404; (vi) *Harvard Business Review* for Table 3.1, from 'Leadership that gets results' by Goleman, D. (March–April, 2000). Copyright © by the Harvard Business School Publishing

Corporation; all rights reserved; (vii) Open University Press, for material from Figure 6.1 and all of Table 6.2 of *Educational Leadership and Learning* by Law, S. and Glover, D. (2000); (viii) Sage Publications Inc., for Hoy, W.K., Tarter, C.J. and Kottkamp, R.B. (1991) *Open Schools, Healthy Schools*, pp. 16 and 133, copyright ©; (ix) Teacher Training Agency of the United Kingdom, for material from: *National Standards for Subject Leaders* (1998); *National Standards for Headteachers* (2000).

Introduction

Change is everywhere; the future is unpredictable. Turbulence rather than stability characterizes the environment in which schools operate and school leaders lead. Why is this? How can we understand this? How can we lead in this climate? What should leaders be doing in schools?

Interest in complexity theory has grown at an exponential rate since the early 1990s. It is being seen as the major theoretical principle which underlies economic systems, biological and evolutionary systems, brain-based research, artificial intelligence, developments in the physical and social sciences, health services and management practices. It has captured the attention of Nobel prize winners and scientists worldwide. More than most management theories, which are not theories at all but only recipes for, or stories of, particular practices, usually written by bosses, complexity theory is a theory *qua* theory, i.e. it has coherence, consistency, comprehensiveness, simplicity, explanatory and generalizable potential, and fecundity. It is not just a management fad.

This book sets out why and how an understanding of complexity theory is important for leadership in education. As educational leadership is a major growth area (e.g. in the National Professional Qualification for Headteachers in the UK and prescriptions for subject leadership), this book applies ideas from management and other literature on complexity theory to education.

Unlike many management books (particularly in the business world) this book draws on *evidence* and is rigorous. The evidence that it uses comes from various sources, for example published empirical research evidence is used extensively; all of the examples in the text are based on real, actual events in schools with which the author has had contact during many years of university work; and the ground has been explored with many groups with whom the author has been working on management and leadership courses of higher education and professional development in different parts of the world. The book combines academic scholarship with immediate practical import. The approach adopted here takes a dispassionate look at empirical literature on organizational behaviour and leadership. It strips out simple advocacy, polemics and anecdotes disguised as scholarship, which characterizes some of the management writing in this field, and presents an introduction to the range of relevant issues. The book is deliberately heavily referenced so that readers can identify the major texts in the field.

The book falls into two sections. Part I (Chapter 1) sets out the key components and constructs of complexity theory in a way which is intended to introduce new readers to the field. Part II (the remainder of the book) addresses the question 'what are the implications of complexity theory for school leadership?', i.e. *if* complexity theory *then* what follows from it? Each chapter addresses the several implications of adopting complexity theory in school leadership; these are not part of the theory itself but are consequences of the theory. To understand the issues readers can take each chapter on its own, but as complexity theory advocates synergy, to understand the book as a whole it is important to appreciate how chapters interrelate.

Part I
The theory of complexity

1 Complexity theory

An introduction to complexity theory

None of us can exist independent of our relationships with each other. 'Complexity' derives from the Latin root meaning 'to entwine'; the notion that an organism interacts dynamically with its environment, influencing and, in turn, being influenced by its environment, is a key principle of the emerging science of complexity. The burgeoning interest shown in this field touches several areas of human life, for example anthropology, biology and ecology. Since the 1970s and 1980s there has been an alignment of complexity theory with business and management practices (e.g. McMaster, 1996; Conner, 1998; Kelly and Allison, 1999), postmodernism (e.g. Cilliers, 1998) and education (e.g. Morrison, 1998). Indeed Fullan (2001: 70) is unequivocal in his view that all schools, if they are to survive, *must* [his term] understand complexity science.

Consider this example: there is a 'teaching' headteacher of a small, four-teacher, rural village primary school in the UK which serves a remote, introverted area, where employment options for adults are largely either farming or nothing. The school enjoys good relationships with parents, but this does not extend beyond formal meetings and visits for 'special events'. The headteacher is disenchanted with recent government reforms of education, as, he argues, they are removing him from those parts of his work for which he came into teaching – working with children, instructional leadership, professional autonomy and informed pedagogical freedom, teaching and a set of values for a liberal arts and humanistic tradition of education. Sensing that the situation of government prescription is unlikely to change he decides to take early retirement.

On taking up her new appointment, the new headteacher decides that the children need to be equipped to take their place in new employment markets, probably outside the neighbourhood. She feels that the horizons of the local population need to be extended, that the curriculum of the school needs to place greater emphasis on ICT, and that the school could become much more of a community resource. To that end she discusses with the teachers in the school and through a series of open meetings with the parents, ways of moving the school forward. This leads to the establishment of a range of 'out-of-hours' classes in IT for adults, the school becomes a centre for job advertising and for Internet links, and the three other teachers in the school together make concerted changes to pedagogy, so that large parts of the curriculum become learner-centred and ICT-driven. A small building programme takes place to convert rooms into a learner-resource suite, and parent-assistants come into the school on a regular, organized basis.

Within one year the school has changed from a slightly sleepy, if well-intentioned and friendly, place, into a vibrant community with links and connections to the outside community and beyond. In the school, teachers 'share' classes and work together far more closely, and involve parents in decision making on curricular and pedagogic matters – the school has moved from benevolent autocracy to participatory democracy. Children and parents have raised aspirations.

What has happened here? The school had reached a critical point where the former headteacher stayed or went (a 'bifurcation point' at the point of self-organized criticality in terms of complexity theory, discussed later in this chapter) – where events had built up until a new resolution had to be found by changing the school. The new headteacher sees that the school is 'out-of-step' with its environment; to bring the school into more developed relations and closer connectedness with its environment requires new networks with the environment to be made (*external* connectedness, see Chapters 5 and 7). For this to operate successfully requires *internal* changes to the school (*internal* connectedness, see Chapter 7). The headteacher's leadership is facilitatory (see Chapter 3), fostering new connections and more developed relations both internally and externally, premised on extensive communication (see Chapter 6). The school has changed through self-organization (discussed in this chapter) with supportive leadership, and a new organization has emerged in the form of team-based teaching (see Chapter 2 and this chapter). Further, the school has become an open system and has impacted on its local environment – it has been affected by the local environment and, in turn, has affected that environment (see Chapter 5); all parties have learned through feedback (see Chapter 4). Complexity theory provides a useful way of explaining the events that took place.

Complexity theory is a theory of survival, evolution, development and adaptation.[1] It has several antecedents, yet it breaks the bounds of these. Hodgson (2000) traces the roots of the concept of emergence to the nineteenth century philosopher Lewes, and the concept of unpredictability to the philosopher Morgan (1927: 112). In the 1930s, the New Zealand economist Souter and the English economist Hodgson discussed the significance of emergence and its unpredictability (Hodgson, 2000). More recently Hodgson cites the work of Polyani in the 1960s on the concept of emergence in the natural and social sciences. Lewin (1935, 1938, 1951) considered the behaviour of individuals and groups to be the interactions between personalities, individuals and their environments, each of which brings driving and restraining forces. He argued that systems are in constant flux rather than stability (De Smet, 1998: 7).

The foundation of Open Systems Theory, a forerunner of complexity, was formulated by Von Bertalanffy – a biologist – from the 1930s onwards (Von Bertalanffy, 1968) and was taken further into Open Systems Theory by Katz and

Kahn (1966, 1978) who, themselves, built on the work of Allport (1954, 1962). Here an open system is dynamic, its members living and exerting agency, and its changes irreversible and self-regulating. Novel changes for an uncertain and unpredictable future emerge spontaneously through the interaction of the organism with its environment.

This is a holistic, connectionist and integrationist view of the individual and the environment, rather than a fragmented, reductionist perspective (Youngblood, 1997: 34). In this view feedback is essential for development and change, and interdependence of the organism and its environment are emphasized. The dynamic flavour of Open Systems Theory is particularly appropriate for the study of turbulent behaviour (Malhotra, 1999: 3), and here the individual and the environment change each other. Katz and Kahn (1978) suggest that open systems import, store and use energy and information from outside so that the system can adjust to its environment; indeed they suggest that systems have an innate propensity towards increasing in size and complexity (see also De Smet, 1998: 8). Complexity theory goes further than Open Systems Theory, for Open Systems Theory is ultimately teleologically deterministic and its consideration of nonlinear systems marginal, whereas complexity theory breaks with this (Stacey, 2000: 296; Stacey *et al.*, 2000: 92).

Complexity theory is the offspring of chaos theory, but, as with Open Systems Theory, moves beyond it. Chaos theory, whilst stressing the unpredictability of the future, the system's sensitivity to initial conditions (which can never be measured precisely, thereby giving rise to unpredictable futures) and the importance of examining nonlinear systems, is premised on the same rationalist teleological determinism as Open Systems Theory (Stacey, 2000: 296; Stacey *et al.*, 2000: 142), as it uses the iterative, recursive process of making the outcome of one calculation the input to the next stage of the system (Gleick, 1987; Stacey, 2000: 322).

By contrast, complexity theory incorporates, indeed requires, unpredictable fluctuations and non-average behaviour in order to account for change, development and novelty through self-organization (discussed later). Chaos theory, Stacey suggests (*ibid*: 296; Stacey *et al.*, 2000: 89–96), has little internal capacity for spontaneous change from one 'strange attractor' to another, whereas complexity theory incorporates, indeed requires, spontaneous reorganization emerging from the interaction of elements. Chaos theory, like other systems theories, Stacey *et al.* (2000: 90) aver, has little room for novelty or creativity; the model implied in the original specification simply unfolds over time. It is a model which cannot apply comfortably to human interaction as human action is not so deterministic (*ibid*: 91).

Complexity theory, as a complete theory, developed from the 1980s, particularly in the work of the Santa Fe Institute in the United States. In some senses the *ancien régime* of chaos theory has given way to the study of complexity as 'life at the edge of chaos'. It is an attempt to explain how open systems operate, as seen through holistic spectacles. In complexity theory a system can be described as a collection of interacting parts which, together, function as a whole; it has boundaries and properties (Lucas, 2000: 3). This interaction is so intricate that it cannot be predicted by linear equations: there are so many variables involved that the behaviour of the system can only be understood as an 'emerging consequence' of the sum of the constituent elements (Levy, 1992: 7). The key elements of complexity theory are set out in this chapter (Figure 1.1).

Complexity theory looks at the world in ways which break with simple cause-and-effect models, linear predictability and a dissection approach to understanding phenomena, replacing them with organic, nonlinear and holistic approaches (Santonus, 1998: 3) in which relations within interconnected networks are the order of the day (Youngblood, 1997: 27; Wheatley, 1999: 10).

In the physical sciences, Laplacian and Newtonian theories of a deterministic universe have collapsed and have been replaced by theories of chaos and complexity in explaining natural processes and phenomena, the impact of which is being felt in the social sciences (e.g. McPherson, 1995). For Laplace and Newton, the universe was a rationalistic, deterministic and clockwork order; effects were functions of causes, small causes (minimal initial conditions) produced small effects (minimal and predictable) and large causes (multiple initial conditions) produced large (multiple) effects. Predictability, causality, patterning, universality and 'grand' overarching theories, linearity, continuity, stability, objectivity – all contributed to the view of the universe as an ordered and internally harmonistic mechanism in an albeit complex equilibrium; a rational, closed and deterministic system susceptible to comparatively straightforward scientific discoveries and laws. The differences between conventional wisdom and the principles of complexity theory are set out in Table 1.1.

Figure 1.1 Components of complexity theory.

Table 1.1 Conventional wisdom and complexity theory

Conventional wisdom	Complexity theory
Small changes produce small effects	Small changes can produce huge effects
Effects are straightforward functions of causes	Effects are not straightforward functions of causes
Similar initial conditions produce similar outcomes	Similar initial conditions produce dissimilar outcomes
Certainty and closure are possible	Uncertainty and openness prevail
The universe is regular, uniform, controllable and predictable	The universe is irregular, diverse, uncontrollable and unpredictable
Systems are deterministic, linear and stable	Systems are indeterministic, nonlinear and unstable
Systems are fixed and finite	Systems evolve, emerge and are infinite
Universal, all-encompassing theories can account for phenomena	Local, situationally specific theories account for phenomena
A system can be understood by analyzing its component elements (fragmentation and atomization)	A system can only be understood holistically, by examining its relationship to its environments (however defined)
Change is reversible	Change is irreversible – there is a unidirectional arrow or time

Table 1.1 signals the paradigm shift that has been heralded by complexity theory. The link between a deterministic view of the universe and the project of modernity is not difficult to discern; both are premised on the same principles for progress, and both are poor at accounting for change in schools (Riley, 2000: 35). The rise of complexity theory captures the contemporary spirit of change, uncertainty, impermanence, openness and unpredictability that began early in the twentieth century (with Heisenberg's uncertainty principle, quantum physics and theories of relativity).

Complexity theory (Waldrop, 1992; Lewin, 1993; Kauffman, 1995) examines phenomena as 'complex adaptive systems', with components at one level acting as the building blocks for components at another. Similar initial conditions can produce largely dissimilar outcomes, e.g. two neighbouring nations with similar initial conditions evolve entirely differently (Merry, 1995: 27). A complex system comprises independent elements (which themselves might be made up of complex systems) which interact and give rise to organized behaviour in the system as a whole (e.g. Åm, 1994). Order is not totally predetermined and fixed, but the universe (however defined) is creative, emergent (through iteration, learning and recursion), evolutionary and changing, transformative and turbulent. Order emerges in complex systems that are founded on simple rules for interacting organisms (Kauffman, 1995: 24); life is holistic and profoundly unpredictable.

Because systems emerge over time, it is not possible to determine with any certainty, in advance, the results of that emergence: the dinosaurs did not know that their days were numbered; the Incas of Peru could not have anticipated their demise, yet they surely died! We cannot know in advance how the brain of a young baby will develop by the time she has reached, say, forty years old. Emergence over time brings new states; old forms die and new forms proliferate.

Through feedback, recursion, perturbance, auto-catalysis (defined later), connectedness and self-organization, higher and greater levels of complexity and differentiated, new forms of life, behaviour, systems and organizations arise from lower levels of complexity and existing forms. These complex forms derive from often comparatively simple sets of rules – local rules and behaviours generating complex global order and diversity (Waldrop, 1992: 16-7; Lewin, 1993: 38; Åm, 1994). Dynamical systems (Peak and Frame, 1994: 122) are a product of initial conditions and are often governed by simple rules for change – the dynamics of change. General laws of emergent order can govern adaptive, dynamical processes (Kauffman, 1995: 27). The basic rules and components can be simple, and give rise to emergent complexity through their interaction simultaneously (Waldrop, 1992: 86).

Waldrop (1992: 241–2) provides a fascinating example of this in Reynolds's computer program Boids, where just three initial conditions are built into a mathematical formula that reproduces the flight of a flock of birds. These are: (a) the boids (birds) strive to keep a minimum distance from other objects (including other boids); (b) the boids strive to keep to the same speed as other boids; (c) each boid strives to move towards the centre of the flock. The example of boids is very fitting: there is no cosmological or teleological 'ghost in the machine' which is determining how the birds should fly; the flock of birds/boids is self-organizing. The complex emerges from the simple (Hartwell, 1995: 8), it is not imposed from outside (Marion, 1999: 29). There is no single leader or central control; rather there is *distributed control* (Lewin and Regine, 2000: 30). It would be an interesting question, perhaps, to ask what is the minimum number of rules required for schools to operate effectively and creatively.[2]

Complexity emerges thus (Figure 1.2):

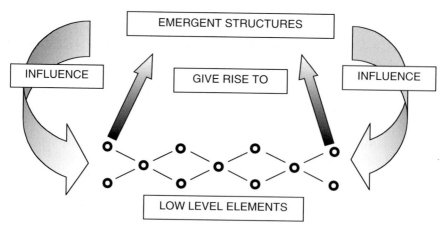

Figure 1.2 The rise of emergence in complexity theory.

In Figure 1.2 the interaction of individuals feeds into the wider environment, which in turn influences the individual units of the network. Bar-Yam (1997) suggests that a complex system is formed from several elements, and that the behaviour of the complex system cannot be inferred simply from the behaviour of the component elements – the whole is greater than the sum of the parts (see also Goodwin, 2000: 42). Bar-Yam (1997) suggests that central properties of complex systems include: the number of their elements, the interactions of their elements (and the strengths of these interactions); their formation and operations; their diversity and variability; the environment in which they operate; and their activities. Organizations move towards greater degrees of complexity and higher orders as they evolve, and new properties appear at each emergent level (Lissack, 1999: 4). For example:

Lower order	→	*Emergent higher order*
Organized	→	Self-organized
Mechanical	→	Humanistic
Directives	→	Empowerment
Hierarchical	→	Networked
Single leaders	→	Distributed leadership
Closed, dissipative system	→	Open, evolving system
Depersonalized	→	Relationship-driven
Demarcated and detached	→	Connected
Inflexible	→	Adaptable
Closed system	→	Open system
Restricted communication	→	Open communication
Enacted organization	→	Learning organization
Transactional leadership	→	Transformational quantum leadership
Passive	→	Active
Low-order thinking	→	High-order creative thinking
Censure	→	Feedback
Sterile environment	→	Rich environment
Private knowledge	→	Distributed knowledge

Out of low-order command-and-control systems of leadership with fragmentation and isolation of teachers, emerge flat management, internally and externally networked schools which operate in multiple teams and matrix structures, distributed leadership and person-centred institutions. This is a result of developments in the internal and external environments of the school.

Systems, however defined, are complex, unstable, emergent, adaptive, dynamical and – significantly – changing. In human terms disequilibrium can be accounted for by intentionality, competition (e.g. Åm, 1994), intelligence, creativity and the independent behaviours of acting individuals. Systems, however defined, are perpetually out of balance (*ibid.*), and order emerges as the system (from ant colonies to economic practices) strives for unachievable equilibrium or homeostasis. Complex adaptive systems are constantly modifying and rearranging their building blocks in the light of prediction, experience and learning

(Waldrop, 1992: 146, 177). They display 'perpetual novelty' (*ibid*: 147). Self-organization is the order of the day. A school moves from a departmental structure to a faculty structure to a community resource to a specialist centre, both in response to the environment and in order to position itself in the environment.

So far the term 'complex adaptive system' has been used, and is in common parlance in complexity theory. More recently Stacey (2000: 368) and Stacey *et al.* (2000) have questioned this term for its system-driven, cybernetic, mechanistic connotations. They prefer the term 'complex responsive process', as it connotes more of human relations, which for them lie at the heart of complexity theory for organizations and management, and combines the agency and mutual influence of individuals and groups. Indeed they argue (*ibid*: 188) that thinking of an organization as a system has to be replaced, within complexity theory, by thinking of the organization as the processes of people relating to, and interacting with, each other over time. Such interaction places communication at its core, and Chapter 6 introduces some of the issues in this field.

Dynamical interaction of elements

Complex adaptive systems comprise many *interacting* elements which must be understood together – holistically; these elements, because of their interactions, cause new elements to form and new phenomena, new structures and new rules of behaviour to occur. Each element influences and, in turn, is influenced by the other elements in the system and, together, they give rise to emergent new forms whose nature and structure it might not have been possible to predict. Institutions, agents and systems co-evolve (Cohen and Stewart, 1995: 331; Stewart, 2001).

For example, in the UK the increasing marketization of schooling causes schools to be placed on a business footing. That, combined with other incentives (e.g. increasing resources for schools which dance to the government's tune), in turn leads to the promotion of some schools (e.g. city technology colleges and specialist schools). It also leads to the demoralization of much of the workforce because increasing competition takes place in an atmosphere of under-resourcing. In order for market forces to work the public needs information about school performance, which gives rise to increased public assessment, inspection, league tables, massive audit systems and significantly more paperwork for teachers. To cope with this, an increasingly managerialist mentality comes into schools, with the latest fad of the day from business entering the school agenda: total quality management, quality development, high reliability organizations, re-engineering the school.

The combination of all of these pressures makes teachers leave the profession, perhaps because what is happening is not why they came into teaching or because of the stress. There is a crisis of recruitment and retention of teachers; experienced teachers leave prematurely, and prospective teachers with high quality first degrees are put off from entering the profession. Senior teachers stop teaching and become managers or cover for absent teachers. The combination of staff absence and poor quality teachers leads to a lowering rather than raising of standards and this heightens the problems of teacher recruitment and retention – decreasing returns.

The consequences of these problems, in turn, lead to massive government advertising campaigns (whose effect is minimal), causing questions to be raised in government circles about the economic rates of return on investment and so on. The 'soup' of multiple factors gives rise to a host of unexpected outcomes. The process is one of fermentation rather than linear cause and effect.

The issue here is that linear causes and effects, which characterized the Newtonian universe, are rendered impossible. Rather, the task is to understand the shifting nature of constantly changing forms – for example the movement of smoke from a bonfire, the movement of water in a cataract, the movement of sand in a desert. Smoke from a bonfire is affected by ambient winds and, in turn, affects the environment; the flow of water in a cataract is affected by rocks in its path and, in turn, affects the rocks; sand in a desert builds up in response to local winds and then reforms the landscape of that environment, causing new wind patterns, and so on; a simple classroom incident escalates into major trouble, involving parents, school governors, even the judiciary. Multiply this phenomenon by the very many components that typically constitute a system and it is not difficult to see why predictability is a chimera: it does not exist.

Fixity in the environment and its components does not exist; stability is the stability of the mortuary. Stable organizations, as Stacey (1992: 40) reminds us, ultimately fail. Indeed April (1997: 26) suggests that change and unpredictability are *requirements* if an organization is to survive: 'a butterfly which flies in a straight line without zigzags – will fall prey very fast'. A heartbeat is marked by regularity immediately prior to cardiac arrest. Organizations must change to survive.

Disequilibrium is vital for survival. The structure of the caterpillar must cede to the structure of the butterfly if the species is to survive. Systems must be open if they are to survive; such openness engages the possibility of importing energy from the external environment and converting it into more complex emergent structures and, by way of balance, exporting entropy (negative energy) into the environment – a process of negentropy (Johnson, 1999). Deterioration and decay – entropy – can be traded and exchanged for positive energy in the environment (Wheatley, 1999: 79). Indeed Johnson (1999: 3) suggests that for a system to be sustainable it needs to be able to convert energy into an increasingly complex structure and must be able to eliminate waste energy. This is an ongoing dynamic process.

Self-organization in connected networks

An infant school in the UK enjoys good relations with the junior school, whose site it shares. There is extensive communication between the schools, and curricular, pedagogic and assessment continuity are strong. The two schools are sited in an increasing popular developmental and residential area in a new town. Each school recognizes that its population is increasing, and that it cannot simply resolve the situation by adding a growing number of portable classrooms. Hence, by mutual agreement, the two schools merge into a single new school, with a building programme to create new permanent rooms. Economies of scale mean that the quality of the learning environment improves for all the children. At a time of perturbation a new system emerges through interaction of its internal and external elements; communication is strong, and the schools self-organize into a new internal structure. Wallace (1996: 264), discussing school mergers in the UK, makes the specific point that mergers often take place in an environment of turbulence, and that interactions of players at different levels in such reform initiatives (e.g. local, central governmental and institutional players) are complex, unpredictable and often contrary. He mentions that the new paradigm of 'dynamic complexity' (*ibid*: 264) rather than linear control is a feature of the complex interactions of contextual factors. Externally initiated policies, he suggests, interact with local contexts to produce a new, unpredicted reality.

A key feature of complex adaptive systems is that order emerges through self-organization of interacting elements and constant self-readjustment of the system (Coveney and Highfield, 1995: 85). Heating ice spontaneously causes it to reorganize itself into water; heating water causes it to spontaneously self-organize as steam. Borrowing from the theories of chaos and dissipative structures (Gleick, 1987; Prigogine and Stengers, 1985), the reorganization, or re-self-organization, takes place at bifurcation points – the point at which an existing organism becomes so unstable that it has the possibility to develop in several different ways, and the new form cannot be predicted (Capra, 1997). Moments of decision occur at the concurrence of problems, situations, participants and choice opportunities (April *et al.*, 2000: 84), i.e. at bifurcation points (Hartwell, 1995: 11).

From a management perspective, Stacey (1992: 183–4) suggest that self-organization is a process in which teams and groups form themselves spontaneously around issues, with the participants themselves (not managers) deciding what their boundaries will be. Indeed he suggests that self-organizing networks might operate against management hierarchies. Self-organization, argues Marsick (2000: 10), occurs through feedback and communication.

Order is not imposed from without or by external constraint; it emerges from within – it is auto-catalytic, emerging spontaneously of its own accord (Cohen and Stewart, 1995: 265). Auto-catalysis describes the ability of elements to catalyse each other, and thereby to generate new forms from within. Order and freedom are thus partners rather than competitors (Wheatley, 1999: 87); control and order are conceptually separate.

Complex adaptive systems possess a capability for self-organization which enables them to develop, extend, replace, adapt, reconstruct or change their internal structure (or *modus operandi*) so that they can respond to, and influence, their environment. A school that is responsive to its environment may reorganize its activities: it may become a community resource; it may involve parents far more extensively than before, for example in policy decision making; it may set up student councils; it may move towards student-centred learning through a massive injection of IT hardware, funded by running courses for the general public.

Prigogine and Stengers (1985: 156–9) provide a fascinating example of self-organization in the lowly slime-mould: the *Acrasiales* amoebas. If the environment of the slime-mould becomes depleted in the essential nutrients needed to sustain life, the amoebas sense this through chemical sensors and cease to reproduce.[3] They collect together and form a 'foot' containing about a third of the aggregated cells and which supports a mass of spores. These detach themselves from the foot and migrate in search of a new environment which is suitable to sustain life, forming a new colony of amoebas.

What has happened here? The organism is responding to the environment by reconfiguring itself and metamorphosing in order to survive; it is an open system responding to its environment. The process involves self-organization, and the slime-mould, reinvigorated, is capable of survival; the whole process is dynamic. The slime-mould demonstrates *auto-catalysis*, a central feature of self-organization: the ability of a system to evolve itself, from within. In this process local circumstances dictate the nature of the emerging self-organization; it is a 'bottom--up' process (Marion, 1999: 31). This is a very simplified example of a central pillar of complexity theory, that of self-organization, and it contains several features: *adaptability*, *open systems*, *learning*, *feedback*, *communication* and *emergence*. Let us examine these a little further.

The slime-mould has to be aware of, and open to, its environment if it is to survive. Without this it would starve; one theory for the extinction of dinosaurs is their inability to adapt – to self-organize – following the influence of a massive meteor impact on the Earth's climate. A system which cannot adapt, which is not nimble enough to change, cannot last (Belasco, 1990); one is either quick or dead. For a system to survive it cannot rely on introspection and closure, it must be open to the environment; sensing it, responding to it and, in turn, shaping it. Closed systems in equilibrium die; systems *need* disequilibrium in order to survive (April, 1997: 9).

Not only is a self-organizing system auto-catalytic; it demonstrates *autopoiesis*. This means that each living system possesses its own unique characteristics and autonomous identity (Kelly and Allison, 1999: 28) which enable the system to perpetuate and renew itself over time – it creates the conditions for its own persistence (Gaines, 1997: 4). For example, a school may become a centre of excellence for the arts, or for sciences. Autopoiesis derives from the Greek, meaning self-production or self-making (Wheatley, 1999: 20), with such creation taking place through engagement with others in a system. The system is self-bounded and self-referenced (aware of its own identity and core properties), self-regenerating (able to sustain that identity even though aspects of the system may change, e.g. staff turnover in a school), and self-perpetuating (able to develop a strong culture or ethos in which the system serves the individual as well as vice versa). Wheatley (1996: 11) suggests that schools need to create their own identity in their local context and community. When an organization is clear on its identity then it is favourably situated to respond intelligently to its environment.

It is no longer possible to rely on linear models of management. Linear models of management, which underpinned the simple linear causality of the command-and-control mentality of hierarchical, bureaucratic organizations, have to be replaced with networked, nonlinear, emergent, mutually informing groups and their management. Groups and institutions are self-organizing and self-managing rather than organized and managed by senior managers, the principles on which this view rests being discussed below. Complexity theory in management moves away from modernistic conceptions of management, leadership and organization and towards postmodernist conceptions (Jameson, 1991; Morrison, 1998). In organizational terms this is represented in Table 1.2.

Change is endemic to survival. Further, *learning* is a critical factor within this ever-changing environment. Systems or organisms which cannot learn from their environment, and environments which cannot learn from constituent elements, simply perish. A school which does not meet local demands, that operates as an island of traditionalism, will die. The brain of a newborn baby is not already full of everything that it will need to know throughout life; the brain must be able to learn and adapt. A baby is not a homunculus. It is unsurprising, perhaps, that the current orthodoxies for education in an ever-changing environment stress the learning society, the learning organization, lifelong learning, learning networks, learner-centred education and brain-based education. As Fullan (1991) and Dalin and Rolff (1993) remark, change *equals* learning. If self-organization is to lead to, or be an effective consequence of, survival then the self-organizing system must

Table 1.2 Modernistic and complex organizations

Modernistic organizations	Complex, postmodern organizations
Large	Small
Hierarchical	Flatter management
Bureaucratic	Teamwork and matrix structures
Departmentalized	Multi-team membership
Closed	Open
Demarcated	Flexible boundaries
Specialized	Multiple abilities/intelligences
Mechanistic	Organic/flexible/changing
Standardized	Flexible/niche-targeted
Inflexible	Flexible/adaptable
Fordist	Post-Fordist
Technocratic/impersonal	Person-centred
Producer capture	Consumerist
Grand plan	No meta-narratives
Similarity/continuity	Difference/discontinuity
Absolutist values	Shared valued/relativist values
Controlling	Self-organizing/autonomy
Command-and-control management	Empowering/facilitatory management
Predictability	Unpredictable
Deterministic	Indeterminate

be constantly learning – the *kaizen* of Japanese industries perhaps, with their emphasis on continuous improvement by participants in the system, often on an incremental and collaborative basis (Morrison, 1998).

At an organizational level, McMaster (1996: 10) suggests that organizational learning involves:

- an ability (within the organizational structures) to receive, understand and interpret, in various ways, signals from the external environment;
- an ability to respond in various ways to those signals, including creating new internal structures and organizational features;
- an ability to influence the external environment both proactively and reactively.

A school needs, itself, to become a learning organization as well as developing the learning potential of its students.

The preceding points on learning are, perhaps, self-evident; what is required is to comment on the nature of, the components of and the processes involved in that learning. A key factor here is that *feedback* must occur between the interacting elements of the system. Complexity theorists (Waldrop, 1992; Cilliers, 1998) have turned to Hebb's (1949) views on learning here. Hebb's view of learning operates on an associationist or connectedness principle ('joined-up thinking'): if X and Y occur together then an association between the two is formed in the brain synapses; if there is recurrence of the association between X and Y then the strength of that connection is increased into strong 'cell assemblies'; if recurrence is minimal or non-existent then the association decays and dies. If each time I encounter the school principal I experience pain, then, naturally, I will tend to associate pain with such meetings, and this will shape my behaviour with her/him. I may avoid the principal, or deliberately stand my ground, or shout, or complain, or take steps to reduce the pain, or absent myself, etc. – I have learned something and it affects my behaviour.

Negative feedback brings diminishing returns (Marion, 1999: 75); positive feedback brings increasing returns (discussed below). Negative feedback is regulatory; it signals deviation from the norm like a thermostat which regulates temperature, causing interventions whenever too much deviation occurs. A thermostat manages to keep the temperature in a room constant only by constantly switching itself on and off in response to its sensing of the air temperature in the room. The implication for schools, perhaps, is to find the appropriate systems, people or resources to act as equivalents to thermostats, sensing the environment and making internal adjustments.

Positive feedback uses information not merely to regulate but to change, grow and develop (Wheatley, 1999: 78). It amplifies small changes (Stacey, 1992: 53; Youngblood, 1997: 54). Senge *et al.* (2000: 84) cite the example of a baby animal whose eating is voracious, and the more it eats the faster it grows; its rate of growth accelerates. Once a child has begun to read she is gripped by reading; she reads more and learns at an exponential rate.

Not only can feedback be positive, it also needs to be rich. If I simply award a grade to a student's work, she cannot learn much from it except that she is a success or a failure, or somewhere in between. If, on the other hand, I provide rich feedback she can learn more; if I only point out two matters in my feedback then the student might only learn of those two matters; if I point out ten matters then the student might learn about ten matters. We have to recall that the root of 'feedback' is 'food'; nourishment rather than simply information.

Feedback is essential if a system is to be in step with itself and its environment (Marion, 1999: 74–5). Learning requires memory; self-organization *requires* memory. If an organism is to learn from experience – even vicarious experience – then it needs a memory; it has a history. A change agent or leader in a school who neglects the significance of the past (and its contribution to the ethos and culture of the school) risks overlooking a key variable in the successful management of the school. An organism or system needs to draw on that memory or, according to Hebb's associationist principle, the association – the accumulated memory – will die. There is a constant threat of entropy. As Cilliers (1998: 93) remarks with reference to memory: use it or lose it!

The collective memory of an organization is used productively to anticipate the future and to make whatever predictions are possible, even if these are tentative, uncertain and pragmatic. Decisions for the future are informed by decisions made about past experience. Complex adaptive systems have to anticipate the future. Schools have to prepare for what they see on the horizon; the sad matter is that the rise of bureaucracy frequently prevents this: the oxen are so weighed down by the plough which they are pulling that they cannot raise their heads to look into the distance (Bottery, 1992).

Connectedness, a key feature of complexity theory, exists everywhere. In schools, children are linked to families, teachers, peers, societies and groups; teachers are linked to professional associations, other teachers, other providers of education, workplace placements for children, support agencies like psychological and social services, policy-making bodies, funding bodies, the courts and police services, and so on. The school is not an island, but is connected externally in several ways. Many schools sink under internal communication and connectedness, through memoranda, meetings, paperwork, assessment data, inspection data, working parties, policy and curriculum development groups, e-mail, intranet and telephonic communication, voice mail and a host of other forms. The price of communication is high in terms of teacher stress.

In a rainforest, ants eat leaves, birds eat ants and leave droppings, which fertilize the soil for growing trees and leaves (Lewin, 1993: 86). As April *et al.* (2000: 34) remark, nature possesses many features that organizations crave: flexibility, diversity, adaptability, complexity and connectedness. Connectedness is *required* if a system is to survive; disturb one element in the connections and either the species or system must adapt or die (see the discussion of fitness landscapes in Chapter 7); the message is ruthless. Connectedness through communication is vital. This requires a *distributed knowledge* system, in which knowledge is not centrally located in a command-and-control centre or the property of a limited set of agents (e.g. senior managers); rather it is dispersed, shared and circulated throughout the organization and its members.

Connected networks rather than islands are the order of the day. As Wheatley remarks (1999: 145), we can learn from the spider and her web; if the web breaks she reconnects it to itself; to strengthen a system we make more connections and stronger relationships, and this is an internal rather than external process. The brain is a mass of neural networks with no single control centre which oversees its functioning. Processing information and feedback for learning is not routed through a central control mechanism; it is *distributed* throughout the system, and information, knowledge and meanings and their control are also distributed throughout the system (Waldrop, 1992: 145–7).

Schools are storehouses of distributed knowledge; it frequently governs the micro-politics of the organization; Morrison (1998) argues that leaders have to understand micro-politics in detail if they are to effect change successfully. On a more formal level, common sense argues that no individual leader possesses all the knowledge stored in an organization. The leader *relies* on distributed knowledge and being able to draw upon it. It is folly for a leader to believe that she has all the knowledge of the organization. The implication of this, as Wheatley (1996: 5) observes, is that self-organization through connectedness *requires* democratic processes; it is inevitable. As she says: 'you can't avoid including people' (p. 5) (cf. Goldstein, 2000: 15).

Connectedness implies relationships, for example between individuals and teams; between teams; between subsystems; between the institution and its environment (Lewin and Regine, 2000: 19). Further, these relationships are mutual, not one-way. On an interpersonal level this suggests an increased need for trust between equal partners – a collaborative rather than a competitive mentality. This creates a win-win situation, a 'both/and' rather than an 'either/or' (*ibid*: 168).

The collective memory of this institution is located everywhere in it; there is, then, a need for careful storage, access to, and retrieval of, this collective memory. This respects the person-centredness of schools: all the participants in the school can make a knowledge contribution to the school; leadership equates with dispersed, distributed leadership. As Yeats (1962) remarked: things fall apart; the centre cannot hold.

Further, in organizational terms the notion of distributed intelligence and information has huge implications, for it argues against hierarchical and bureaucratic command-and-control approaches to management and leadership and, instead, argues for the realization that systems are more fittingly conceived to be networks (just as the brain is a series of neural networks) – loosely coupled or more tightly coupled.

The ramifications of this are to suggest that leadership is not the preserve of the senior figure of the school; everyone everywhere can exercise leadership. The leader is simply the one who goes first and shows the way, not necessarily the boss! Leadership is no longer the activity of gatekeeping and directing but of enabling and empowering. Decentralizing control requires a flexible, adaptable system which, itself, is co-ordinated if it is to survive. This argues against boundary-driven, controlled, inflexible, rigid systems and organizations. The school leader is the facilitator of information exchange rather than its gatekeeper.

If learning through feedback is to take place, if connectedness is to work successfully, and if knowledge is to be collected from a distributed, dispersed system, then an essential requirement will be an effective communication system (see Chapter 6). Communication in schools is a key variable in their success and their person-centredness (cf. Peters, 1989; Cilliers, 1998). The amount of feedback and communication is frequently inversely proportional to its capability for predictability. The greater the amount of feedback given, be it as data, information or knowledge, the less it is possible to predict what the results of that high information content might be. The balance has to be struck between selective (and inadequate) information for predictability and control, and a necessary high amount of information for self-organization to occur.

Communication is central to complexity theory, and to organizational and leadership theory that draws inspiration from complexity theory. Significant, open-ended and lateral communication must replace vertical or bilateral forms of communication, in which directions, decisions and instructions descend from on high in a hierarchical bureaucracy, and information ascends to the top of the hierarchy – the nature or contents of the communication are different. Complexity theory suggests that, in a networked structure for self-organization, communication must take multiple forms, be through multiple channels, and be open.

The emphasis on networks is reflected in the view that an organization which is to meet the demands of constant change has to have a particular 'fitness landscape' (Kauffman, 1993, 1995), where the contours of the elements of the organization can be mapped as a suitable terrain for adaptability (discussed in Chapter 7). Weick (1976) suggests that fit organizations are characterized by loose coupling and that there are seven principal benefits of loosely coupled organizations, in that they:

- allow sections of the organization to continue and evolve separately;
- can be, and are, more sensitive to the demands of the environment;
- enable local responses (i.e. within selected sections of the organization) to be made to local environmental demands;
- permit sections of the organization to experiment with new structures;
- are able to isolate problems and, thereby, to prevent wholesale breakdown or total collapse of the organization (the domino effect) (Community Intelligence Labs, 1999: 4);
- enable flexible, sectionally self-determined responses to be made to unpredictable environments and circumstances;
- are cheaper to run than tightly coupled organizations.

In several senses schools may be loosely coupled (Dalin, 1998: 45), containing elements which are loosely connected and which may not be entirely consistent with other parts of the organization. They may be comparatively unco-ordinated, and possess very few rules; they may be places where people disagree (Weick, 1976). Rather than being detrimental to innovation and growth, the relative freedom that this brings may actually foster innovation, flexibility, adaptability and growth (Peters and Waterman, 1982; Fullan, 2001). One department might be developing whilst another is stable, so that the whole system does not suffer from innovation fatigue. The move towards organizing schools as loosely coupled or 'loose-tight' organizations (a core of central values which the various groupings in the school then interpret) receives support with regard to openness to change (e.g. Hargreaves and Hopkins, 1991; Dalin and Rolff, 1993; Dalin, 1998).

A self-organizing system, then, if it is to demonstrate fitness, needs to abide by principles of internal connectedness yet loose coupling – where the individual elements of the organization have freedom and autonomy to organize themselves in a participatory way within an overall framework of the goals, incentives and values of the organization and can thereby learn and change (Johnson, 1999: 32). In this respect organizational learning is akin to searching for fitness (Marion, 1999: 174).

Stacey (2000: 333–4) cautions against equating self-organization with individualism, complete democracy, anarchy, the empowerment of all the junior members of staff and the disempowerment of the senior staff. Rather, he suggests that self-organization is not a 'constraint-free form of behaviour' (*ibid*: 334) but has to take account of differentials of power, influence, constraint, competition, limited consensus, differential capabilities and capacities to respond. Hence senior managers can still enable and constrain actions and behaviour (*ibid*: 335–6). It is the interaction of these factors that produces self-organization. Indeed Stacey *et al.* (2000: 124) expressly indicate the limits to individual choice within power structures and argue that conflicting constraints ('power relations') (*ibid*: 155) are essential for genuine novelty to emerge. Power is a central issue, and one cannot behave as though it is not present (see also Stacey 1992: 189). Complexity theory is not licence; it operates within boundaries.

Emergence

A primary school is situated in a multiply-deprived inner-city area in the UK. Drug-related crime is high, one-parent families abound, the school grounds are regular sites for prostitutes and drug addicts at night, vandalism is rife, unemployment is widespread, and ethnic tensions frequently flare up into physical violence. The results of a school inspection are poor; the school is identified as a 'failing school' and is placed into 'special measures'. The inspectors have particularly identified children's low achievements in public assessments, low expectations by the staff, an undemanding curriculum and an over-reliance on didactic teaching in an effort to control large numbers of disruptive and disturbed children.

The school staff is shattered; each teacher had been working tirelessly and under enormous stress, and now they have been 'kicked in the teeth' by an insensitive and under-informed inspection. As a result the morale in the school plummets; teachers leave *en masse* and are unable to be replaced, as the 'tag' of a 'failing school' turns away potential applicants. Despite the installation of a new, temporary headteacher whose style is assertive and directive to the point of aggression, there is little perceptible change. The school closes. A new school re-opens, with a large injection of funding, additional premises, increased allowances for teachers, a range of support mechanisms, additional staff to attend to the social and psycho-logical needs of the families and children, large numbers of small-group work on a withdrawal basis for particularly disturbed students, and considerable provision of additional resources by a range of funding agencies. The nature of the new organi-zation is established by all the participants, and the task of the new headteacher is facilitatory, providing whatever support is possible to 'make things happen'. Concerted efforts are made by the new staff to consult with each other, to achieve consistency of approaches to handling difficult children, and there is extensive teamwork in the support provided for such children. The curriculum is redesigned to move towards student-centred learning rather than teacher-centred teaching, and several rooms are designated as resource areas for a range of learning activities. Improvement abounds.

The example is of emergence: the old system is unable to adapt and so it dies, and a new system emerges from its ashes, which is better suited to the situation being faced. The efforts to change the system simply by changing the leadership (a new form of control) do not work; self-organization cannot be mandated – it emerges spontaneously and of its own accord. The new system is internally restructured, and, significantly, works because it relies on human relations, dis-tributed leadership, servant leadership by the headteacher (discussed in Chapter 3) and team-based approaches, together with appropriate support mechanisms. The school is self-organizing.

Emergence is the partner of self-organization. Systems possess the ability for self-organization, which is according not to an *a priori* grand design – a cosmo-logical argument – nor to a deliberately chosen trajectory or set of purposes – a teleological argument. Rather, the self-organization emerges of itself as the result of the interaction between the organism and its environment (Casti, 1997), and new structures emerge that could not have been envisioned initially (Merry, 1998), for example Figure 1.3.

Changes are irreversible – a butterfly is not simply 'more caterpillar', it is something completely different. A frog is not simply more tadpole nor can it ever revert to being a tadpole. New, higher, evolved forms emerge as a consequence of preceding events. A flock of birds flying in V-formation can fly further and faster than an individual bird (Santonus, 1998: 1; cf. Jacobson, 2000: 1); the whole is greater than the sum of the parts (Lucas, 2000: 3; Cilliers, 1998). New properties appear at each successive level of emergent complexity; each successive level has its own rules, key structures, concepts and generalizations (Waldrop, 1992: 82). Individual teachers become a department; departments combine to form a faculty or division; faculties combine to form an organization or institution; institutions combine to form partnerships, and so on. At each level constant changes occur to accommodate the new situations, and new rules, procedures and structures emerge for each level.

The role of leaders, then, is to change the perceptions of a situation, which articulates closely with complexity theory. It was Einstein who remarked that 'our thinking creates problems which the same level of thinking can't solve' – we can-not solve a problem by examining it from the same frame of reference or

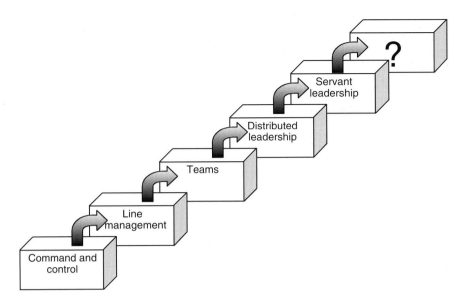

Figure 1.3 A sequence of emergence.

consciousness that created it (Sherman and Schultz, 1998: 9; Lissack, 2000: 10); we need to look at the situation in a new light.

Not only are systems complex and adaptive, there is a natural, inbuilt movement towards greater complexity in systems (Lewin, 1993: 132). They naturally and spontaneously evolve towards a critical point at the edge of chaos, a point in which they are at their most diverse and creative (Goodwin, 2000: 46–7), wherein the richness of connectivity, networking and information sharing is at its most fecund, before tipping over into chaos. They are, using Hock's words, 'chaordic' (Youngblood, 1997: 35; Stewart, 2001: 3), on the boundary of chaos and order.

Youngblood (1997: 29) and Brown and Eisenhardt (1998) suggest that organizations at the edge of chaos balance too much structure (which inhibits diversity and responsiveness to the environment) with too little structure (which moves towards chaos and is too sensitive to the environment). It happens of its own accord; as Kauffman (1995: Chapter 4) says, order is for free.

The movement towards greater degrees of complexity is a movement towards 'self-organized criticality' (Bak and Chen, 1991), in which systems evolve, through self-organization, towards the edge of chaos (Kauffman, 1995). Take, for example, a pile of sand. If one drops a grain of sand at a time, a pyramid of sand appears. Continue to drop another piece of sand and a small cascade of sand runs down the pyramid; continue further and the sand pile builds up again in a slightly different shape; continue further and the whole pyramid falls down like a house of cards. This is chaos, and complexity theory resides at the edge of chaos, at the point just before the pyramid of sand collapses, between mechanistic predictability and complete unpredictability (Karr, 1995: 3):

| Linear systems | $\rightarrow$ | Complexity | $\rightarrow$ | Non-linear chaos |

Stacey (2000: 395) suggests that a system can only evolve, and evolve spontaneously, where there is diversity and deviance (*ibid*: 399) – a salutary message for command-and-control leaders who exact compliance from their followers. Similarly Fullan (2001: 42) suggests listening carefully to dissenters and resisters, as they may have an important message to convey, they may be critical to the effectiveness of change, and build in difference; leaders must not simply have like-minded innovators.

The exact movement, reconfiguration and subsequent catastrophic destruction of the sand pile mentioned above are largely unpredictable. At the point of self-organized criticality the effects of a single event are likely to be very large, breaking the linearity of Newtonian reasoning wherein small causes produce small effects (the straw that breaks the camel's back, or a small cause with a massive effect) – a single grain of sand which destroys the pyramid. Change implies, then, a move towards self-organized criticality.

A significant factor here is that, the closer one is propelled towards the edge of chaos, the more creative, open-ended, imaginative, diverse and rich are the behaviours, ideas and practices of individuals and organizations, and the greater is the connectivity, networking and information sharing (content and rate of flow) between participants (see the discussion of fitness landscapes in Chapter 7) (Stacey *et al.* 2000: 146). The message appears to be that if an individual or organization wishes to become creative and imaginative in order to survive, then it may have to expect to be pressed towards self-organized criticality. This is not a euphemism for unmitigated stress and pressure; rather it suggests that people need support and space to develop and, importantly, to change, and to be creative and imaginative. Simply pressurizing people is ineffectual.

Self-organized criticality also suggests that systems and organizations have an inherent propensity, through their dynamic interactions, to 'power themselves up' and move towards this critical state, just before the total shipwreck of chaos. In education this sounds remarkably like the intensification thesis (Hargreaves, 1992, 1994) and the experience of many schools, where pressure builds on the system until that system explodes: staff leave or are on stress-related absence; senior managers depart; new management structures are brought in for failing schools; new practices ensue. Whilst *something* catastrophic might have been expected (at a bifurcation point), it might have been impossible to predict what it would be (e.g. the headteacher has a heart attack, the school closes, the school has a massive injection of funds, parents protest to the government, the media closes in on the school and saves the day!).

That connectedness and self-organized criticality can lead to the Red Queen effect is charted by Lewin (1993): the Red Queen effect (from Carroll's *Alice Through the Looking Glass*) is the effect of running faster to stand still. A rabbit has to run faster to escape the fox; the fox runs faster to catch the rabbit; the rabbit runs faster to escape the fox, and so on;[4] this is the intensification thesis in nature. In schools many teachers' only reward for increased paperwork seems to be more paperwork: the more they provide the more they have to do; it is as if the paperwork they provide fuels the thirst for more paperwork – it provides more 'ammunition' for those who demand paperwork. The Red Queen effect reminds us that people do not lead isolated lives but instead are interwoven inextricably with others (Lewin, 1993: 58); this reinforces the comments earlier on the necessity for feedback (see the discussion of fitness landscapes in Chapter 7). In the example of the pile of sand in the discussion of self-organized criticality (Bak and Chen, 1991), Michaels (1995) suggests that the pile of sand would be nothing if the grains did not relate to each other and hold each other together, i.e. relationships and mutual support are the key to successful building.

As systems move toward greater complexity so new structures emerge through competition and collaboration amongst elements of the systems (Waldrop, 1992; McMaster, 1996; Cilliers, 1998). On the one hand competition for limited resources leads to new structures of self-organizing systems wherein only the fittest survive. Competition is essential for learning. On the other hand, collaboration is frequently a requirement of systems if they are to survive: if only a few elements survive in a competition the resulting structure of the system might be too simple for rich or new forms of self-organization to evolve (Cilliers, 1998: 95).

Recalling Hebb's account of learning earlier, if association is to be strengthened then this *requires* collaboration. Learning requires competition in order that the most pressing items are learnt and reinforced and the least pressing are extinguished (cf. Kauffman, 1993), and it requires collaboration so that neural networks and cell assemblies (or their macroscopic equivalents) form and are reinforced. Complex systems evolve as systems and structures are subjected to the selection pressures of specific environmental factors, be it through competition or collaboration. The increased competition between schools (and thereby the creation of 'magnet' schools and 'sink' schools) has led to strengthening partnerships between schools and parents, schools and communities, schools and local education authorities, schools and schools, schools and industry.

As new systems and structures emerge, often in unpredicted ways, so they themselves generate new environments. The argument for emergence here is that innovations and changes rarely happen in isolation, but in tandem. Take, for example, the replacement of horse-drawn technology by automobiles. Along with the demise of horse power went stabling, feeding and watering arrangements, horse services and servicing. In their place sprang up a whole new system of structures or technologies – hard road surfaces, service stations, out-of-town shopping, motels, traffic crime and new employment prospects, at a new level of emergence, with whole new networks together. This is most clearly demonstrated in the meteoric shift from industrial societies to information societies, from muscle workers to knowledge workers (Sivanandan, 1979). In schools the provision of new facilities can bring increased demand for places (Senge *et al.*, 2000: 84–5).

Emergent systems create diversity, multiplicity, heterogeneity – in short, complexity. What is being suggested here is that emergent systems can create vastly new opportunities – 'increasing returns' (Arthur, 1990) – so that to them that hath shall be given, and where one small change can effect massive change and returns, akin to the butterfly effect in chaos theory (Gleick, 1987; Stewart, 1995: 130, 143). This is the amplification effect of positive feedback.

Increasing returns support co-evolution (Kauffman, 1996: 12; Stewart, 2001) – the system affects the environment and the environment affects the system. The rise of automobiles saw the demise of saddlers, smithies, stage coaches and coaching inns, and their replacement with garages, motels, fast-food services, traffic lights, paved roads, tickets, etc. Increasing returns can be seen everywhere. For example Silicon Valley came into being because of its proximity to the major research centres at Stanford and Berkeley, with their supply of highly skilled workers. Silicon Valley emerged; nobody ordered it (Tetenbaum, 1998).

In schools a clear example of increasing returns is in the nature of school choice; children from wealthy homes enjoy a range of advantages, for example parents can move house into wealthier areas with 'better' schools where there is the opportunity for their children to receive education alongside other positively motivated students and teachers; there is increased opportunity and ability to undertake a range of educationally worthwhile extra-curricular activities; access to greater educational resources may be improved; there is an opportunity for high take-up of the academic knowledge that many schools offer.

This latter is well documented by Bourdieu's (1976) cultural capital thesis, which argues that students' economic and social capital, translated into cultural capital, ensures differential take-up of the knowledge that schools formally offer, in principle, to all. Already-privileged students possess the wherewithal, the cultural capital and *habitus* (e.g. background, positive attitude to school, supportive and educated parents, a home background of learning, access to books and educational stimulation) to take up what the school offers, and so are advantaged in comparison to those for whom school represents an alien culture. Increasing returns also underpins the notion of 'magnet schools' in which successful schools attract better teachers, better students and better resources than do 'sink schools'.

Schools as complex adaptive systems

Schools exhibit several features of complex adaptive systems, for example:[5]

- they require organization and have distinguishing structures and features that change over time;
- they are dynamical and unpredictable organizations;
- they are nonlinear organizations: causes do not always straightforwardly produce effects (the industrialist Senge (1990: 57) commented that yesterday's solutions are today's problems!); it is difficult to infer causes from effects or outcomes;
- small changes can have massive effects;
- they are complex, complicated and constantly changing;
- they are a human service and rely on people;
- relationships are highly important in their work (echoing Vygotsky's, 1978,

often quoted maxim that all higher order thinking is socially transmitted and learnt);

- they have to adapt in response to macro- and micro-societal change;
- the environments (external and internal) in which they operate are largely unpredictable and mutable;
- they have to maintain 'relative autonomy' from the wider society, i.e. they have to position themselves in relation to the wider society, deciding where they wish to be in relation to it (e.g. Cilliers, 1998: 99);
- they exert pressure on their members;
- they have a range of methods of communication and rely on communication and effective networking;
- the synergy of their several parts is greater than any individual or smaller combination of individuals;
- new properties emerge at every level of the organization (Lissack, 2000: 8);
- they are learning organizations;
- they have a proclivity to instability and operate at the edge of chaos.

The problem is that many schools as they are currently construed are, *par excellence*, modernistic institutions, displaying all the features of such institutions set out earlier. Even the language of discussion is imbued with metaphors from a bygone age (Hartwell, 1995: 2). We speak of the *machinery* of governance, of *re-engineering* schools (West-Burnham and Davies, 1996), and metaphors of control, order, structure, consistency and uniformity abound (Morrison, 1989). Wheatley (1999) comments that the whole notion of 're-engineering' institutions is fundamentally misconceived, as it is entirely mechanistic and dehumanized; rather, she suggests, institutions need to be 'de-engineered', i.e. rendered human (Finley, 1994: 2).

Metaphors of engineering assume that people are insentient and uncreative; naturally people will resist this (April, 1997: 63; Katz, 1997: 20). Organizations have to 'unlearn' mechanistic, engineering models (Fisher and Fisher, 1998: 105; April *et al.*, 2000: 54–5). An ideal organization does not conform most fittingly to a machine; it is organic, dynamic, humanistic and sentient; it has a heart. As Youngblood (1998: 2) observes: machines break down whilst people creatively evolve. The language of machines (Fisher and Fisher, 1998: 112), which comprises 'redesign', 'structure', 'drive', 'mechanisms', 'steer' and 're-engineer', has to be replaced by human-centred language: 'nourish', 'adapt', 'nurture', 'grow', 'cultivate' and 'organisms'.

What is needed, perhaps, is a paradigm shift to countenance new forms for schools in an emerging new world. Such a move places a heavy responsibility on leadership; the leaders of the schools are in the vanguard of changing schools to become complex adaptive systems or complex responsive processes. The remainder of this book suggests the tasks of leadership here.

The key areas identified from complexity theory for school leadership so far are:

- the elements of schools as self-organizing learning systems;
- the school and the environment;

- emergence;
- positive fitness landscapes in schools;
- self-organized criticality;
- communication and information;
- relationships, connectedness and networked structures;
- new forms of leadership.

The subsequent chapters of the book address these key elements. In looking at the implications for school leadership which are taken up later in the book, and by way of summary, one can suggest several issues to be raised in connection with each of these key elements of complexity theory and leadership. For each issue several questions can be raised which will be addressed in subsequent chapters, for example:

The elements of schools as complex self-organizing learning systems

- What are the key elements, structures and 'cell assemblies' (groups) in schools which contribute to their self-organization?
- How can disequilibrium be introduced, supported, managed and led in the school to produce new forms of organization?
- What is the role of information management in the process of creating and coping with disequilibrium?
- What needs to be put out of balance if disequilibrium and its consequent learning is to occur?
- How can schools become organizationally intelligent?
- How can the existing/new/emergent structures be identified in the school which are important for self-organization and emergence?
- What has to compete with and collaborate with what in the school in order for the organization to learn?
- How will the competition between and collaboration amongst elements of the school be managed and led so that organizational learning is promoted?
- How can the 'cell assemblies' for organizational learning be strengthened in the school?
- How can schools become more agile, flexible, adaptable and capable of changing?
- What are the 'knock-on' effects of new structures, forms and technologies on schools?
- How can schools become autopoietic, i.e. to develop, manage and sustain their own identity and fitness landscapes?
- What are the leadership tasks, roles, styles and processes in this area?

The school and the environment

- What are the internal and external environments with which the school must interact?

- How can the internal structures of the organization be changed in order to respond to the environment and to influence the environment?
- How can schools become more open to the environment, and how can these moves be managed and led?
- How can schools be enabled and supported to adapt to changing environments and to change their environments?
- How can schools sense and scan their environments and anticipate the future?
- How can schools become nimble and adept at change?
- How can schools receive, process and interpret messages and signals from their environments?
- How can schools restructure themselves in light of the information received from their environments?
- How fit is the school to cope with change, flexibility and adaptability?
- What are the leadership tasks, roles, styles and processes in this area?

Emergence

- What existing structures can be utilized to facilitate emergence in the school?
- What new structures have to be established in order to facilitate emergence?
- How can emergence be managed and led in the school?
- What are the simple elements that must interact in the schools to create new self-organized systems?
- What has to be transformed for the new school?
- What are the simple local rules/protocols/procedures/structures in the school which can give rise to new forms/structures/contents/procedures for schools?
- How can a balance be struck between too few and too many interacting elements in schools, too few leading to impoverished organizations and too many leading to inertia?
- What is the nature of strategic planning for an unpredictable future?
- How can schools cope with unpredictability and modify plans in the light of emerging information?
- How can schools anticipate the future?
- What are the conditions for emergence in the school, how can these be identified, developed, supported and sustained?
- What are the platforms for emergence in the school and what is the role of leadership in developing these?
- How can the school learn?
- What is required to feed and sustain the school as a learning organization?
- What auto-catalyzes the school?
- How can leaders catalyze change and innovation?
- How can increasing returns be developed and managed in the school?
- What are the leadership tasks, roles, styles and processes in this area?

Positive fitness landscapes in the school

- What is the fitness landscape of the school?
- What constitutes the peaks in the school (what are they, e.g. departments, individuals, subjects, achievements, etc.)?
- How close are the peaks to each other (tight or loose coupling)?
- What are the highest peaks in the school?
- How effective are the roads/passes/communications in the school?
- What are the support structures in the school to manage the scaling of the peaks?
- How well matched are the inhabitants of the landscape to their area of the landscape?
- What are the leadership tasks, roles, styles and processes in this area?

Self-organized criticality

- How can the move to self-organized criticality be led?
- How can self-organized criticality be identified in school? What are its signs?
- How can school staff be sustained at the level of self-organized criticality?
- How can self-organized criticality become a creative force in the school – imagining and realizing diverse possibilities?
- How can self-organized criticality be prevented from tipping over into chaos or over-intensification in the school?
- What are the leadership tasks, roles, styles and processes in this area?

Communication and information

- What feedback can be given and to whom in the organization?
- What feedback loops exist in the school and how can these be extended and utilized?
- How can communication become multi-channelled, multi-directional and open?
- How can the contents of communications be disseminated, and to whom?
- How can the communication systems be managed in the school?
- How can a balance be struck between too little and too much feedback?
- How can the memory/knowledge/information of the school be generated, distributed, stored, accessed, retrieved, shared and used? How can the efficiency of these be ensured?
- How can the memory of the school be managed (i.e. what should the school remember and what should it forget or disregard)?
- What are the leadership tasks, roles, styles and processes in this area?

Relationships, connectedness and networked structures

- How can relationships and interactions be developed, facilitated and supported between people, 'cell assemblies' (groups) and sections?

- How can schools become networked/matrix organizations (within and externally)?
- How can networking sustain schools in an unpredictable environment?
- How can schools become more person-centred?
- What are the connections that have to be made in the school to facilitate self-organization? How can this be led?
- What are the leadership tasks, roles, styles and processes in this area?

New forms of leadership

- What are the new leadership tasks/roles/behaviours/styles for the emergent, self-organizing school as a complex adaptive system?
- How can distributed leadership be ensured (i.e. so that leaders are throughout the organization, not simply in the head teacher's office)?
- How can leaders energize the school?
- How can leaders facilitate the emergence of a new complex, adaptive self-organizing system?
- What is the nature of leadership in a decentralized, empowered organization?
- How can leaders emerge and new models of leadership emerge?
- What are the leadership tasks, roles, styles and processes in this area?

It can be seen that the final question in each subsection here is the same, drawing together the issues and to ask their significance for leadership. These issues are addressed in detail throughout the remaining chapters, and the focus throughout will be on determining the implications that the issues have for effective school leadership. The questions above are introductory; the remaining chapters set out key elements of each of the topics covered.

Figure 1.4 takes these elements and converts them into self-assessment questions which leaders and schools can use in considering the extent to which they embody central elements of complexity theory. Clearly these are at a high level of generality. They have been placed on a five-point rating scale; simple frequencies can be calculated, which will enable an analysis of strengths and weaknesses to be conducted.

Complexity theory enables us to: (a) regard schools from a dynamic rather than static perspective; (b) understand how schools adapt to external and internal contexts; and (c) find effective ways to benefit from individual creativity and innovation within a school-wide framework (cf. Santa Fe Center for Emergent Strategies, 1999).

Figure 1.4 A self-assessment questionnaire to judge the school's fitness for complexity.

| *1 = very little* | *2 = a little* | *3 = quite a lot* | *4 = a lot* | *5 = a very great deal* |

Question	[1]	[2]	[3]	[4]	[5]
1 How far is the school a complex adaptive system?	[ ]	[ ]	[ ]	[ ]	[ ]
2 How far is the school able to cope with unexpected or unpredictable change?	[ ]	[ ]	[ ]	[ ]	[ ]
3 How positive are the interpersonal relationships in the school?	[ ]	[ ]	[ ]	[ ]	[ ]
4 How far does the school enable groups to organize themselves?	[ ]	[ ]	[ ]	[ ]	[ ]
5 How rapid is the school's responsiveness to change?	[ ]	[ ]	[ ]	[ ]	[ ]
6 How comfortable is the school with unpredictability?	[ ]	[ ]	[ ]	[ ]	[ ]
7 How open is the school to the external environment?	[ ]	[ ]	[ ]	[ ]	[ ]
8 How far has the school moved away from a command-and-control style of management?	[ ]	[ ]	[ ]	[ ]	[ ]
9 How far has the school moved away from hierarchical models of management?	[ ]	[ ]	[ ]	[ ]	[ ]
10 How far does the school rely on networks and groups?	[ ]	[ ]	[ ]	[ ]	[ ]
11 How far is order imposed in the school?	[ ]	[ ]	[ ]	[ ]	[ ]
12 How far is order emergent in the school?	[ ]	[ ]	[ ]	[ ]	[ ]
13 How far does the school rely on feedback – internal and external?	[ ]	[ ]	[ ]	[ ]	[ ]
14 How far is the school self-organizing?	[ ]	[ ]	[ ]	[ ]	[ ]
15 How far is the school able to influence its external environment?	[ ]	[ ]	[ ]	[ ]	[ ]
16 How rich is the feedback that the school gains from its environment?	[ ]	[ ]	[ ]	[ ]	[ ]
17 How rich is the feedback that the school gives to its environment?	[ ]	[ ]	[ ]	[ ]	[ ]
18 How successful is the school in learning from its experiences?	[ ]	[ ]	[ ]	[ ]	[ ]
19 How connected is the school to its several environments?	[ ]	[ ]	[ ]	[ ]	[ ]
20 How far is control/decision making distributed throughout the school?	[ ]	[ ]	[ ]	[ ]	[ ]
21 How easy is it for the school to cope with the departure of teaching staff?	[ ]	[ ]	[ ]	[ ]	[ ]
22 How easy is it for new staff to be inducted in the ways of working in the school?	[ ]	[ ]	[ ]	[ ]	[ ]
23 How far is the school moving, rather than static?	[ ]	[ ]	[ ]	[ ]	[ ]
24 How capable is the school at identifying and solving problems in its internal and external environments?	[ ]	[ ]	[ ]	[ ]	[ ]
25 How collaborative are the groups and networks within and outside the school?	[ ]	[ ]	[ ]	[ ]	[ ]

Part II

The practice of complexity in schools

2 Schools and self-organization for complexity

Chapter 1 suggested that complexity theory underlines the importance of self-organization, and that self-organization appears, autocatalytically, through the interaction of its component elements. The task of this chapter is to tease out implications of this principle for schools, for example how to:

- develop and sustain self-organization and emergence, and ensure that components of the school catalyze each other and are regenerative;
- make schools adaptable, flexible, open and differentiated systems;
- enable schools to adopt flatter management and flexible internal boundaries;
- develop the person-centred school;
- develop networking and connectedness within the school;
- develop self-organizing groups and teams for emergence to occur in the school;
- increase people's motivation for involvement in self-organizing groups;
- develop the role of the leader in addressing these issues in the self-organizing school.

This chapter will focus on the *internal* aspects of self-organization, leaving for Chapter 5 the *external* pressures for self-organization and the nature of the internal response to them. Further, Chapter 6 will address the issue of *feedback* in schools.

This chapter argues that, informed by complexity theory, schools should be regarded as self-organizing, complex, emergent, nonlinear organizations, within which different forms of differentiation occur (horizontal, vertical, spatial). Even though horizontal networks embody complexity theory, the matter is not simply a structural one for school leaders, i.e. setting up structures and watching them 'roll out' to a prefigured future. Rather, complexity theory sees the future as uncertain and emergent, and the school as a tangle of micropolitics which affect the directions of development. The leadership task becomes the management of the micropolitics and of moving the members of the school from a competitive, secretive, isolationist and procedures-driven mentality to a collaborative, interdependent, group- and team-based network, with devolved decision making and its accompanying responsibility and accountability. To achieve this is a matter of commitment and group development, in which motivation, incentives and rewards play an important role. This agenda requires the leadership of the school to consider the balance of specialist and generalist teachers, and the degree of loose or tight coupling within the school. Running through the discussion is the need for communication to feed and nurture interdependence.

Foundations of self-organization in the school

It was suggested in Chapter 1 that self-organization emerges from within an institution; it is neither imposed nor mandated; 'order is for free'. Each system is *already* organized (Kelly and Allison, 1999: 33). Hence the management of self-organization must commence with the identification of the existing self-organization if it is to be effective (see Chapter 7 on fitness landscapes).

It is important to identify the components of the self-organizing school, its individuals, groups (formal and informal), departments, faculties, cross-school groups, the nature of the interdependencies and interactions between them, and their principles, models, rules and behaviours (Sherman and Schultz, 1998: 7). This is because changes in any of the latter impact on the infrastructure of the organization.

There is a need, then, to identify the number of groups which exist in the school (for example, Wickens, 1995; Kauffman, 1993, 1995 and Marion, 1999: 105, give a rule of thumb which says that it is the square root of the number of participants in the organization). So, for a school of around eighty staff, one would expect the number of naturally forming groups to be around nine. Attempts at self-organization should respect the naturally forming groups as well as the more formally structured groups or subsystems. As West (1999: 191) remarks, there is a natural tendency in organizations towards informal groups, and indeed schools cannot prevent the formation of informal groups, like it or not.

It is important to take into account, in planning, the micropolitics of the school, and to work with it rather than against it. If people cannot work together then why force them to unnecessarily? Careful leadership is acutely aware of informal groups as well as formal groupings, will look for informal groupings and at their membership, and will be aware that informal groupings can exert stronger effects than many formal groups (Hoyle, 1986). Indeed Wheatley (1999: 45) suggests that 'critical mass' is less important than 'critical connections'.

Micropolitics is an inevitable as well as advisable consideration in the school (Lindle, 1999: 171). The micropolitics of the school embraces informal networks within the school and between the school and its external environment (Iannaccone, 1975). Micropolitics concerns itself with relationships, interactions and dialogue (Mawhinney, 1999: 162), key features of complexity theory. One can contrast the formal side of schools with their informal side thus (cf. Hoyle, 1986):

Formal	*Informal/micropolitical*
Goals	Interests
Authority	Influence

Departments	Coalitions
Institution	Groups
Procedures	Strategies
Acting	Mobilizing

Mawhinney (1999: 168) argues that micropolitics is concerned more with conflict than consensus, competition rather than collaboration, bargaining and persuasion, influence and coalitions and, significantly, suggests that the power of the micropolitics of the organization can be significantly greater than formal power in the school. West (1999: 193) suggests that informal groupings tend to serve a purpose of inhibiting, frustrating or resisting, whilst formal groupings are used to initiate or develop. As argued in Chapter 1, resistance, deviance and disagreement are all valuable spurs to change, perturbation, self-organization and emergence (Fullan, 2001); we need antithesis as well as thesis in order to reach synthesis.

Marion (1999: 88–9) suggests that self-organizing institutions also need to consider their forms of *differentiation*. *Spatial differentiation* refers to the geographical situation within the organization – its arrangement of units, buildings and rooms. Most schools have shared spaces, with specialist facilities and private rooms (the headteacher's office, technicians' rooms, administrative offices, staff rooms), i.e. there is not a clear match between spatial differentiation and tasks. This argues, perhaps, for an audit of rooms, their usage in the school and the location of resources for teaching. Just as important, perhaps, it suggests the need for attention to timetabling for room usage, and indeed for movement between rooms. This is a particular problem for schools with dispersed/split sites. This is not a new phenomenon: the balance of dedicated specialist rooms (e.g. laboratories, gymnasia, music rooms, IT rooms) to generalist rooms has long exercised school planners.

Vertical differentiation refers to the number of tiers or layers of management; the suggestion is to reduce the number to an absolute minimum, replacing a hierarchy with a 'flatocracy' of networked units. The potential for this already exists in schools by dint of their departmental structures. The larger the size of the school, the greater is the chance of a bureaucracy. Perhaps they are inevitable in larger organizations (though Jaques, 1990 argues for their desirability on the grounds of management abilities, responsibilities, accountability and efficiency).

The number of layers of an organization might increase, commensurate with its size, reaching a maximum of maybe seven (Blau and Schoenherr, 1971). This is a difficult matter, for not only does it suggest that schools could re-examine their organizational levels (e.g. department heads, faculty heads, pastoral heads, senior managers) to reduce them to a minimum, but that this needs to be balanced with the need for a promotional ladder, career development structure and reward system. It also requires careful attention to lines of accountability in the school.

This is not necessarily to suggest the removal of hierarchy, as hierarchy can move a school forwards more rapidly than a networked matrix (see Chapter 7 and Stewart, 2001). Complexity theory is not *intrinsically* against hierarchy (Stacey, 1992: 180), though the frequent alliance of hierarchy and command-and-control mentalities is antithetical to complexity theory. Stacey (2001) argues that power and constraint are realistic boundary delimiters in complexity theory. Hierarchies may be essential for short-term efficiency and stability, whereas informal networks are more needed for change and development.

Horizontal differentiation refers to how tasks are divided and the number of people and operations involved in achieving the tasks. This is difficult in schools, as teachers have to have a more holistic understanding and operation of their tasks, including, for example, expertise in pedagogy, curriculum planning and assessment, child development, psychology, relations with a range of people, policy and decision making, classroom management and organizational management and welfare issues. What is being suggested is that there is no straightforward match between a single task and a single teacher; rather the situation is one teacher, many tasks.

Horizontal differentiation tends to fragment and separate tasks whilst vertical differentiation requires them to be co-ordinated or integrated. Indeed one of the advantages of increasing vertical organization is its capacity for creating an 'aligned organization' (Wickens, 1995; Coleman, 1999), with all networks and players moving in the same direction. In this sense vertical organization may help to produce fractal self-similarity from chaos theory (Stewart, 1990), where individual elements of the networks reproduce the features of each other, albeit in microcosm (e.g. the shape of each leaf of a fern is a miniature replication of the whole fern and the shape of each part of each fern's leaf is a miniature replication of the whole leaf). Wheatley (1999) suggests that fractal organization is characterized by adherence, across units of the network, to a common set of guiding principles. This, of course, may be too closed, teleological, controlled and deterministic than complexity theory would support.

Teamwork, here, is less about units within schools doing the same things; it is more about them moving in the same direction. That this suggests the need for a shared common purpose or mission becomes apparent here. Lewin and Regine (2000: 253–4) coin the expression 'the buttercup effect' to describe the processes at work here: a buttercup sends out runners along the ground which, in turn, root and develop their own flowers, whilst still being attached to the former buttercup. There is self-similarity between buttercups but they are also autonomous and have their own lives; the complex organization is the whole series of linked buttercups. This is the essence of the fractal school, wherein teams within the school see how their work fits in, and contributes to, the work and shared values of the rest of the school. Each team possesses characteristics of the whole organization which, clearly, requires an articulation of the values which are driving the organization. Indeed Merry (1998) suggests that functioning at the edge of chaos is achieved better in an organization with a fractal networked structure. That said, self-similarity of groups argues against the diversity of complexity theory.

The key issue from the discussion of horizontal differentiation, perhaps, is the need to regard schools as networked institutions. If flexibility is required in a complex, self-organizing school then this, in turn, suggests decentralization, distributed decision making and control, and keeping the number of prescribed procedures and regulations to the minimum. The move is from a pyramidal organization to a web (Figure 2.1).

This, of course, might argue against regarding the school as a high reliability organization which is driven by standardized procedures (Bierly and Spender, 1995; Stringfield, 1997). This is not to argue that schools should be empires, anarchies or balkanized departments (a fragmented school where the whole is less than the sum of the parts) (Hargreaves, 1994). Rather it argues for 'fitness for purpose': there are some schools where reliability through procedures and consistency of practice and behaviour is a powerful device for raising achievement (bureaucracies lift the trailing edge of organizations to an acceptable minimum) (Lieberman, 1990), to provide a foundation from which to move toward a more open-ended, self-organizing institution.

This might be the case for 'failing schools', where the absence of procedures or consistency contributes to their weakness. Here high reliability might be a useful concept, in that it involves (Reynolds, 1995; Stringfield, 1997: 152–7):

- massive investment in training;
- detailed identification and rectification of weaknesses;
- a limited number of explicit goals;
- standard operations which are applied consistently;
- adequate resources for the school's operations;
- the alignment of management, administrative, curricular, pedagogic and cultural subsystems towards achievement of the school's goals;
- a blend of centralization and controlled delegation;
- efficient and extensive communication;
- extensive backup facilities and knowledge about the operations;
- close monitoring of activities and people.

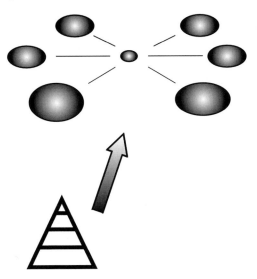

Figure 2.1 Moving from a pyramidal to a web structure.

For other schools the procedures-driven mentality undermines their excellence (and bureaucracies can undermine excellence) (Lieberman, 1990). This is not to argue for incoherent disparity within schools; rather it is to take seriously Wickens's (1987: 95) point that teamwork does not rely on people replicating tasks (the weakness of self-similarity), but on everybody moving in the same direction towards the same aims and objectives. That this long-range determinism sits uncomfortably with complexity theory has to be recognized.

The self-organizing complex school will be built on units (e.g. subject groups, pastoral groups, year groups, development groups, whole school management groups) which are autonomous, networked and connected, with rich communication. Indeed, using the analogy of Reynolds's 'Boids' from Chapter 1, Lewin and Regine (2000: 296–7) suggest that there are three lessons to be learned from the Boids:

1   Stay close to each other (with mutual trust, respect and the opportunity to influence each other, learning to be a team player).
2   Keep up (ensure that each person has the opportunity to be the leader).
3   Avoid collisions (by avoiding obstacles, by pooling resources and support).

In a school, this argues for close communication, staff development and being proactive respectively. This is, perhaps, platitudinous. The task of the leader is to identify how these might be realized more effectively, for example by addressing questions such as:

•   how to render communication unavoidable and central to the organization;
•   how to ensure that people have the opportunity to work with each other, and that those who wish to work with each other are able to do so (e.g. through fluid, inclusive, cross-boundary team membership) (Jackson, 2000: 64);
•   how to ensure that curriculum integration is managed through teamwork;
•   how to ensure that problems are anticipated and solved collaboratively;
•   how to pool and access resources.

These factors are designed to ensure that the human side – the *people* subsystem – features just as strongly as the technical and administrative subsystems (Leavitt, 1964) in the school; their development is a leadership responsibility. Jackson (2000), himself a headteacher, provides an interesting example of this in a 'school improvement group'. This group is led by two co-leaders and breaks down into 'trios' of staff (*ibid*: 64), each trio being involved in its own activities of finding out about the work of the school and identifying areas for improvement, as a result of which partnerships are formed for development and improvement which involve others in the school and outside, and the group provides ongoing feedback to itself and to others (Rules One and Two of the Boids example). All staff of the school are involved, regardless of level, and the group is mutually supportive of its members and communicates internally and externally extensively (Rules One, Two and Three of the Boids example). It looks for suggestions and provides development activities for the members of the school (Rule Three of the Boids example).

These principles suggest the possibility of rotating school leaders and devolved and distributed leadership, which will be discussed in Chapter 3. They also suggest the need for support mechanisms, which in turn rely on developed interpersonal relations, i.e. schools as human, people-centred organizations.

Networks, groups and teams for emerging self-organization

The ICT department of a secondary school in the UK is responsible for serving and servicing all the other departments, faculties and administration of the school. To do this requires great sensitivity on the part of the ICT staff, as they have to sense and respond to differing needs, personalities, levels of seniority, demands and micropolitics in the school, and all within budgetary constraints that set limits to the scope of their operations. To accomplish this, the head of the ICT department places high on her agenda the fostering of positive working relations with all the groups in the school, and she convenes weekly meetings with the ICT staff, at which they share their feedback on the implications of their work for other members of the team.

At one meeting the ICT team indicates that the mathematics department requires additional technical support, that the business department needs more up-to-date software, that the art department's Internet connections to museums and galleries are very slow (particularly when calling up pictures), and that this slows down the internal network at times of peak usage. Decisions are taken to link more closely the work of, and ICT support for, the mathematics and business departments (which will require the two departments to collaborate more), and to ask the art department to indicate those times when it will need extended Internet access, so that other departments restrict their usage, i.e. so that internal communication and collaboration between the departments (which affects their planning and teaching) is increased. Networking is crucial.

Networking and the development of collaboration between groups, teams and departments is a sensitive, human affair, not simply a planning exercise. It is commonplace to read that trying to create an aligned organization with a group of individual professionals whose values may differ, and within an organization whose aims are heterogeneous (like a school), is like trying to herd cats. The strength of a school is its tolerance of internal difference, not its ability to produce teachers who are robotic clones. The task is to create interdependence of the diverse aspects of school life and populations. Leadership concerns boundary setting and maintenance (Fisher and Fisher, 1998: 197), fostering networks and connections, interdependence and collaboration.

Within different components of organizations, the key feature of the self-organizing, complex institution is *interdependence*. People fulfil a range of different tasks in schools; they sit on different committees and teams. A major task of the leaders, therefore, is to attend to relationships and interpersonal communication, teamwork and the fostering of positive communication within the network. There are several formal networks within schools, for example:

- the *departmental* network (usually by subject);
- the *pastoral* network (usually by school class and the pastoral team in the school);
- the *faculty* network (where inter-departmental discussions take place and where faculty heads meet to discuss cross-faculty issues);
- the *whole school curriculum planning* network (which is separate from departmental or subject planning and which sets out overarching curriculum issues in the school);
- the *monitoring* and *assessment* network (where teachers have responsibility for the conduct of the formal and informal assessment requirements);
- the *age group* network (where teachers have responsibility for whole age groups or phases, for example a Key Stage in the UK, or a primary phase, or a sixth form phase);
- the *management* network (where issues concerning leadership, management, decision making, policy and strategy are discussed);
- the *school improvement* network;
- the *external relations* network;
- the *information technology* and *knowledge management* network.

Teams may be 'natural work teams' (brought together through the everyday work), 'cross-functional teams' (whose members are drawn from across the 'natural work teams'), 'small project teams' (for temporary tasks) and 'special purpose teams' (whose work is similar in its temporary nature to the work of the small project team, but whose projects are bigger and whose work draws on several 'natural work teams') (Fisher and Fisher, 1998: 50–5). Teachers are normally members of several networks simultaneously. Whilst this facilitates communication, the fact that teachers are members of several networks at once requires clear communication lines to be established and used, and accountability to be clarified (complexity theory does not mean the abandonment of accountability). The recognition that teachers belong to several networks exacts its price, for it suggests that planning for school development needs to look at the impact of developments on all the networks, for example a change in the assessment aspects of a teacher's work will have 'knock-on' effects on her curriculum planning, use of information technology, age-group planning, and so on; units do not exist in isolation. The question then becomes: 'what effects will this proposal have on the other activities of teachers?'

If the school is to emerge and develop most effectively and smoothly, then the networks can become the platforms or scaffolding for that emergence; hence it is essential for adequate information sharing between the networks to be complemented by careful task specification of the networks, and the prevention of overload (i.e. to prevent self-organized criticality from breaking into chaos).

Networking relies on teamwork and group development. The rise of interest in teamwork and group development coincides with the emergence of complexity theory (e.g. Katzenbach and Smith, 1993); but perhaps it is no coincidence. As Tetenbaum (1998) suggests, self-directed teams are an element of self-organization.

Morrison (1998: 182–3), emphasizing the human and interpersonal aspects of teams, defines a team as

> 'a group of people with a common objective, whose members possess different areas of expertise, skills, personalities and abilities that complement one another, and who are committed to working together cooperatively on a common, shared task and a common purpose … A team is aware that it is a team and individuals work towards team cohesiveness and positive interpersonal relations'.

It is a social group and not just a device for getting tasks done. Membership of a team and a group is a matter of commitment and positive interpersonal relations, not just of procedure. Some teams and groups are formal, others are informal; some are permanent some are transitory, for example (Table 2.1).

Formal groups, West (1999: 192) argues, are those through which the work of the school is achieved, e.g. planning, resourcing, organizing, coordinating, administering and problem solving. Informal relationships are just as significant. Teachers seek fulfilment through relationships, not just work (*ibid*: 191).

It is commonplace to see informal groups and cliques established in schools, indeed in the case of large schools with several staffrooms, members frequently segregate themselves along informal lines and appropriate their own staffroom territory. As with the discussions of differentiation above, such groups/cliques might be 'horizontal' (comprising members of equal status), 'vertical' (comprising members of different levels in a hierarchy) or 'mixed' (*ibid*: 191). The task of school leaders, aware of territoriality and group identity (and strong group identity might lead to competition between, or hostility to, other groups, *ibid*: 193), might be to promote collaborative, inter-group relations.

In informal groups, West avers, leaders are those who establish or articulate the norms or identifying behaviours or attitudes of the group. Membership of groups, particularly of informal groups, satisfies several motives which are largely person-related rather than task-related (Riches, 1993; Morrison, 1998: 191; West, 1999: 192–3):

- affiliation needs (opportunities to socialize);
- security needs (emotional support);

Table 2.1 Formal, informal, temporary and permanent groups

	Temporary	*Permanent*
Formal	Specific project/ team	Departments
	Task force	Senior management team
	Development team	Permanent committees
	Select committees	External relations groups
Informal	Induction partner	Friendship groups/cliques
	Mentor/support	Professional associations and
	Coalition/alliance	relationships
	Social meeting groups	Intra-departmental groups

- esteem needs (promoting self-respect through positive feedback);
- self-fulfilment needs (achieving potential);
- reduction of tension (through mutual support);
- sense of identity (and status that this brings);
- increased job satisfaction (through a sense of belonging and involvement);
- commitment to the organization;
- task accomplishment.

The informal group offers both psychological and interpersonal support. It can be the hotbed of resistance which, as Fullan (2001) suggests, can be an important catalyst for change (see Chapter 1). West (1999: 192) makes it clear that the demarcation between formal and informal groupings is unclear – they impact on each other; micropolitics impacts on formal as well as informal groupings. Hence networking and teamworking have to take account of the informal as well as the formal groupings in the school. For example, this might imply that leaders of formal groups might be those who are informal leaders, as they already have followers. Further, it suggests that both informal and formal groups have to concern themselves with the personalities, emotions, group dynamics and leadership behaviours of their participants (cf. Stacey, 1992: 120).

For a network to operate effectively it can learn from group and team development studies and, indeed, Leonard *et al.* (1998: 294) reinforce the notion that teams need to be *developed* before they embark upon too many tasks. Youngblood (1997: 183–5) suggests that the leadership requirements for leading teams through change, transitions and development place heavy emphasis on nurturing relationships, ensuring a rich flow of information, promoting ownership and communication of both fact and feeling (*ibid*: 262). For him, the development of a successful relationship relies on a commitment to make the relationship and the shared vision succeed, trust and empathy, recognition and respect for differences, self-disclosure, communication and peace making.

The frequently cited example of team development (e.g. Robbins and Finley, 1998b) by Tuckman (1965) derives from a meta-analysis of patient groups in clinical settings. Even though this might confound the applicability of the findings to non-clinical settings, nevertheless, taking the example as a critical case, i.e. bearing all the hallmarks of other institutions but with heightened sensitivity, it is possible to identify the link between relationship forming and task performance in group and teamwork.

Tuckman identified four stages of group self-organization, itself an example of emergence, perhaps. Stage One – the *forming* stage – is characterized by testing and dependence (p. 386). Members discover the boundaries of acceptability in the group by developing interpersonal relationships. Orientation to task is minimal; Robbins and Finley (1998b: 42) suggest that, at this stage, the team faces the critical decision of deciding how to decide! The leadership task becomes one of moving the group towards establishing positive interrelations in order for consensus on 'deciding how to decide' to emerge, and for really developing trust between participants (Tschannen-Moran, 2000).

Stage Two – the *storming* stage – reflects the fact that, as the barriers of politeness fall in the group, hostility and intra-group difference surface: trial by fire. Emergence for self-organization can be painful. Stress is high, and leadership, therefore, should be about conflict management and stress management and reduction. Storming should be seen as a positive sign rather than a problem, for it suggests that the individuality of people is emerging and the nature of power in the group (or indeed its leadership) is becoming important. Indeed Fullan (1991) suggests that conflict is inevitable if change is to occur. Participants invest emotions in the group activities, which is an important factor in building commitment (discussed later). Task accomplishment may be minimal at this stage.

Stage Three – the *norming* stage – is characterized by the development of group feeling, cohesion and consensus, i.e. self-organization. Cohesion and consensus, then, are achieved through the surfacing and working-through of disagreement and conflict rather than imposed, 'contrived collegiality' (Hargreaves, 1994). Differences between participants are accepted and the commitment to the group's success *qua* group/team is strong. Participants focus their emotional energy less on disagreeing with each other and more on working together collaboratively to complete a task. Here, at last, are the beginnings of task achievement in self-organization. Tuckman (*op. cit.*) indicates that a characteristic of this stage is the extended sharing of information – distributed knowledge.

Stage Four – *performing* – is where the task is accomplished and the group/team becomes a problem-solving network, both at optimum performance level and optimum interpersonal relationships. With unconscious foresight, perhaps, Tuckman writes that this stage sees the '*emergence* of solution' (p. 387) [my italics]. Role behaviour settles and contributes towards task achievement, and 'interpersonal structure becomes the tool of task activities' (p. 396).

These stages can be represented as shown in Table 2.2.

Each stage brings problems; indeed, a group or team might regress at any stage, and it may be necessary to re-enter previous stages. Problems and solutions can be set out as shown in Table 2.3.

In a later paper, Tuckman and Jensen (1977) added the final stage of *adjourning*, when the group's or team's work is complete. Here the focus shifts from task

Table 2.2 Leaders' tasks in stages of team development

	Forming	*Storming*	*Norming*	*Performing*
Interpersonal relationships	Finding boundaries	Challenging behaviours	Achieving consensus	Harnessing consensus
Task achievement	Very limited; deciding how to decide	Limited; challenging how to decide	More extensive; sharing for achievement	Completed; using energies and teamwork to achieve task
Leader's task	Building relationships and setting clear agendas, building trust	Conflict management; role clarification; building trust	Providing feedback; pressing for task achievement	Providing feedback; celebrating achievement

Table 2.3 Leaders' problem solving in team development

Stage	Problems	How to Address Them
Forming	Perceptions of each other/task	Brainstorming
	Dynamics of team	Open-endedness
	Micropolitics of team	Opening up to each other
	Status of members	Negotiating status through discussion
	Trust-building	Building informal relationships
	Prior experiences of members	Sharing experiences
	Clarifying roles	Role allocation
Storming	Conflict	Constant clarification of roles
	Insecurity	Mutual support
	Negative reactions	Sharing anxieties and talking
	Confrontation	Conflict management
Norming	Fluidity of roles	Re-evaluating roles to manage them
	Complacency	Feedback, presenting new challenges
	Free-sharing	Understanding of roles and tasks
Performing	Complacency	Greater autonomy and feedback
	Knowing when to stop	Re-form the group

to socio-emotional factors, and the group or team disbands. What is important here is that self-organization emerges not at the start of bringing people together, but after a while – it spontaneously (even though with difficulty, perhaps) achieves the 'norming' stage when the circumstances and conditions are propitious.

Tuckman's work regards group development in a quasi-linear fashion, whilst Banet (1976) sees linear development of groups as only one of three models. In a helical model he describes the development of groups in terms of increasing deepening of relationships in the groups over time, and in the cyclical model the focus is sharply on the present, with several perspectives circling around the group.

Cacioppe (1999: 325) reports research which indicates that groups do not develop in a simple or universal sequence of stages. Rather, he suggests, groups work in 'punctuated equilibrium'; by this he means that the normal tendency for many groups is towards inertia which is punctuated by explosions of activity (see also Cohen and Stewart, 1995: 333–4, who discuss gradual changes with occasional larger changes). The first meeting of the group often sets up its general direction, general assumptions and behaviours for achieving the task. These, Cacioppe argues, remain relatively intact for the first half of the group's life. He reports one universal law: the transition from inertia to activity occurs at the same point in the group's life span – halfway between the first meeting of the group and its official deadline to complete the task (pp. 325–6), irrespective of whether the group has one hour, one week or months before its deadline.

The theory of punctuated equilibrium is not without its critics. For example, Brown and Eisenhardt (1997) suggest that it does not represent the experience of many organizations, particularly those experiencing multiple, rapid changes.

Rewards, motivation and incentives for group development

Cacioppe (1999) suggests powerfully that teams need incentives in order to max-imize their development and achievements, and that these team rewards should take place at every stage of the team's work and development (see also Tan, 2000: 37). Team-based compensation can be based on the achievement of the objectives set for the team(s), and rewards for efficiency and commitment.

The notion of incentives takes very seriously the issue of motivation, a factor which is surfacing as a crucial element in the recruitment and retention of teach-ers in the UK. Indeed Coleman (1999: 42) suggests that self-organization, a central feature of complexity, is, at root, a 'process of human motivation enabled by empowerment practices'. For too long schools have simply ignored motivation rather than taking it seriously, developing and rewarding it. Indeed, as discussed in the work of Goleman in Chapter 3, for institutions to 'get results' they must con-sider motivation as a central plank of management for self-organization. As Cacioppe (*op. cit.*) says: 'rewards are one of the loudest and clearest ways leaders of an organisation can send a message about what they consider important' (p. 322). If teams are the order of the day then teamwork, rather than individual work, needs to be rewarded (Tjosvold and Wong, 2000: 353).

Rewards should be linked to tasks which can only be achieved through collab-oration (Coleman, 1999: 40), preferably cross-boundary collaboration. Cacioppe (*op. cit.*) suggests that up to 20 per cent of team-based developments have foundered because of lack of team pay, a figure which increased the longer the team was in existence. Rewards can cement a team together; they provide the nec-essary 'glue' for a team (p. 323).

Cacioppe suggests that rewards can be used in four main ways, to reward:

1   *direction* (task setting, clarifying objectives, developing positive interper-sonal relations);
2   *support* (those activities which members undertake to support each other and to develop team identity);
3   *reinforcement* (accomplishment of the task);
4   *celebration* (of outstanding individuals and team performance).

He classifies rewards into three types: monetary (M) (which includes money, prizes and gifts), recognition (R) (which includes praise), and development (D) (which includes empowerment) (p. 326). The different kinds of reward are set out in Figure 2.2.

Clearly many of these are unsuitable for schools (they derive from business), not least because some of them have no place in not-for-profit organizations for a public good. Some of them are manipulative, the mentality is instrumentalist in the service of a command-and-control mentality (and complexity theory replaces

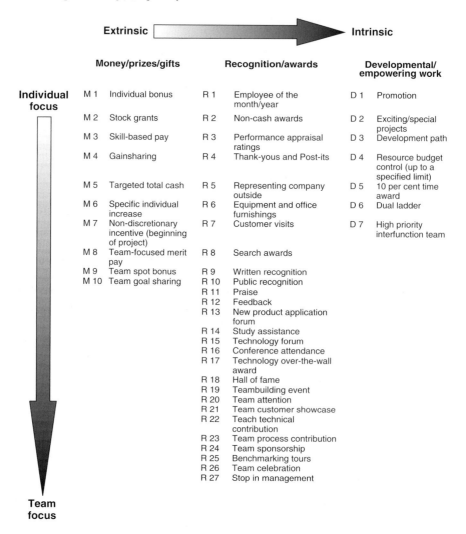

Figure 2.2 Incentives and rewards for motivating people.

such teleological determinism with a more open-ended, non-manipulative and non-directive, non-controlling, emergent, unpredictable set of principles), and because some of the suggestions in the table might be insulting and demeaning to teachers. Nevertheless they suggest strongly that greater attention needs to be paid not only to rewards but to rewarding teams and team development in schools. This is a serious agenda for leaders in the school.

For example, a secondary school in the UK recruited a large number of newly qualified teachers, who were working in several different departments in the school and who were under the care of four different mentors. The notion of mentoring was comparatively new to the school, and the mentors were nervous of their abilities to accomplish their tasks competently. They recognized that they would need a degree of consistency in their approach to the demands of the new teachers, and the headteacher asked the mentors to become a 'mentoring team' in the school. The mentors were initially fearful of exposing to each other what they considered to be their lack of expertise in mentoring, and felt that they needed development time and support to be able to succeed here.

In response to this, at the outset the headteacher agreed to sponsor the teachers from the school budget (M3, M7) in order to attend development courses at a local institution of higher education, to fund 'supply teacher' cover so that the mentors could meet together to develop their work, and to provide additional payment for one year to the four individuals (M1, M6). Depending on the outcome, evaluated by the mentors and their mentees, the headteacher was prepared to give a team-based bonus (M8). As the team of mentors developed their work, they recognized that their work would unavoidably impact on that of their colleagues, hence they ran a short series of formal and informal meetings with colleagues in order to apprise them of their own work and to develop working links with those colleagues. As a result this was formally recognized (R9, R10, R11, R12, R20) by the headteacher and school governors. Further, the four mentors completed higher degrees at their local university, specializing in mentoring, and, indeed, worked closely with that university in the development of other mentors on programmes offered by that university (D3). Team development was matched by team as well as individual rewards.

Different rewards might be useful for different stages in a team's life (Cacioppe, 1999: 328) (Figure 2.3).

Team's life stage	Direction	Support	Recognition	Celebration
Stage 1 Starting *(forming)*	M3, M7, M10, R3, R7, R12, R27, D7			
Stage 2 Establishing itself *(storming, norming)*		M6, R8, R9, R11, R12, R14, R17, R19, R20, D3		
Stage 3 Performing the task *(performing)*			M1, M2, M5, M6, R1–R21, R25–R27, D1, D2, D4–D7	
Stage 4 Ending *(adjourning, disbanding)*				M4, M8–M10, R2–R4, R9–R14, R17, R18, R22–R24, R26

Figure 2.3 Rewards at different stages of team development.

The suggestion that team rewards can match different stages of team development is an important implication for fostering emergence in the self-organizing institution (see also Lawler, 1991; Gross, 1995; Flannery *et al.*, 1996).

What is also clear from the preceding discussion is that motivation ('incentivization') moves beyond simply being a matter of paying people more, involving, perhaps, moves to the higher stage of Maslow's hierarchy of self-actualization. Employees look to the organization's reward system to detect its central values (Gilsdorf, 1998). Gupta and Shaw (1998) suggest several important considerations in the use of financial incentives (pp. 150–1):

- relate them to valued behaviours;
- use effective measurement systems (accurate and transparent);
- have effective communication systems (so that people know accurately what is required to gain the financial benefit);
- make the system complete (covering all the aspects of the performance);
- use them to supplement other rewards simultaneously;
- make meaningful differentiations (give large rewards for large behaviours);
- set realistic goals (achievable yet challenging);
- provide skill training and resource support;
- emphasize long-term as well as short-term success;
- be realistic – make sure that the incentives are motivating;
- be systemic – make sure that everybody has the opportunity to benefit from a financial incentive scheme.

Kohn (1998) argues against incentive payment schemes, arguing that claims in their favour are overstated and that, in fact, they do not motivate. They might elicit temporary compliance but, he argues, the more they are used, the more people lose interest in whatever they were required to do in order to receive the reward. Incentive schemes which focus on rewarding behaviour, rather than developing and involving sentient people, simply 'miss the point' (*ibid.*). If the starting point is not behaviour but people then, suggests Kohn, issues like autonomy, the quality of the job, the conditions of work and taking people seriously are more important than money; simply paying people for behaving in certain ways is a diminished view of their value. As Hertzberg (1987: 30) puts it: if we want people to be motivated to do a good job then we have to give them a good job to do. Kohn suggests that it is necessary to pay people well and fairly, and then do everything possible to take money off people's minds.

Pfeffer (1998) argues that group-oriented compensation schemes can improve teamwork, without increasing the amount of 'free-riding' (lazy people cashing in on the group benefit). He suggests that organizations which pay on a collective basis outperform those that do not. If teamwork is required then leaders should reward teamwork.

Leadership and teams

The leader of the team is in a pivotal position to motivate and reward the team; here the tasks of leadership might include (Katzenbach and Smith, 1993; Gibbs, 1995; Cacciope, 1999: 323–4; Stacey, 2001):

- ensuring that tasks are distributed equitably;
- focusing on shared goals;
- ensuring that the team works together smoothly, effectively and with positive relations;
- communicating and providing adequate information and positive feedback;
- facilitating interpersonal relations;
- leading by example;
- developing the leadership and development potentials of members;
- communicating trust.

Clearly these are not exclusive to team leadership. The team leader has to communicate the rewards that are available and should ensure that support mechanisms and development programmes are in place to enable these to be achieved.

Teams are not an unmitigated good. Morrison (1998: 184–5) suggests that they can possess many drawbacks in schools, for example they might:

- be slow, cumbersome and create much paperwork;
- enable a small minority to exert a disproportionate effect on the whole organization;
- make unrealistic demands on members;
- risk 'group think';
- become a euphemism for constant surveillance by peers (Garrahan and Stewart, 1992; Steingard and Fitzgibbons, 1993);
- produce high stress levels;
- require compliance rather than creativity;
- be resistant to external influences (intra-group membership overrides inter-group membership);
- create role overload and role conflict;
- create problems of coordination.

Hoy *et al.* (1992) suggest that it is counter-productive to include every teacher in every decision. Further, Robbins and Finley (1998b: 14–15) suggest that teams can suffer from several problems which, it can be suggested, provide an agenda for leaders, as shown in Table 2.4.

It is noticeable in the column of 'Tasks for leaders' that many of these concern attention to communication, information sharing and the building of relationships through shared decision making. The message is clear: leadership in the networked group or team is an interpersonal rather than solely a task-based matter.

An essential requirement for effective teamwork is that the fundamental elements of teamwork must be built into everything that the team has to do. Leonard

Table 2.4 Teamwork problems and leaders' solutions

Problem	Solution	Tasks for leaders
Mismatched needs	Expose hidden agendas; ask people what they would like from the team	Supporting, facilitating and managing discussions
Confused goals and cluttered objectives	Clarify goals and outcomes, and keep them to a minimum	Articulating and developing shared goals, outcomes facilitating the management of the focusing
Unresolved roles	Clarify expectations of roles	Manage the discussion of roles and role conflict; reduce role overload and role conflict; be sensitive to emerging human problems in managing roles
Bad decision making	Decide decision-making process	Facilitate and negotiate decision-making process
Bad policies and procedures	Rewrite the rules!	Formulate new policies through group involvement and decision making
Personality conflicts	Surface differences and see how they can be used productively	Provide neutral, safe territory for discussions and move towards negotiated agreements
Bad leadership	Act on feedback from the team or replace the leader	Learn from feedback or resign
Bleary vision	Improve or replace the vision	Articulate the vision and how it can be achieved; inject new insights
Anti-team culture	Voluntary team membership; match tasks to members	Facilitate communication and information sharing; ensure that benefits of teamwork appear quickly and are valued
Insufficient feedback and information	Generate information flow and communication everywhere	Instigate and sustain communication flow and information sharing; render them unavoidable
Ill-conceived reward systems	Ensure effective reward systems (e.g. find out what rewards people value); reward team and individual effort	Know people's motivations and values; ensure that rewards match people and teams
Lack of team trust	Foster trust through openness and honesty	Lead by example; facilitate discussions of how to improve trust
Unwillingness to change	Identify inhibiting and facilitating factors; reduce resistances and increase facilitating factors	Provide incentives; explain; communicate; share decision making; negotiate goals and practices; listen and act with people
The wrong tools	Provide appropriate resources	Support by appropriate human, material, temporal, administrative, financial, spatial resources

et al. (1998: 289) suggest that team-learning skills through extensive communication are an important ingredient. Team formation relies on working through human relationships in order to accomplish tasks. This is important, for it suggests that the attempt to accomplish tasks without paying attention to the human factor is misdirected. Leadership for team development, then, becomes a matter of fostering the promotion of positive relationships, promoting positive feedback, the open exchange of ideas and a willingness to listen (Tjosvold and Wong, 2000: 350–3); as these authors remark: if one wishes to be listened to by others then one should listen to others.

Specialists and generalists

The picture that emerges so far is that schools, as networked institutions, have to be seen holistically, because demarcation is comparatively limited. Vertical, horizontal and spatial differentiation are limited, as schools are characterized by overlap rather than boundary maintenance in most areas; teachers are members of multiple networks and have to be both specialists and generalists: specialists in their subject fields and management responsibility, and generalists otherwise, or perhaps it is truer to suggest that they have multiple specialisms.

The notion of generalists, or possessors of multiple specialisms, is useful, for it suggests that in a developed, self-organizing school there will be considerable interdependence in the sense that there is potential for overlap of tasks. This enables the school to be buoyant rather than brittle. In a brittle institution a chain of events or set of educational activities is reliant on individuals, and the institution or set of activities is only as strong as the weakest link, with no overlap. Consider, for example, the sole chemistry teacher in the school; if she is absent it is extremely difficult to replace her. Her specialist expertise is not duplicated. In a buoyant organization the potential for overlap is stronger; the potential for duplication of expertise is high. If an institution is to be robust in times of uncertainty then it is perhaps advisable for it to restrict its number of specialisms and to move towards increasing its generalisms (or multiple specialisms). The implications here are for schools to identify those areas where specialism is required and where it is not.

Marion (1999: 208) argues that the generalist organization is more suited to unstable conditions whilst a specialist organization is more suited to stable conditions. If the unstable conditions are short-lived then specialist organizations can survive, though if the conditions persist then they will probably not. The generalist tends to be a better survivor in an unpredictable world (*ibid*: 209). If this is the case, then it seems that schools, even though in many cases they are elephantine, slow-moving institutions, may be better survivors than organizations which run until exhausted – calm elephants live longer than nervous gazelles! This is, perhaps, a dangerous scenario, for it argues against change and innovation at a time when change and innovation are frequently topmost on the agenda, where flexibility is at a premium and where emergence requires change. Further, it might imply that schools reduce their activities to those which are served by generalists, and this might be dangerous in a time when schools are required to produce specialists. For schools, the implication might be that they need to select carefully their areas of development and their areas of maintenance, which is the stuff of development planning (Hargreaves and Hopkins, 1991), and to ensure that the specialist developments are adequately resourced.

The more complex the organization is, the slower it is to change. Large, complex organizations move slowly; like a sponge, they can absorb pressure without changing. This echoes Pfeffer and Salancik (1978) who argue that it is harder to change large, loosely coupled organizations than tightly coupled organizations, because loosely coupled organizations simply absorb perturbations.

Leadership for loosely and tightly coupled schools

A leadership decision needs to be taken on the tightness of the coupling of the elements of the school. For example, a tightly coupled school, like a high-reliability school, may be useful for levering up poor performance, but this may be at the cost of personal and interpersonal autonomy and relations respectively. On the other hand, too loose a coupling might result in drift and a lack of innovation.

The leader(s) in the school have to decide which elements of the network (e.g. its subsystems and units) will be loosely or tightly coupled, which held together and which kept separate, and how this will occur (e.g. through communication, working together, integration of activities, collaborative planning, separate and coordinated planning). For example, if the science and mathematics departments are going to be more closely coupled than the science and music departments, then how will this closer coupling take place? For example, will there be joint curriculum and assessment planning so that areas of work are related; will there be joint projects or topics; will reporting systems be similar; will there be shared resources (including teachers, rooms and students); will they work together on school improvement topics; will staff attend the same professional development activities; will the two departments agree joint aims and objectives, etc.?

The self-organizing, complex school, then, will need to consider itself in terms of the ways in which it organizes itself formally and informally and, centrally, its mechanisms for communication and collaboration. In this respect a fitness landscape is a useful means of approaching this task (see Chapter 7).

Conclusion

This chapter has addressed several issues:

- schools should be regarded as self-organizing, complex, nonlinear organizations;
- systems and structures in the school should be horizontal networks rather than vertical hierarchies;
- micropolitics is a significant contributor to regarding schools as complex organizations;

- micropolitics should shift from a competitive to a collaborative focus;
- regarding schools as high-reliability organizations might stifle emergence and self-organization;
- developing interdependence is of prime concern for schools;
- group work, teamwork and network development are essential features of the self-organizing school;
- the development of groups, teams and networks requires increased attention to motivation and incentives at each stage of development and tasks of the team;
- the balance between generalists and specialists in the school needs to be considered for team-based activities;
- the extent of loose or tight coupling is an important feature of the self-organized school, with loose–tight organizations being appropriate for much of the time;
- effective communication is essential for the self-organizing school.

The principles of complexity theory support responsible and accountable devolution of operations and decision making to groups and teams in a networked school. Yet it is the willingness of senior managers to slacken the reins in order for self-organizing groups and teams to run freer and faster that could be problematical. The issues of developing motivation, incentives, responsibility and support for self-organizing groups to develop is difficult to the point of impossibility in a climate of overwork, intensive demands on teachers, demoralization, rampant indiscipline in schools, exhausted and overburdened staff, and massive recruitment and retention problems – where even finding a teacher, regardless of whether she or he is a specialist or a generalist, is a major accomplishment. This chapter has presented a formidable agenda, perhaps, for leadership in the school, and it is to this that the next chapter turns.

3 Leadership for self-organization and emergence

Replacing command and control leadership

The head of the science department of a secondary school in the UK is concerned to find ways of attracting more older girls to take chemistry in the upper end of the school. To this end she discusses the matter with the headteacher, who shares the same concern and who is keen to promote this. The head of science takes a lead in developing links with a local petrochemical company for work placements for her students, and staff from that company are involved in teaching those students in school, curriculum development in the school, supervision of students' work-related activities, and assessments for public examination.

In the same school the teachers of business studies and food technology wish to promote the vocational training of those students who are interested in developing a career in hotels, catering and tourism. The heads of the business and food technology departments discuss the matter with their colleagues and the headteacher, who supports the idea of increasing the amount and duration of work placements and their related curriculum implications in school for those students who are keen to follow such careers.

For all of this to be successful requires considerable timetabling adjustments within the school, so that students are able to have substantial blocked time out of the school premises, so that departments (business and food technology) collaborate, so that the 'knock-on' timetabling effects are agreed with other teachers, and so that the curriculum development and assessment teams in the school are able to work in closer collaboration on these initiatives, together with the involvement of those outside the school staff.

The headteacher, concerned to support these developments, takes active formal and informal steps to promote positive working relations with the local companies and groups external to the school, in order to smooth the situation. She secures funding from local industries, careers development agencies, the government and the European Union. The money enables meetings to take place during school, resources and equipment to be purchased, teaching 'supply cover' to be purchased, and the costs of transport for students and communication to be funded. The outcomes of this are that a new department of tourism and hotel management studies is formed, a new team called the 'external relations' team is formed in the school, the curriculum and assessment teams merge, and representatives drawn from local employers join the curriculum team in the school.

In this example the school has self-organized, and reorganized, its internal systems, structures and practices to respond to external and internal developments and requirements; new forms of organization emerge. The leadership is distributed throughout the school (discussed below), and the role of the headteacher is to be supportive, facilitatory and enabling rather than directive; the headteacher assumes the role of the servant leader (discussed below).

This chapter suggests that leadership for self-organization and emergence has to move away from command-and-control and towards democratic, person-centred and relational styles of leadership. In this respect, the chapter argues, though transformational leadership is an improvement on transactional leadership, in that it embraces person-centredness and relational aspects, nevertheless it is still fundamentally technicist, trapping participants in the agendas of senior controlling managers, and therefore sits uncomfortably with the notions of emergent order and self-organization of complexity theory. Rather, this chapter suggests, transcendental, distributed, servant leadership and quantum leadership might be more fitting styles of leadership for the complex school, as they stress open-endedness, unpredictability and interpersonal relations.

Leadership in the emergent, self-organizing school, it is argued, requires considerable emotional intelligence in order to foster the positive interpersonal relationships required for self-organization. Leadership moves away from being coercive and authoritarian and adopts more humanistic principles, promoting the organizational health and climate of the school, and building on mutual trust. More specifically, it is suggested that leadership replaces coercion and pacesetting with authoritative, affiliative, democratic and coaching styles; it creates a safe environment for experimentation and risk taking and promotes interdependence, communication, cooperation, diversity and self-organization. For all of this to be successful, the chapter contends that leadership must attend to the human side of the organization, both personally and interpersonally.

Leadership within the nonlinear, self-organizing school is remote from the hierarchical command-and-control mentality of bureaucratic organizations in which compliance is the watchword (Riley, 2000: 29). Change and emergence can occur anywhere in the organization, often in an unpredictable way (Beeson and Davis, 2000: 183). Hierarchical leadership takes insufficient account of the fact that change occurs everywhere, often not by mandate from above; complexity theory catches this notion that change activities are everywhere in the organization. Chains of command are replaced by webs of influence and networks (Wheatley, 1999: 109). Indeed 'holarchies' (flat management structures) rather than hierarchies are advocated (Community Intelligence Labs, 1999: 2). Leadership in the decentralized organization can start at the bottom (Malone, 1998: 278).

There are several worries about the command-and-control style of leadership, for example it:

- creates resentment and resistance within the organization;
- absolves followers of individual responsibility;
- pushes a more natural self-organization underground, thereby making it harder to manage (Kelly and Allison, 1999: 66);
- promotes mutual distrust;
- assumes that the leader is completely competent, possessed of all the facts and answers and, therefore, is dangerous in the hands of an incompetent leader;
- is insulting to the creative, self-disciplined, self-organizing intelligence and integrity of participants (cf. Riley, 2000);
- misrepresents the actual nature of institutions, which are complex and peopled by informed participants who, themselves, change the organization from within;
- is mechanistic and linear;
- assumes that leaders are the ultimate authority;
- leads to blaming junior members when things go wrong and taking credit when things go right (Lloyd and Trapp, 1999: 332–3);
- falsely assumes that institutions can, in fact, be controlled;
- misrepresents the complexity of the environment (internal and external);
- is inappropriate for knowledge work (Fisher and Fisher, 1998: 197);
- assumes that leaders have massive effects on the organization.

Complex organizations have their own, internal dynamic which is not always contingent on leaders (consider the example of Reynolds's Boids in Chapter 1). Indeed Wheatley (1996: 3) suggests that one can 'have order without control' (see also Goodwin, 2000: 43), or as Marion (1999: 169) remarks, bad administrative decisions rarely bring down an organization. Gronn (2000: 319) suggests that it is an exaggeration to believe that leaders can exert too much agency. Control, suggests Stacey (2000: 411), is replaced by an identification of constraint, and leadership concerns facilitating procedures which will encourage high quality, creative experiences in participants (Goodwin, 2000: 47–8).

Youngblood (1997: 110) argues against the command-and-control mentality found in hierarchical organizations. For him such organizations are powerless, for the senior figures (who have all the power) do not do the work, and yet those who do the work have no power. Indeed, in schools, Senge *et al.* (2000: 58) suggest that there is a 'structural blindspot' because the views of students carry little weight, and yet they are the very people who have the most meaningful knowledge of the school.

McMaster (1996), like management critics Micklethwait and Wooldridge (1997), argues that many of the trappings of leadership (e.g. mission statements, vision statements, in-depth and detailed strategic management) are entirely unnecessary as the organization organizes itself. Mission statements and vision statements risk narrowing down the activities of diverse groups and people into mind control and thought police – hardly the opening-up of minds for which education stands. Indeed Stacey (1992: 126–39) mounts a robust critique of the

value of vision statements within complexity theory-driven organizations, arguing that they:

- are only able to state the obvious because the future is uncertain and unpredictable;
- cannot prevision the future reality of the organization;
- are dangerous guides to standardized practice in turbulent times;
- are unable to take account of, or to act as a referent for, specific actions;
- are unclear on the difference between healthy sharing and 'group-think';
- can lead to collective organizational suicide;
- place unrealistic demands on leaders and followers;
- do not take account of what participants are actually doing *in situ*;
- do not work in practice.

Leaders (Stacey, 1992: 146) should replace the setting of objectives in mission
and vision statements with 'developing agendas of issues'.

There are two important implications that flow from the need to replace the
command-and-control mentality. First, an alternative style of leadership is
required; second, leadership becomes distributed and devolved – instead of one
leader there are many, each exercising leadership roles in their fields.

With regard to an alternative style of leadership, leaders become influencers,
facilitators and shapers rather than commanders; the move is from being isolated,
controlling and secretive leaders to being relational, open and honest, from pos-
sessing omniscience to being human and concerned for relationships (Lewin and
Regine, 2000: 84–6). Indeed Fullan (2001: 5) finds that improved relationships is
the common factor in successful change, and he advocates considerable attention
to it by leaders; people come before products (*ibid*: 55). Recognizing that their
authority is both earned and limited, leaders must listen, respond, encourage,
build relationships, acknowledge, support and keep out – letting go in order to let
others achieve what they can do better than the leader (Gross, 1998).
Communication must be open and multi-directional.

Leaders have to create the environment for ideas and practices rather than
mandating prescriptions. In this style they trust the collective expertise and wisdom of participants and support the development of this, creating the conditions
for change and attending to the relationships involved, and then giving space for
the institution to evolve from there onwards. Leaders support experiments and
demonstrate genuine concern and care for their colleagues (i.e. they are ethical in
their behaviour), developing and respecting the human side of organizations.

Leaders, then, cultivate *conditions* rather than direct practice; they create disturbance and the need for innovation, but in a safe environment, maintaining an
overview of where the institution is going (without being directive) and recognizing and fostering connections and relations within the institution; they reduce
disconnections, blind spots and constrictions in the institution (Lewin and Regine,
2000: 271). The consequence of this is that leaders are inclusive in their work with
colleagues, they demonstrate reciprocity, and they foster empowerment, flexibility and adaptability in participants, i.e. 'leaders by not leading' (*ibid*: 272).

Such a view of leadership replaces compliance (Kelly and Allison, 1999: 85) with fostering synergy, collaboration, relations and commitment; and attending to relationships, teamwork and the development of positive communication within and between networks, working with, and for, people rather than doing things to them. Clearly the giving up of control or, more precisely, recognizing that they never really had control, autonomy or absolute knowledge, is an important and sometimes difficult task for leaders.

Marion (1999: 268) suggests that if innovations are required, together with the identification of new problems and new solutions, then the answer is to turn the organization loose and let it move itself. Leadership moves away from personal aggrandizement and self-importance and towards providing the opportunity for others to demonstrate and develop leadership – a much more enabling role. This is a signal characteristic of empowerment – releasing the self-motivation of others to exert autonomy, responsibility and ownership in their work (Coleman, 1999: 41). This suggests Senge's (1990: 340) view of leadership as stewardship, and April's (1997: 38) and Greenleaf's (1995) notion of servant leadership (discussed below).

McMaster (1996: 215) sees the move to new styles of leadership as the move from the left-hand column to the right-hand column below:

Closed	→	Open
Secretive	→	Accessible
Exclusion	→	Inclusion
Impersonal	→	Expressive
Authority-based	→	Self-responsible
Bureaucratic	→	Accountable
Direct control	→	Trust in processes
Hierarchical	→	Interconnected
Rule-bound	→	Value-based
Tightly controlled	→	Loosely coupled
Produced	→	Directed

(From: *The Intelligence Advantage* by M. McMaster (1996), reprinted by permission of Butterworth-Heinemann).

In a school the message here is ambitious, for it argues for increased democracy (Apple and Beane, 1995). Peterson (in Apple and Beane, 1995) suggests that a key lesson to be learned for leadership here is the need for grassroots involvement (p. 77), multi-racial unity, time for reflection and learning (Schön, 1983), extended parental involvement, and the promotion of structures for change. Essentially leadership concerns the divestment of power.

These kinds of leaders address three As (McMaster, 1996: 272–8):

1   they *allow*: (a) matters to emerge; (b) connections to grow; (c) ambiguity, uncertainty and paradox; (d) experimentation (and their possible failure); (e) errors to be made without needless blame; (f) freedom and autonomy amongst the participants as individuals and groups;

2   they are *accessible* (e.g. formally, informally, cognitively, communicatively, emotionally, psychologically) but not intrusive;

3   they are *attuned* (capable of listening, responding, intuiting, deliberating, putting trust in people).

This moves away from the headteacher or leader as stentorian guard to a person who is sentient, humanitarian and supportive. It can be seen that the model of leadership that is being suggested here is that which is focused on people rather than on formal procedures. Indeed Coleman (1999: 42) suggests that an essential feature of leaders is that they treat others with dignity.

As leaders step off their pedestals so they become members of a flatter management, networked system. This entails being prepared to become as human as their colleagues. Indeed Lewin and Regine (2000: 307) and Lindle (1999: 173) suggest the need for relational leaders to be authentic (open with information, even if that information is not good news), to acknowledge others, to be accountable and to be attentive to people. This is both the heart of trust and the recognition that leadership is a moral contract to bring out the best in everyone for the good of the school. Further, Stacey (2000: 400) suggests that leadership, as a relationship rather than simply an individual competence, has to take seriously the emotions of all participants. In this chapter this is discussed in relation to emotionally intelligent leadership, a feature which is significant if diversity and even deviance are to be encouraged for emergent self-organization and change to occur. Stacey (1992: 198) suggests that leaders should positively encourage counter-cultures in organizations as stimulants to change.

For example, the results of a school's inspection may be demoralizing for the staff who have been working hard and devotedly under serious stress from difficult students. One response to this might be a 'blame' strategy from the leader, berating the staff for misdirected effort, for lack of effort, for tolerating bad behaviour in classrooms, for inadequate application of school rules, for failing to set high enough standards or adhering to them. In this scenario staff may simply quit the school, leaving it in a worse state than before. An alternative strategy might be for the headteacher simply to recognize the work of the teachers, to share the problem with them and, with them, to try to formulate a response and a way forward, in an atmosphere of collaboration, support and the absence of blame.

McDaniel (1997) suggests several tasks of leadership for promoting emergence and self-organization in the complex school: (a) making sense of situations and making connections; (b) planning for diversity; (c) promoting self-organization; and (d) increasing the emphasis on cooperation and interdependence. Indeed April *et al.* (2000: 39–40) suggest that leaders of complex organizations should 'allow for multiple goals, embrace the concept of multiple effects and multiple causes within fluid and flexible frameworks, forms in which understanding interrelationships, rather than just cause-and-effect operate' (see also Pettigrew and Whipp, 1993).

The task for the leader then becomes that of coordination, monitoring and developing the overall health of the system (Baskin, 1998). These are demanding for many leaders, as they are required to:

- be outstanding role models;
- provide opportunities for learning and development of relationships;
- know when to stand back;
- set policy and yet be prepared to modify it;
- be an excellent communicator;
- avoid reliance on power hierarchies;
- recruit and retain autonomous, creative participants;
- energize and sustain the organization;
- foster consensus and commitment;
- develop team players and team leaders;
- recognize and develop expertise in the institution;
- have expertise as well as generalist abilities.

On top of all of these requirements (Kelly and Allison, 1999: 170–1) they must be human and be seen to be human, they must be able to foster respect, to mentor and coach, to be active listeners and counsellors, to be experienced in their role, and to be non-threatening team players. They must be 'people' people.

This change of mentality argues against the rigidity of high-reliability schools, set out in Chapter 2. This is not to argue that high-reliability schools are impersonal or inhumane; that need not be the case. Rather it is to question whether there is a risk of high-reliability schools becoming too mechanistic, inflexible, goal oriented and teleological to sit comfortably within complexity theory, which stresses openness, evolution, emergence and relations.

Chapter 1 suggested that organizations have to change, have to be out of equilibrium, and that there is an inbuilt propulsion within organizations towards self-organized criticality. Hence systems need to be constantly energized. The implications here are that leaders have to be energizers, creating disequilibrium in order for the organization to survive. The task of leaders, then, as Heifetz and Lawrie (1997) argue, is to regulate stress – turning up the heat whilst at the same time enabling steam to escape, and avoiding innovation overload (Lloyd and Trapp, 1999: 336).

The issue concerns self-organized criticality. People and institutions naturally move towards a peak of creativity at the edge of chaos. The task is to ensure that the self-organized criticality works *for* individuals and the organization rather than *against* them. This suggests that leaders in schools have to be sensitive to sudden changes, for example by asking themselves: 'why is there a sudden rapid turnover of staff?' (how many schools have a 'leaving' interview for departing staff, as well as a recruitment interview?), 'why are things suddenly changing in the school?', 'why is such-and-such a person suddenly happy or unhappy in the organization?', 'what are the pressures that are being placed on staff, and with what likely result?' The implication here is that one sees in sudden changes in the school a *human* response to an *organizational* issue, and it is one task of leaders to be alert to the human side of the enterprise. Sudden changes, as Chapter 1 remarks, may indicate that a new form of self-organization is emerging.

For example: a senior teacher in a school has been there for some ten years and has established herself as a key figure in the school, being approachable, popular and efficient in terms of the students, teachers and parents. She has enjoyed working hard and demonstrating considerable commitment to the school, both in school and out of hours. However, she finds that the pressure of conflicting demands on her results in her feeling that she is constantly compromising her integrity (role conflict) and her ability to complete a job satisfactorily (role overload). She feels that students are suffering because of her inability to keep up with her main task of improving their learning and achievement.

Further, the headteacher is constantly setting forward new initiatives without considering the resource base required to support them, and the headteacher's response to any question about this is to rage and blame, so staff avoid telling him anything so as not to invite this response. The headteacher brooks no disagreement. New initiatives are introduced in unrealistic time frames for suitable development, and the results are that the senior teacher's home life and health suffer seriously. The response to external pressure on the school is greater and greater diversification on an increasingly reducing resource base (because the resources are being spread too thinly) rather than consolidation or 'sticking to the knitting' of the organization's primary purposes and core activities.

The senior teacher finds that the headteacher constantly makes decisions without consultation, resulting in contradictory messages leaving the school, which undermines her own position. The combination of these factors causes her to question, for the first time in the school, whether she can usefully continue. After putting up with the situation for three years, and after a particularly heated dispute with the headteacher, she leaves for a new job; at the same time as she leaves, four other experienced colleagues leave.

The example shows that self-organized criticality should have been managed through perceptive intervention by the headteacher but that the leadership style involved worked counter to this, exacerbating rather than alleviating the situation. The message is clear: if self-organized criticality is an unavoidable feature of complex organizations, it does not follow that this should be counter-productive. The secret is to harness this for the good of the organization as well as the good of the individual concerned – a win-win situation. It concerns providing support for creativity rather than beating people into acceptance.

In the example there is a striking absence of feedback (from the senior teacher to the headteacher) or positive feedback from the headteacher to the senior teacher. In the absence of positive or adequate feedback the move towards self-organized criticality takes a negative turn, and the member of staff leaves. The school has de-formed the potential of self-organized criticality for positive advantage into negative hostility until the intervention of the 'straw that breaks the camel's back' – the heated dispute with the school headteacher. Referring to the example of the pile of sand in Chapter 1, this is the equivalent of the grain of sand which causes the whole pile to collapse. The message is clear: self-organized criticality must be developed, recognized and, perhaps most significantly, turned to positive effect.

Transformational leadership

Leadership of the emergent, self-organizing school resonates with certain aspects of transformational leadership (Burns, 1978; Bass, 1990) as the emergent organization transforms itself over time. Here the leader provides *platforms* for change and self-organization. In a school these might be (Kelly and Allison, 1999):

- articulating the vision and identity of the school and aligning the organization to achieve them;
- being a role model;
- creating a sense of urgency;
- seeing and articulating opportunities for learning and development;
- developing partnerships and working relationships within and outside the school;
- creating new initiatives in the school;
- increasing positive feedback and reducing negative feedback;
- increasing communication providing information;
- developing individuals and networks through devolved and collaborative decision making;
- building on, and developing, the expertise in the school, e.g. providing appropriate staff development programmes;
- rewarding new behaviours.

The transformational leader is contrasted with the transactional leader. The transactional leader operates on the principle of exchange theory (Blau, 1964; Homans, 1971; Dansereau *et al.*, 1975), where the leader will exact certain performance or behaviour from others on the basis of what those others will obtain in return. A headteacher might ask for support for a particular innovation from the head of the mathematics department, to which the head of mathematics agrees, on the understanding that she obtains increased funding for her own department. The transactional model, a bartering or bargaining model (Blau, 1964), is designed to enable the leader to further her or his own agenda. As Lindle (1999: 175) remarks, leaders have to balance the costs and benefits in making educational decisions in terms of who wins and who suffers.

Morrison (1998: 133) suggests that whilst headteachers have many properties to exchange, for example material resources, promotion, esteem, autonomy, application of rules, teachers, too, have many valuables to be used in the exchange or barter, for example support, opinion leadership, conformity and reputation. Major (2000: 357–61) suggests that senior managers might expect flexibility, adaptability, continuous learning and self-development, information sharing and teamwork; other employees might expect, in return, personal and social meaningfulness in their work, opportunities for personal and professional growth and development, and a recognition from their employers and senior managers that they, as employees, also have family life and leisure time as well as work time.

Transactional leadership is also based on expectancy theory (*ibid*: 132). This states that people will involve themselves in a project if they expect it to be worth their while and to lead to personal benefits; the higher the perceived benefits, the greater will be their willingness to be involved. This has major implications for the nature of the transactions that leaders will suggest, and indeed for the significance of incentives and rewards, which were discussed in Chapter 2 (Bass, 1990; 1998). Expectancy theory and exchange theory are both instrumental and teleological, designed to further the strategic objectives of leaders.

For example, in a school a transactional headteacher might approach the head of science to gain her support for a proposed new initiative, let us say a new recording system for assessment results; the department head's response might be to promise support on the condition that the headteacher supplies the department with appropriate IT equipment both to undertake the initiative and also to provide greater IT resources for the science department.

Transformational leadership comprises several factors (Bass, 1990, 1998; Bass and Avolio, 1994; Hinkin and Tracey,1999: 109). Amongst these are: *idealized influence* (charisma and vision, which inspire followers to want to follow the leaders); *inspiration motivation* (the communication of high expectations and clarity of vision, inspiring participants to be involved, to change and to embrace the vision, motivating followers and engendering team spirit); *intellectual stimulation* (including problem solving and deliberately seeking new ideas, being innovative and creative and rising to new challenges); and *individualized consideration* (attention to people as individuals and to their need to experience success and personal development).

Tichy and Devanna (1986) suggest that transformational leaders regard themselves as change agents, are courageous, believe in people, are driven by a set of values, are lifelong learners, are able to handle ambiguity, uncertainty and complexity, and are 'visionaries'. In similar vein, Bennis and Nanus (1985) and Duke and Leithwood (1994) found that transformational leaders articulated a vision for the future, emphasized individual and organizational learning and developed commitment and trust.

In the context of schools, Leithwood (1994) suggests that transformational leaders: (a) support teachers in developing and sustaining a professional school culture; (b) promote the professional development of teachers; and (c) improve problem-solving processes. Harris (2000: 83) suggests that transformational leaders in schools (headteachers or, indeed, heads of departments) not only manage the structure but the culture of their contexts. Leithwood and Jantzi (2000: 3) suggest that transformational practices are effective in developing commitment and capacity. They suggest six dimensions of transformational school leadership (p. 5):

- building the vision and goals of the school;
- providing intellectual stimulation;
- offering individualized support;
- symbolizing professional practices and values;
- demonstrating high performance expectations;
- developing structures to promote participation in school decisions.

For example, in the UK a secondary school appointed a new headteacher whose prime concern was to improve the standards of achievement of the students. The school had a reputation for traditionalism and an inability to keep up with the vocational demands of education. The headteacher commenced by holding a full staff meeting at which he made it clear that his driving concern was to improve students' learning and achievement. He followed this by conducting one-to-one interviews with each teacher, posing the simple statement: 'Tell me, in priority order, what you need in order to be able to improve students' learning and achievement and how you will evaluate the achievement'. Each teacher named the 'shopping list' of items, and was then asked to cost out these items. For *every* teacher, the headteacher promised to 'deliver' the money, which ran to a huge sum.

At the same time, the headteacher was very busy in putting in bids to as many external providers of sponsorship and income as possible, for example: (a) a 'teaching and learning initiative' bid to the Department for Education and Skills; (b) a bid to the European Union for money to develop language teaching; (c) another bid to the Department for Education and Skills to be given recognized 'specialist' status as a centre for language; (d) a bid to local community groups to develop community languages using the school; (e) bids to loyal employers for sponsorship to create partnerships for vocational placements from school; and (f) a bid to the Department of Trade and Industry for specialized IT resources for language development. The headteacher was a model of diligence, working immensely hard and on several fronts; he was completely accessible to the staff, shared problems and successes, made demands but met these with support. Several staff who could not keep up the pace resigned, and they were replaced by other teachers who were committed to the vision of improving learning and achievement.

Through these funding initiatives the school succeeded in raising a huge sum of money in additional income, so that all the teachers' 'shopping lists' were able to be funded. The teachers, seeing that the headteacher had been able to keep his word, were motivated to achieve their wishes for student achievement.

A renewed vigour was observable in the school; the school received a huge injection of IT equipment, which became a widely used local resource, often after hours. Short training courses were run for the public, which brought in greater revenue that was used to purchase more IT equipment.

One problem in raising student achievement was the low expectation and disruptive behaviour of several teenage boys in the school. The headteacher operated a 'no nonsense' policy of temporary school exclusion for persistent troublemakers. During their periods of exclusion, the students would be loaned a laptop computer from the school in order to maintain correspondence with the school, to send the students work, and to receive new instructions from the teachers. This meant that home tutoring services were not required, which saved money, indeed the laptop computers were seen as a renewable resource, which contrasted with the use of non-renewable resources of home tutors' time. The policy worked, and indeed was heralded in the neighbourhood as a success story for motivating disaffected students, and was copied by other schools and used as a flagship project by other educational providers.

After two years the students' academic performance was lifted appreciably, the motivation of staff and students was increased, the school was noted for its entrepreneurial and positive atmosphere coupled with caring concerns for its students, and its efforts were praised by local employers who began to approach the school deliberately to recruit as employees those students who had been in work placement with them. It is a striking example of 'increasing returns' coming to a school which was prepared to commit itself to a vision.

Transformational leadership is concerned with a vision-driven, values-based, structural, cultural and systemic change in an organization. Bass (1990: 21) suggests that transformational leadership both broadens and elevates participants' interests, and enables participants to look beyond the immediate and self-interested towards the mission of the organization which is realized through group participation. It is achieved through commitment, positive example, empowerment of participants and fostering their ownership, rich communication and energizing, and enthusing participants (Stewart, 1990; Coleman, 1994; Morrison, 1998). It is inspirational, motivating, stimulating and characterized by concern for individuals (Barling *et al.*, 2000: 157). In many respects it relies on charisma of the leader and the willingness of followers to participate in the collective pursuit of improvement and innovation (Burns, 1978: 3). The vision is an enabling structure rather than simply a goal (April, 1997: 38), supportive of synergy and collaboration.

The nature of relationships between leaders and participants is based less on exchange and more on the shared transformation of the organization, with leaders as catalysts for change (Collins, 1999). The nature of leadership is relational (Silins *et al.*, 1999), and has a strong sense of moral purpose (Fullan, 2001). Leadership is about followership (Blank, 1995); one is not a leader unless there are followers.

Transformation, McMaster (1996: 185) suggests, embodies emergence; it is a process which creates new relationships within an organization, and between the organization and its environment. It does this by reorganizing its activities and by drawing upon, increasing and (re)distributing its knowledge. In school terms, Leithwood *et al.* (1996) found that transformational leadership impacted on major dimensions of schools, bringing benefits as follows:

- charisma/inspiration/vision;
- goal consensus;
- individual consideration;
- intellectual stimulation;
- modelling;
- high performance expectations;
- culture building;
- structuring;
- management by exception;
- contingent reward.

The results report particular benefits in terms of (a) charisma/inspiration/vision; (b) intellectual stimulation and; (c) individual consideration. Transformational leadership exerts a positive effect on those aspects of the school which foster its potential to learn. Charisma is inspirational, articulating a shared vision which moves and stimulates participants.

Rowden (2000: 30) suggests that charisma involves vision and its articulation, sensitivity to people's needs, environmental sensitivity, perhaps unconventional behaviour, risk taking, and preparedness to upset the *status quo*. Charisma evokes in followers deep feelings of loyalty, trust, respect, affection, acceptance and a sharing of excitement in the leadership. Further, Rowden reports several studies which have found strong positive associations between charisma, organizational commitment, job satisfaction and a leader's sensitivity to participants' needs.

Kelloway *et al.* (2000) found that transformational leadership enhanced followers' cognitive and affective commitment to the organization, and their individual and group performance, and that feedback exerted an important effect on this. Leithwood *et al.*'s (1996) results for schools suggest that transformational leadership has positive effects in five main areas:

1   effects on the perceptions of the leader (the leader's effectiveness and participants' satisfaction with the leader);
2   effects on the behaviour of followers (bringing increased effort from them and their contribution to the organization);
3   effects on followers' psychological states (their commitment, concern for professional development and changes in attitudes and behaviour, morale and job satisfaction);
4   organization-level effects (organizational learning, improvement, effectiveness, climate and culture);
5   effects on students (teachers' perceptions of student effects; students' participation and identification).

Organizational learning is discussed in Chapter 4.

The limits of transformational leadership in complexity theory

Transformational leadership resonates with key features of emergence and self-organization but, as Allix (2000) argues, there are limits to transformational leadership. He argues powerfully that:

- transformational leadership is just as instrumental and manipulative as transactional leadership because leader-determined needs are privileged over others' subjective wishes (p. 15);
- it relies on persuasion, influence, indoctrination and micropolitics;
- that it is morally blind (see also Cardona, 2000), unable to differentiate between the Ghandi-like leader and the Hitler-like leader. Indeed he suggests that it is little more than an emotionally, charismatically charged version of transactional leadership, whose intention is dominatory (p. 18).

Similarly Beeson and Davis (2000: 181), Stacey *et al.* (2000) and Stacey (2000, 2001) suggest that there are limits to the applicability of transformational leadership within complexity theory, as transformational leaders treat nonlinear systems as if they were linear, predictable and controllable. Leaders, they argue, in fact may be unable to engineer transformations in the organization.

Transformational leadership is technicist, trapping followers into the agendas of the leaders. In transformational leadership, the intention is still to seek the control and compliance of the followers, whatever the rewards might be. The transformational leader is simply an enriched version of the transactional leader (Bass and Avolio, 1994: 3), topping up transactional leadership with a dose of vision and charisma. Both transactional and transformational leaders are, at source, variants of a teleological determinism, and command-and-control mentalities.

These are powerful criticisms of transformational leadership, and suggest the need to move beyond transformational leadership to genuine democratic, distributed, transcendental, quantum and servant leadership within complexity theory.

Transcendental and servant leadership

Transcendental leadership (Cardona, 2000) appeals to participants' motivations and agendas. Transcendental leaders look at the needs of collaborators and centre their work on addressing those needs, though not in a manipulative way. In particular, transcendental leaders are less concerned with their own agendas and more concerned with developing participants', i.e. to contribute to others' personal development and to meet their needs, to seek their well-being, so that they can transcend themselves. They put others first. In this sense leaders have a democratic, non-technicist basis that is lacking in the notion of a transformational leader.

April *et al.* (2000) support the notion of 'servant leadership' in complex organizations, where a major role of the leader is to synergize and develop a sense of community in the institution, with shared power and decision making and group-oriented approaches (Greenleaf, 1995: 196, 1996). Servant leadership (April *et al.*, 2000: 100–4) has a long pedigree in religion (Berry and Cartwright, 2000: 344), and involves a sense of servanthood, with leadership as a state of being (a sense of vocation). It also implies stewardship (a recognition of shared ownership and interdependence rather than personal ownership of an organization), one consequence of which is a sense of citizenship and community (a shift from leadership to being a citizen who is a member of a community). The servant leader facilitates the surfacing of others' ideas and networks, and helps to create their futures.

Servant leadership is designed to promote a sense of community and a sharing of power in decision making (Brookshire, 2001). Servant leadership presupposes a degree of democracy. Greenleaf (1995) suggests that servant leaders need to ask themselves:

1   As a result of your leadership, are those whom you serve growing as persons?
2   Are they, while being served, becoming healthier?
3   Are they becoming more autonomous, freer, wiser and more capable?

4   Are they, themselves, more likely to become servant leaders?
5   What is the effect on the least privileged in society; will they benefit from my leadership?

Spears (2001), the Chief Executive Officer of the Robert K. Greenleaf Center for Servant-Leadership, indicates ten characteristics of servant leaders:

- listening (to oneself as well as to others);
- empathy (with others, however different they may be);
- healing (making people whole);
- awareness (of self and others), and Greenleaf, echoing the value of perturbation in complexity theory, indicated that awareness is a disturber and an awakener, rather than the giver of solace;
- persuasion (rather than reliance on positional power);
- conceptualization (to 'think big');
- foresight (which includes the use of informed intuition);
- stewardship (of the organization);
- commitment to the growth of people (personal as well as professional);
- building community (particularly in large organizations).

Servant leadership in schools can be practised by every teacher, not just the senior managers or headteacher. It argues for a degree of humility in one's leadership behaviour; this moves away from the 'hero innovator', aggressive and ego-serving model of leadership, and toward a much more facilitatory style of leadership (Fisher and Fisher, 1998: 194). It is premised on extensive and effective communication (see Chapter 6). It does not seek personal aggrandizement; servant leaders ask questions of teachers such as: 'how I can help you to enable the students to learn and to achieve more effectively and successfully?', 'how can I help you to develop you as a teacher?', 'how can I help the school to benefit from your work with other teachers?', 'how can I enable you to enjoy, and learn from, your work with students?'

Servant leadership is not without its problems (April *et al.*, 2000: 115; Berry and Cartwright, 2000: 344). For example, it suffers from the same difficulty as earlier normative theories of leadership in supposing that there is 'one best way' for leaders to act rather than, for example, suggesting that leadership behaviour changes with, and adapts to, the situation, and it may be 'hopelessly idealistic' (Berry and Cartwright, 2000: 344). Nevertheless, the move away from directive leadership to servant leadership signals an important paradigm shift in leadership thinking.

Quantum leadership

April *et al.* (2000: 64–8) suggest that complex, self-organizing institutions rely on 'quantum leadership' (see also Quigley, 1997; Youngblood, 1997). Quantum physics focuses on the subatomic, particle-level world (micro-management perhaps!), and finds that particles exist only *relationally* rather than independently

(Zohar, 1990); they are constantly in motion and turbulence, and this turbulence is a function of their interdependence (Wheatley, 1999: 11). Quantum organizations (Youngblood, 1997: 31–2; 1998) are organizations which thrive on complexity, uncertainty, creativity, wholeness, autonomous action, flexibility, change, personal leadership and relationships. Quantum physics lays emphasis on relationships and uncertainty; none of us exists in isolation (McNamara, 2001: 3).

From quantum physics can be derived tenets for leadership in which emphasis is laid on a shift of leaders' tasks from directing to the creation of rich environments for self-organization to take place (Wheatley, 1999). Quantum leaders clarify a shared vision, enrich the culture of the organization, develop alignment and understanding by promoting ownership, nurturing relationships in the school, encouraging, supporting and disseminating learning, and nurturing people and the person-centred organization. For Youngblood (1997: 112–6), quantum leadership is a process rather than a position, a verb rather than a noun. Quantum leaders are active in connecting the organization with its environment, disturbing and perturbing the system in order to stimulate change, ensuring the rich flow of information, and promoting organizational learning.

Quigley (1997) suggests that quantum leaders are forever looking for new ways in which the core competencies of an organization can interact more effectively to make more creativity possible, and they ensure that the system has a sense of direction, an aim and a purpose, as well as a plan of action. Quantum leaders recognize the talents available in staff, and are concerned with facilitating and enabling staff to interact in new ways. Built into effective quantum leaders is an understanding that motivation is important, and that positive human interaction is built on a foundation of moral principles, so that the leader is part of a moral contract and preserves moral integrity in his/her behaviour. In quantum leadership freedom requires order just as order requires freedom.

Distributed leadership

The notion of *distributed leadership* is a *sine qua non* for the emergent organization (Fisher and Fisher, 1998: 194; Morrison 2001a). Schools concern knowledge work and knowledge-based institutions, and Fisher and Fisher (1998: 215) argue that distributed leadership is the corollary of knowledge-based institutions. Knowledge, they aver, lies in each worker's head, at whose discretion it is shared or not. Distributed leadership is, in effect, 'collective self-leadership', as this respects the notion of discretionary disclosure of knowledge.

Leadership in the complex organization is not concerned only with the power of senior figures and with hierarchy. For example, Miami University's Department of Educational Leadership includes in its set of sixteen principles for school leadership the requirements that leadership should not be equated with one's position in a hierarchy, and that leaders may be found anywhere in the organization, because leadership concerns a 'quality of practice' rather than 'organizational position' (University of Miami Department of Educational Leadership, 2001: 5). Its authors argue for leadership to be separated from hierarchical relations, as it is about 'power-sharing' rather than 'power-imposing' (*ibid*: 5). Echoing the spirit of complexity theory, the authors comment that diversity is a necessary component of education, and that such diversity comes through engagement with others (p. 6) (see also Senge *et al.*, 2000: 317–21).

Leadership is best thought of as a behaviour rather than as a role or position in a hierarchy (Wheatley, 1999: 24), and no single person can be expected to display leadership in all contexts. Rather, Riley (2000: 46) regards leadership as 'a network of relationships among people, structures and cultures' rather than the preserve of a sole school headteacher. Leadership is not an individual matter but spreads throughout an organization (Barnes and Kriger, 1986: 16; Morrison 2001a), with leader roles overlapping, complementary, and shifting from person to person; it is shared (Méndez-Morse, 1999: 3) and can be exercised by several people (Slater and Doig, 1988). Fullan (2001: 10) suggests that good leaders develop other good leaders at all levels of the organization, which is a way to 'bring on' the next generation of school leaders, and that there is a need for leaders at all levels of the organization (*ibid*: 122).

Leaders can emerge anywhere in the organization (Morrison 2001a) and already exist everywhere in the organization (Brandon, 1992: 32), though, of course, not everybody is a leader. As Janov (1994) suggests, leadership is less about role and more about behaviour, and leadership can be satisfied by many people, not just one person (see also Cashman, 1998: 20; Spillane *et al.*, 2000). Gibb (1954) comments that leadership is best conceived as a group quality, and leadership naturally passes between individuals in light of different and changing circumstances. People sometimes take leadership roles and other times adopt followership roles (Kelley, 1988).

Nickse (1977: 5) suggested that teachers are in ideal positions to be leaders in schools because not only do they have a vested interest in what takes place, but also they have a sense of history of the organization and of their colleagues, they know the community and are in a position to implement change. Kiel (1994: 216) underlines the importance of having several leaders in organizations within complexity theory, arguing that because, in complexity theory (as in chaos theory), small actions can have large effects, individual actions can produce large consequences.

Gronn (1999, 2000) argues powerfully for distributed leadership in schools; it is, he avers, an 'evolutionary concept' (Gronn, 2000: 323) and is a 'fluid and emergent' phenomenon (p. 324). Indeed there can be leadership by a team rather than by an individual (*ibid*: 332). Distributed leadership, he suggests, is 'an idea whose time has come' (*ibid*: 333), a view which echoes Rost's (1991) advocacy of collaborative and shared leadership.

Anyone can exercise leadership (McMaster, 1996: 70) provided he/she has followers, i.e. the essence of leadership is a relational matter. As Fullan (2001: 13) remarks, leaders who do not treat others well have no followers. Leaders, managers, other teachers are all equal but simply do different work. Indeed, in a complex organization leadership is actually required to be distributed throughout the institution. Leaders in school, for example, can be curriculum planning leaders, management leaders, timetabling leaders, pastoral leaders, pedagogical leaders, resource leaders, IT leaders, community relations leaders, assessment leaders, subject leaders, relationship- and team-building leaders. At particular times or for particular purposes different leaders take centre stage.

Collier and Esteban (2000) also term this 'systemic leadership'. Systemic leadership, they suggest, is a 'diffused view of leadership' (p. 207) which is grounded in the free, autonomous creativity of participants, hence it is emergent and developmental (see also Senge, 1997 who regards leadership as distributed throughout teams in the organization). It is characterized by openness and extensive communication (Collier and Esteban, *op. cit.*) as well as by accountability and autonomy. The authors argue that such a view of leadership emphasizes communities of commitment, discernment and practice; indeed the notion of community itself is a key element in emergent, self-organizing schools that have to adapt, and adapt to, their environments. Riley (2000) argues powerfully that reforms in education hinge on the commitment of teachers in order to guarantee success, and that this requires engagement, collaborative respect, and distributed responsibility and decision making, rather than compliance and directiveness.

There are, then, *several* leaders in a complex school. Leadership does not evaporate in complexity theory; rather it is everywhere in the organization. As Coleman (1999: 38) suggests, leadership can be everywhere and everybody can be a champion of change. Change leadership in schools requires several leaders (Lakomski, 2000).

Distributed leadership in the school will require each 'cell assembly' or unit in the networked organization to possess its own leader, whose roles, tasks and purposes will be agreed and who will be able to work with colleagues to improve curricula, pedagogy, assessment and the gamut of activities in her/his purview. The leader will be responsible, for example, for strategy formation, improved teaching and learning, planning and coordination, producing policies and schemes, managing resources, monitoring, evaluation and improvement, managing change, and involving and engaging participants (Bell and Ritchie, 1999). Many of the leadership tasks here are curricular and pedagogic; that is intentional, for a prime purpose of schools is to improve learning and achievement.

The task of distributed leadership in the self-organizing school frequently becomes one of managing and developing relationships, developing opportunities for new working relationships to be formed, celebrating diversity in people and cultures, working towards conflict resolution (and, as Tuckman, 1965 argues, this is inevitable in a healthy organization), and developing inclusive and collaborative work in the organization (cf. April, 1997; Riley, 2000: 4).

Identifying the leadership potential of each participant is, itself, a key management or leadership skill (Crom and Bertels, 1999). In a primary school this practice might be to ensure that the teacher who is particularly talented in art has the opportunity to develop art through the school, advising students and other teachers alike. Or the practice might be to approach a novice teacher who has expressed an interest in whole-school planning to join the curriculum-planning team so that, in the future, she has developed some expertise in the area.

The development of the National Standards for Subject Leaders in the UK (Teacher Training Agency, 1998: 10–12) sets out some key areas for development here for distributed leadership:

A strategic direction and development of the subject;
B teaching and learning;
C leading and managing staff;
D efficient and effective deployment of staff and resources.

The listings of requirements here resonate with the key areas and types of distributed leadership discussed in this chapter. With regard to strategic direction and development of the subject, it is suggested that 'within the context of the school's aims and policies, subject leaders develop and implement subject policies, plans, targets and practices' (p. 10). This includes attention to the human side of organizations. Further, distributed leadership, in subject terms, involves attention to teaching and learning, in which 'subject leaders secure and sustain effective teaching of the subject, evaluate the quality of teaching and standards of pupils' achievements and set targets for improvement' (p. 10). In this they 'establish a partnership with parents to involve them in their child's learning of the subject, as well as providing information about curriculum, attainment, progress and targets' (p. 11), and 'develop effective links with the local community, including business and industry, in order to extend the subject curriculum, enhance teaching and to develop pupils' wider understanding' (p. 11).

Subject leaders lead and manage staff, providing 'to all those with involvement in the teaching or support of the subject, the support, challenge, information and development necessary to sustain motivation and secure improvement in teaching' (p. 11). To do this they 'sustain their own motivation and, where possible, that of other staff involved in the subject' (p. 11). Distributed leadership, exemplified here in subject leadership terms, devolves power throughout the school and requires leaders to be servants and motivators.

Harris (1998, 1999, 2000) suggests that leaders play a key role in departmental success. Effective departments in schools, she avers (Harris, 2000: 88) reinforce values, involve students, provide external support, take risks, and celebrate and share successes. The head of department has a key role in developing these areas. By contrast, she suggests that 'stuck' departments (ineffective departments that are unable to change) require interventions including (*ibid*: 85) changes in leadership, immediate external support, data and diagnosis, early visible changes, a focus on learning, staff development, and collaboration. It can be seen that these resonate closely with the recommendations for subject leaders from the Teacher Training Agency.

Lakomski (2000) argues that organizational learning requires distributed leadership and knowledge. Distributed leadership is a partner to distributed knowledge in a complex, learning organization (Lakomski, 2000; cf. Putnam and Borko, 2000). Schools are, *prima facie*, learning institutions and, if they are to keep pace with change and to learn, then they need to harness the creativity of their participants and their shared, collective knowledge (e.g. through intranet services). They need to become learning organizations (Fullan, 2001).

Further, if creativity is to be maximized then it needs to be *shared* and to contribute to a synergistic organization (Hong and Kuo, 1999: 207). Knowledge management becomes an important feature of organizational learning, integrating internal and external knowledge within and outside the organization (see Chapters 4 and 5). The learning environment of the school must maximize its human resources (Chattel, 1998). Emergence and self-organization require learning and, therefore, human resource management.

Hong and Kuo (1999: 208–9) suggest that human resource development involves: providing participants with challenging work; changing existing patterns of understanding, perception and thinking; and supporting differences in practice. Providing challenging work is addressed, the authors suggest, through:

- *job enlargement* (widening the scope of the work undertaken, which is addressed by learning through instruction and support programmes);
- *job rotation* (taking on different tasks, which is addressed by learning through sharing and mentoring); this can extend to rotating leadership (Fisher and Fisher, 1998: 212) as, for example, in many universities, where heads of department are appointed for a three- or four-year term, and to shared leadership (*ibid*: 213);
- *job enrichment* (increasing the depth of the work content, which is addressed largely by self-learning).

In schools, job enlargement might be addressed by attendance at courses and membership of additional committees. It would also require attention to incentives, promotion and additional responsibility payments. Job rotation suggests that posts (e.g. course directorships, headship of departments, assessment responsibility) are for a fixed term, maybe three years. Rotating membership of groups in the school might increase mutual understanding, bring a necessary degree of destabilization to the institution to ensure that it learns and grows – emerges – and minimize the strength of intra-group identification at the expense of inter-group collaboration (West, 1999: 195). Job rotation also brings with it job enlargement, as the degree of expertise gained increases. Job enrichment is frequently a matter of developing reflective practice (Schön, 1983) and 'extended professionalism' (Hoyle, 1975). This may be supported by the school sponsoring course attendance.

Changing existing patterns of understanding, perception and thinking, then, requires changes to mental models and, Hong and Kuo (1999) suggest, is addressed through instruction, sharing and self-study. The authors suggest that job enlargement, rotation and enrichment are strategies that push people to learn, and are more coercive, whilst instruction, sharing and self-study are less coercive strategies for learning (p. 209); they are 'pull' strategies.

Robbins and Finley (1998a: 18–32) suggest that 'push' strategies are useful for short-term learning, whilst 'pull' strategies take longer but are more deep-seated. Push strategies, they contend (p.30), are useful for efficiency and ensuring compliance, whilst pull strategies are more person-centred and are useful for effectiveness and integrating participants in the organization – they cultivate participants (cf.

Hong and Kuo, 1999: 210). Pull strategies may bring longer-term benefits in terms of organizational learning (Eisenbach *et al.*, 1999: 82).

Though distributed leadership in schools is a major implication of complexity leadership, its limits are signalled by Silins *et al.* (1999). They found, for example, that distributed leadership impacted only indirectly and in small amount on student outcomes. Further, they caution about the dangers of distributed leadership, suggesting that it might distract teachers from their 'core work' of teaching and learning by involving them in wider school issues, and that the law of diminishing returns applied, in that the greater the involvement of teachers in too many aspects of the school, the more this may detract from their central tasks.

Developing leadership in schools

The efforts made by the Teacher Training Agency (2000, 10–15) in the UK to prepare headteachers for leadership roles in areas resonate with some of the key principles outlined so far, in five main areas:

A   Strategic direction and development of the school;
B   Teaching and learning;
C   Leading and managing staff;
D   Efficient and effective deployment of staff and resources;
E   Accountability.

Their constituent elements echo some of the principles set out in this chapter. For example, with regard to 'strategic direction and development of the school', it is argued that 'headteachers, working with the governing body, develop a strategic view for the school in its community and analyze and plan for its future needs and further development within the local, national and international context' (p. 12). In this headteachers are to

> lead by example, provide inspiration and motivation, and embody for the pupils, staff, governors and parents, the vision, purpose and leadership of the school ... create an ethos and provide educational vision and direction which secure effective teaching, successful learning and achievement by pupils and sustained improvement in their spiritual, moral, cultural, mental and physical development ... they secure the commitment of parents and the wider community to the vision and direction of the school ... ensure that all those involved in the school are committed to its aims, motivated to achieve them, and involved in meeting long, medium and short term objectives and targets which secure the educational success of the school
>
> (p. 12)

This resonates with Fullan's (2001) view that leaders need to address five components: moral purpose; an understanding of the change process; the development of, and ability to develop, relationships; the fostering of knowledge building; and the striving for coherence (including prioritizing and focusing) with vitality, enthusiasm and optimism.

With regard to leading and managing staff, headteachers are to 'lead, motivate, support, challenge and develop staff to secure improvement' (p. 14), to

> maximize the contribution of staff to improving the quality of education pro-
> vided and standards achieved and ensure that constructive working
> relationships are formed between staff and pupils … motivate and enable all
> staff in their school to carry out their respective roles to the highest standard,
> through high quality continuing professional development based on assess-
> ment of needs [and] sustain their own motivation and that of other staff
>
> (p. 14) (words in brackets mine)

Headteachers, it is argued, need to be adept at the 'efficient and effective deployment of staff and resources … deploying people and resources efficiently and
effectively' (p. 15). With regard to accountability, they are to

> account for the efficiency and effectiveness of the school to the governors
> and others, including pupils, parents, staff, local employers and the local
> community … create and develop an organisation in which all staff recognise
> that they are accountable for the success of the school … and ensure that par-
> ents and pupils are well-informed about the curriculum, attainment and
> progress
>
> (p. 15)

That is, accountability is relational.
   One can see here that several key elements of servant leadership are addressed.

Leadership style and emotional intelligence

Effective leadership, devolved on human relations in complexity theory, requires
emotional intelligence. Goleman (2000) provides an analysis of leadership which
catches the person-centredness and emphasis on interpersonal relationships and
new forms of democratic and distributed leadership within the complex organization. He recognizes that much of the leadership agenda concerns establishing the
appropriate ethos or climate of the organization.
   Effective leadership for developing strong relations and connectedness, and
to facilitate communication for emerging self-organization, requires considerable emotional intelligence (Palmer *et al.*, 2000), and Goleman's notion of
'emotional intelligence' (Coleman, 1995, 1998a, 1998b) permeates his view of
effective leadership. Emotional intelligence is an important sequitur of leadership in the complex school (the root word of emotion is the Latin *emovere* – 'to
disturb') (Tolle, 1999: 24), and Fullan (2001: 71) argues that, in complex times
and in complex organizations like schools, emotional intelligence is required in
plenty.
   Emotional intelligence comprises the ability that participants have to handle
themselves and relationships sensitively and effectively (Beatty, 2001). The term's
originators, Salovey and Mayer (1990), suggest that emotional intelligence is the
ability to monitor one's own and others' emotions and feelings and to use this to

guide our behaviour. The emotionally intelligent person is skilled in identifying, understanding, using and regulating emotions (Mayer and Salovey, 1993). They suggest that emotional intelligence includes self-awareness, managing emotions, motivating oneself (channelling emotions into reaching a goal, self-control, delayed gratification), empathy, and effectiveness in handling relationships.

In Goleman's (1995) work emotional intelligence is devolved onto five areas (cf. also Barling *et al.*, 2000; Stein and Book, 2000):

- *self-awareness* (emotional self-awareness, accurate self-awareness and self-confidence);
- *self-management* (self-control, trustworthiness, conscientiousness, adaptability, achievement orientation and initiative);
- *social awareness* (empathy, organizational awareness and service orientation);
- *social skill* (visionary leadership, influence, developing others, communication, catalyzing change, conflict management, building bonds, teamwork and collaboration);
- *motivation* (working for reasons other than money or status and an ability to pursue goals tirelessly).

McCluskey (1997) suggests that emotional intelligence can be developed in schools, and is a key feature in regarding schools as 'organic wholes that grow and develop', in which all participants and their knowledge are interrelated, and where this interaction extends to the 'surrounding environment' (p. 1); this matches very closely some central features of complexity theory.

There is a burgeoning literature to suggest that emotional intelligence should be taught in schools, and that this should not simply be confined to leadership (Goleman, 1995; *ibid*: 3; AbiSamra, 2000; Committee for Children, 2000), a factor which is becoming increasingly important in light of the problems of escalating violence in schools. Loader (1997) and Beatty (2001: 8) suggest that a leader's emotional intelligence also concerns the ability to foster a safe environment in schools and to put 'emotions on the agenda' of schools (p. 19); indeed Beatty sees emotions as playing a significant role in the emergent [her word] co-construction of meaning in schools. In her view emotions should not be marginalized to the periphery of leadership, never to be displayed and always to be denied (p. 24); rather they are central in schools and school leadership.

Goleman (2000) characterizes six styles of leadership:

- *coercive* leaders (who demand compliance: 'do as I say', and who are poor listeners) (Fullan, 2001: 42);
- *authoritative* leaders (who mobilize people towards the achievement of a vision: 'come with me', and who may not be good listeners) (Fullan, 2001: 42);
- *affiliative* leaders (who create harmony and strong interpersonal relationships in the organization: 'people come first' (often useful in overcoming people's fear of change)) (Fullan 2001: 41);

- *democratic* leaders (who build consensus and participation: 'let's decide how to move forwards', and who may listen too much) (Fullan, 2001: 42);
- *pacesetting* leaders (who expect self-direction and high-quality performance from participants: 'keep up with me', and who are poor listeners) (Fullan, 2001: 42);
- *coaching* leaders (who develop participants for the longer-term future: 'let's see where you are and how you can develop', often useful to overcome fear of change) (Fullan, 2001: 41).

He then reports an interesting set of correlates between leadership style and aspects of the climate of the organization (Table 3.1) that resonate with emotional intelligence:

Clearly it is dangerous to infer too much from these data, as the sample size and significance levels are unreported. Nevertheless the coercive and pacesetting styles, i.e. those styles which are more 'push' than 'pull' styles and that demonstrate least emotional intelligence, correlated negatively with the overall impact on the climate and its constituent elements, i.e. the greater the reliance on these styles, the worse was the climate of the institution. On the other hand, the authoritative, affiliative and coaching styles, i.e. those which placed greater stress on interpersonal relationships and emotional intelligence, correlated positively with the climate of the organization. Overall, the authoritative style demonstrated the strongest positive relation with the climate of the organization. Further, in terms of the key elements of leadership for self-organization – flexibility, responsibility, commitment and clarity (e.g. of communication, of vision, of direction):

- the greatest degree of flexibility (0.32) was found in the authoritative style and the lowest (−0.28) was found in the coercive style;
- the greatest degree of responsibility (0.23) was found in the democratic style and the lowest was found in the coercive style (−0.37);

Table 3.1 Leadership style and organizational climate

Aspects of climate	Leadership style					
	Coercive	Authoritative	Affiliative	Democratic	Pacesetting	Coaching
Flexibility	−0.28	0.32	0.27	0.28	−0.07	0.17
Responsibility	−0.37	0.21	0.16	0.23	0.04	0.08
Standards	0.02	0.38	0.31	0.22	−0.27	0.39
Rewards	−0.18	0.54	0.48	0.42	−0.29	0.43
Clarity	−0.11	0.44	0.37	0.35	−0.28	0.38
Commitment	−0.13	0.35	0.34	0.26	−0.20	0.27
Overall impact on climate	−0.26	0.54	0.46	0.43	−0.25	0.42

- the greatest degree of commitment (0.35 and 0.34) was found in the authoritative and affiliative styles respectively and the lowest was found in the pacesetting style (–0.20);
- the greatest degree of clarity (0.44) was found in the authoritative style, and the lowest was found in the pacesetting style (–0.28).

It is clear that flexibility suffers under the top-down decision making of the coercive and pacesetting styles and they are damaging to the 'rewards' aspects of the climate. The highest positive correlation was between the 'authoritative' style and rewards (0.54), the highest negative correlation was between the coercive style and 'responsibility' (–0.37) and the least correlation was between the coercive style and 'standards' (0.02). Authoritative leaders, it appears, even though they make clear the ends, give people freedom and confidence for manoeuvre, experiment and risk taking (Brown and Eisenhardt, 1997; Coleman, 1999: 35; Goleman, 2000: 84).

Of course, a coercive style might be effective in energizing a stagnant organization or implementing major changes of policy, and it might be necessary to use such styles with participants for whom all other forms of motivation have failed. The coaching style, which is strongly supportive, turns out to be limited in flexibility; perhaps too supportive a style is constricting. The affiliative style, in emphasizing praise and the promotion of the positive, might overlook poor performance or fail to support colleagues who are unsure about how to move forward on their own.

Further, whilst the democratic style might make for greater commitment and high morale, too much democracy can lead to the inertia of endless meetings, dissensus, and airings of ignorance and incompetence on the part of participants. The pacesetting style might be useful for rapid benchmarking but may turn out to lead to participants trying to 'second-guess' the leader. The coaching style is humane and builds on diagnosis of strengths and weaknesses towards furthering personal goals and personal development, yet it requires constant dialogue, time for which may be scarce, and it assumes that participants are not resistant to change. The authoritative style may be ineffective if one is working with a group of highly expert or more expert colleagues. Indeed, the authoritative leader suffers from the same risk as the transformational leader, i.e. imposing an agenda and manipulating/influencing participants towards realizing it. In this respect the affiliative and democratic styles may sit most comfortably with the notion of the school as a complex self-organizing institution.

Goleman (2000: 84) suggests that the affiliative style may be most suitable for building team harmony, increasing morale, improving communication and building trust, all key areas of emergence and self-organization. On the other hand it also can produce 'rudderless' behaviour – drift in an organization or steering towards failure (*ibid*: 85); hence, to prevent this, Goleman suggests that it might be beneficial to link the affiliative style with the authoritative style.[1]

Goleman (2000: 87) also indicates that different styles are best for different purposes (cf. Fullan 2001: 41). Leaders need to call on many styles, particularly the authoritative, democratic, affiliative and coaching styles (cf. the different styles of leadership at different stages of team formation, discussed in Chapter 2). Goleman suggests that it is necessary for leaders to understand the emotional intelligences underlying the leadership styles. For example, the affiliative leader emphasizes empathy, building relationships and communication, whilst coercive and pacesetting styles might be more starved of emotional intelligence than others.

In schools, Morrison *et al.* (1989) found that in the early stages of an innovation a more authoritative, directive leadership style characterized the early stages of a successful innovation, and this was appreciated by all participants, as it inspired them with confidence in the leader. In the middle and later stages of an innovation a more democratic and less directive style of leadership was valued, once the participants had developed their own expertise in the innovation, and felt less insecure about it.

Barling *et al.* (2000), using the attributes of transformational and transactional leadership set out by Bass (1990, 1998) and the notion of emotional intelligence from Goleman, chart the relationships between emotional intelligence and transformational and transactional leadership (see Table 3.2). High emotional intelligence, including empathy and interpersonal relationships, they suggest, is found in transformational leaders. They report correlations between emotional intelligence[2] and key aspects of transformational and transactional leadership.

It can be seen that transformational leadership correlates positively with emotional intelligence and negatively with transactional leadership. The message is clear: emotional intelligence is bound up with three key aspects of transformational leadership, viz. idealized influence (charisma), inspirational motivation and individualized consideration. Barling *et al.* (2000: 159) suggest that leaders who are high in emotional intelligence are regarded by followers as displaying more leadership behaviours. Causality is not inferred here, so, for example, it may be that transformational leadership increases emotional intelligence and/or vice versa.

It has been argued that emotional intelligence is an important element of effective leadership. Indeed it may be the deciding factor in leadership in schools

Table 3.2 Leadership style and emotional intelligence

Aspects of transformational leadership	Emotional intelligence
Idealized influence	0.12
Inspirational motivation	0.56*
Intellectual stimulation	0.35*
Individualized consideration	0.49*
Aspects of transactional leadership	
Contingent reward	0.44*
Management by exception: active	−0.01
Management by exception: passive	−0.18
Laissez-faire	−0.27

* = $p<0.01$

(cf. Gibbs, 1995; Tran, 1998). That said, Gibbs cautions against too easy an acceptance of emotional intelligence as the solution to leadership. She argues that missing from the discussion is the moral dimension (cf. Fullan, 2001). Emotional skills, she avers, could be used to inspire people or to exploit them; emotional intelligence can be a force for good and evil. What is required, she suggests, is a moral debate on the values that govern the use to which emotional intelligence is put – it is a necessary rather than sufficient aspect of leadership.

Further, Young (1996) suggests that there are several problems of validity in the notion of emotional intelligence, particularly concerning construct, content, criterion-related, concurrent, convergent and discriminative validity. She suggests that measures of emotional intelligence still require validity testing by correlational analysis with other measures of related factors (p. 18), i.e. that the notion of emotional intelligence is attractive but requires more stringent validation procedures than have currently been undertaken.

Leadership and organizational climate for emergence

The effective school, for Miles (1975), has robust organizational health, comprising:

- clear goals;
- excellent communication channels;
- democratic power sharing decision making;
- effective use of human resources;
- collaboration and a sense of belonging;
- high morale;
- innovativeness;
- autonomy from the environment;
- adaptability to changing demands;
- problem-solving adequacy.

The partner to organizational health is organizational climate. The concept of organizational climate is not new (e.g. Halpin, 1966). Gilmer (1966), Litwin and Stringer (1968) and Tagiuri (1968) suggest that organizational climate refers to the particular characteristics of an organization, its social systems and structures, its working practices, its defining qualities, its distinguishing features (from other organizations), the perceptions that employees have of the organization, all of which combine to impact on work and achievement.

Halpin (1966) uses the concept of organizational climate to identify those types of organization where change is more or less likely to occur. He suggests that if the climate is not propitious for change (emergence) then change is unlikely to be successful. He sets out six climates on a continuum from openness to closure, arguing that the more open is the climate the more conducive it is to change (and complexity theory is a theory of open systems).

The climate that is most conducive to change is the open climate. Here the distinguishing features are high morale, openness, cooperation, the minimum of bureaucracy and records, high job satisfaction and motivation, mutual respect for all employees and a feeling of genuineness. The leader is a model of appropriate behaviour and runs a loose–tight organization. Collegiality abounds. Indeed social relationships extend outside the organization.

Slightly less conducive to change is the autonomous climate. Here the distinguishing features are a very high level of autonomy that is accorded to employees, often to the neglect of coordination or alignment with the organization. The satisfaction of social needs often overtakes the achievement of the task. The leader adopts a 'hands-off' approach, being impersonal and sometimes aloof, and guidelines for procedures replace 'the personal touch'.

Less conducive still to change is the controlled climate (and complexity theory advocates order without control), in which the thrust is towards task achievement at all costs, with a highly directive, dominating and often authoritarian leader, and inflexibility and lack of autonomy in work practices. That this might cause resentment and be counter-productive is noted by Senge (1990) and Wickens (1995).

Halpin suggests that a familiar climate is yet more closed to change. This is distinguished by the emphasis on the 'big happy family', with morale and job satisfaction being average, with everybody trying to tell each other how things ought to be done, where social interaction is extensive and involvement is high. This climate embodies both the best and worst of family life (many families are dysfunctional and damaging).

Concomitant with the familiar climate is the paternalistic climate, of which attempts (often vainly) by the leader to control the organization and the people are the hallmarks. The organization is characterized by low morale, it is riven with factions, and the leader is highly intrusive, thereby causing overt resistance. Because it is a divided institution it does not augur well for sustained change; the micropolitics of the organization undermine attempts at change.

Finally Halpin's closed climate is the least conducive to change. Everything stagnates. There is low morale, little incentive for change, little sense (or indeed practice) of involvement. Workers simply 'go through the motions' of work with minimum commitment, with the leader giving generalized exhortations to work, without setting a good example. Inflexibility and a divisive organization in which participants are apathetic, controlled and intolerant are the hallmarks of this type of organization.

Halpin's work is useful in providing heuristic tools for analysis. One has to be cautious, perhaps, in adopting any typifications of organizations because they are typifications rather than actualities – and are possibly over-reductionist. Nevertheless, Halpin's identification of degrees of openness and closure to change at an organizational level is helpful, and indeed his placement of the familiar and paternalistic climates at the closed end of the continuum is perhaps salutary.

Hoy *et al.* (1991) apply Halpin's work to the educational context and identify four climates in education that are conducive to change and emergence. They, too, set these out on a continuum of openness to closure, and identify the open, engaged, disengaged and closed climates along this continuum from openness to closure to change respectively. They identify eight components of organizational climate (pp. 14, 133). Four of these refer to the teachers' behaviour, thus:

- *disengagement* (where teachers are out of touch with that which is happening in the school);
- *hindrance* (where the teachers feel that the principal is burdening them with routine, bureaucratic, unnecessary work);
- *esprit* (morale, which develops with successful task accomplishment and social needs satisfaction);
- *intimacy* (the extent to which teachers enjoy good social relations with each other).

Signalling the importance of principal behaviour in the promotion of a positive school climate, the remaining four are:

- *aloofness* (where the principal is distant and relies on procedures);
- *production emphasis* (where the principal is directive and reluctant to act on feedback);
- *thrust* (where the principal strives to move the organization forward through personal example);
- *consideration* (where the principal demonstrates warmth and humanity).

Using these terms, Hoy *et al.* (1991: 16) construct six typologies of Halpin's climates, and indicate the levels of each component, as shown in Table 3.3.

The positive climate is characterized by concern for people, freedom from bureaucracy, developed social relationships, and limited emphasis on 'getting the task done'– the task is achieved as a consequence of other matters. The inter-correlations between the components of a positive school climate demonstrate that, on key areas

Table 3.3 Typologies and components of organizational climate

Climate dimension	Climate type					
	Open	Autonomous	Controlled	Familiar	Paternal	Closed
Disengagement	Low*	Low	Low	High	High	High*
Hindrance	Low	Low	High	Low	Low	High
Esprit	High*	High	High	Average	Low	Low*
Intimacy	Average	High	Low	High	Low	Average
Aloofness	Low	High	High	Low	Low	High
Production emphasis	Low	Low	High	Low	High	High
Thrust	High*	Average	Average	Average	Average	Low*
Consideration	High	Average	Low	High	High	Low

*Salient characteristic of the open and closed climates.

Source: Hoy, W.K., Tarter, C.J. and Kottkamp, R.B. (1991) *Open Schools, Healthy Schools*, p. 16, copyright ©, reprinted by permission of Sage Publications Inc.

of self-organization (a major area of complexity theory), climates of openness are the most productive for self-organization (p. 133) as shown in Table 3.4.

One can observe the high correlations between organizational commitment and almost all the other factors except intimacy and academic achievement. Trust in the principal had high correlations with almost all factors except resource allocation, directive behaviour and academic achievement. The high correlation (0.58) between 'initiating structure' and 'principal influence' signals clearly the importance of leadership to support emergence. Similarly the high correlations between 'trust in principal', and 'supportive behaviour' (0.56) and between 'trust in principal' and 'commitment' (0.66) indicate, perhaps, the significance of these aspects of leadership. This is reinforced by the high correlation between 'trust in colleagues' and 'commitment'. The high correlation (0.64) between 'supportive behaviour' and 'consideration' and between 'supportive behaviour' and 'trust' (0.56 and 0.24) emphasizes the importance of interpersonal matters in self-organization, a factor which is emphasized, perhaps, by the high negative correlation between 'trust in colleagues' and 'frustration' (–0.31); it seems that interpersonal relations cluster together and constitute key elements of the emergent organization. The highest set of negative correlations are between 'frustration' and variables 1–3, 5–10 and 13–16; frustration, it seems, has to be expected in the self-organizing school, echoing the 'storming' stage of Tuckman's group development (see Chapter 2).

'Directive behaviour' had a negative correlation with 'morale' (–0.03), 'supportive behaviour' (–0.09), 'engagement' (–0.21), 'commitment'(–0.22) and the two categories of 'trust' (in the principal, and in colleagues) (–0.17 and –0.03). This suggests strongly the negative effects of a command-and-control mentality.

In a study which builds on the work of Halpin and Hoy *et al.*, Tam and Cheng (1996) identify four types of primary schools with different degrees of positive organizational climate. The authors use several of the terms from Hoy *et al.*, for example: esprit, intimacy, disengagement and hindrance.

In the 'synergistic school' they report a low level of organizational formalization and hierarchical authority, high esprit, low disengagement and low hindrance, and a high level of participative decision making. There is high morale, high cooperation, participation and cohesiveness, and all of this within a climate of support from a visionary and charismatic principal who encourages professional development (pp. 243–4). The 'synergetic school' possesses the most positive climate and is characterized by strong principal leadership.

By contrast, the 'headless school' is characterized by weak leadership, limited participation in decision making, low esprit and high hindrance. The school lacks direction and the principal appears powerless and displays little concern for the professional development of the teachers. Routine and paperwork predominate here, with the teachers being passive and compliant. This is, the authors aver, the least positive climate. Between the two extremes lies the 'mediocre type' and the 'disengaged' school type, with average performance in the several areas of organizational climate.

The results indicate the benefits of strong leadership and synergy, participation and person-centredness in developing a positive school climate. The synergistic

Table 3.4 Organizational climates for complexity theory

Variable by number	1	2	3	4	5	6	7	8	9	10	11	12	13	14	15
1 Institutional integrity															
2 Resource allocation	0.19														
3 Principal influence	0.40**	0.47**													
4 Initiating structure	0.33*	0.23*	0.58**												
5 Consideration	0.35**	0.25**	0.30*	0.39**											
6 Academic emphasis	0.11	0.41**	0.45**	0.46**	0.36**										
7 Morale	0.44**	0.39**	0.33**	0.34**	0.42**	0.45**									
8 Directive behaviour	0.01	-0.02	0.14	-0.06	0.38**	-0.32**	-0.03								
9 Supportive behaviour	-0.29**	-0.01	-0.20*	0.35**	0.64**	0.15	0.16	-0.09							
10 Engagement	0.29**	0.30**	0.39**	0.16	0.36**	0.35**	0.35**	-0.21*	0.39**						
11 Frustration	-0.26*	-0.41**	-0.38**	-0.16	-0.38**	-0.39**	-0.38**	0.41**	-0.31**	-0.52**					
12 Intimacy	-0.11	-0.04	-0.07	-0.15	0.02	-0.04	0.11	-0.04	0.05	0.22*	0.01				
13 Academic achievement	-0.34**	0.33**	0.18	0.10	0.11	0.63**	0.21	-0.11	0.01	0.21	-0.31**	0.02			
14 Organizational commitment	0.28**	0.31**	0.44**	0.30**	0.36**	0.44**	0.40**	-0.22*	0.29**	0.45**	-0.36**	0.13	0.20		
15 Trust in principal	0.39**	0.12	0.18	0.27*	0.51**	0.09	0.28*	-0.17	0.56**	0.27**	-0.24*	0.10	-0.08	0.66**	
16 Trust in colleagues	0.31**	0.11	0.32**	0.27*	0.36**	0.30*	0.52**	-0.03	0.24*	0.47**	-0.31**	0.27*	0.07	0.65**	0.44**

* = p <0.05 ** = p <0.01; N = 72

Hoy, W.K., Tarter, C.J. and Kottkamp, R.B. (1991) *Open Schools, Healthy Schools*, p. 133, copyright ©, reprinted by permission of Sage Publications Inc.

school is characterized by an absence of bureaucracy and the presence of a positive social climate. The results reaffirm the need to promote the positive school climate, and leadership is a critical factor here. This is echoed in the work of Sergiovanni (1998), who argues that leadership should also move beyond being bureaucratic, visionary and entrepreneurial, and towards being pedagogical, i.e. by enabling schools to become human and humane communities which emphasize both social contracts and capacity building in teachers.

Trust is a key feature of the leadership model in the flat network, in which interpersonal relations figure highly (Malone, 1998: 271–2).[3] Southworth (2000: 276) reports that, in primary schools, not only do collaborative cultures develop trust, but where trust is present, it produces support, encouragement, security and openness, which creates organizational resilience, flexibility and strength. Trust, he avers (p. 277), enables individuals to be valued.

If responsibility is to be shared then it requires trust to be placed in all participants. As Fairholm and Fairholm (2000: 102) suggest, leadership is a collective and relation-based rather than individual activity, and it requires a climate of mutuality, coordinated action and, chiefly, trust (see also Bennis, 1993: 166). A major task of leadership, then, is to build a *culture of trust*.[4] Tschannen-Moran (2000) found a series of statistically significant links between:

- collaboration with the principal and trust in the principal ($r = 0.32$, $\rho < 0.05$);
- collaboration between teachers and trust between them ($r = 0.30$, $\rho < 0.05$);
- collaboration with parents and trust in them ($r = 0.79$, $\rho < 0.01$).

Collaboration and trust, she affirms (p. 314), are reciprocal. Building trust requires attention to several important factors (cf. Fairholm and Fairholm, 2000; Luke, 1998; Tschannen-Moran, 2000), including: positive and genuine interpersonal communication; involvement rather than alienation; putting others before oneself (echoing notions of servant leadership); leaders being sensitive to followers' needs; having flat organizational structures rather than complicated hierarchies; honesty with people; freedom for participants to control their work within a shared vision; and trust that teachers have the expertise and will to make decisions in the interests of the school. Trust, suggests Tschannen-Moran (2000: 314), requires people to be benevolent, reliable, competent, honest and open. Clearly, trust also requires people in whom trust can be placed, e.g. their expertise and moral sense; it would be senseless to place trust in the hands of ignorance or innocence. The corollary of this is that trust requires the development of expertise in all staff. Together these authors aver that trust is a central condition for effective leadership, and it underpins much of Goleman's emotional intelligence set out earlier.

Putting together the elements of these studies, Watkin (2000) reports an important study of headteachers of schools, which uses Goleman's six styles of leadership and his notion of emotional intelligence, and links them to organizational climate and the requirements and characteristics of effective headteachers. Understanding and developing the organizational climate was a key to effective leadership. The study was of the Leadership Program for Serving Headteachers

(LPSH) in the UK. Leadership effectiveness was a function of individual characteristics and competencies, meeting the requirements of the job, improving the school and its climate, and leadership style. Highly effective headteachers, he found:

- were driven strongly by a set of personal values which supported students' achievement (which included respect for others, and balancing challenge with support);
- created a vision for the school and planned the realization of that in practice (which included strategic thinking and the drive for improvement);
- built commitment and support (which included impact, influence and holding people accountable);
- regarded situations (e.g. lack of resources) as opportunities rather than problems;
- cultivated and valued feedback and used it formatively (gathering information and gaining understanding, including social awareness and scanning the environment);
- drew on networks within and outside the school in order to achieve their goals;
- set clear expectations and clear limits of acceptability;
- demanded 'delivery', i.e. set performance standards, and planned for such 'delivery', including analytical thinking, taking the initiative, transformational leadership, teamworking, developing potential, and understanding others;
- challenged poor performance.

These are key areas in regarding schools as complex, self-organizing institutions.

Watkin (2000) reports that, of the six styles of leadership from Goleman, no single style was uniformly right or wrong; rather the styles varied according to 'fitness for purpose'; the skill was in the selection of the most appropriate style for the situation. He reported that headteachers of high-achieving schools possessed all the key characteristics listed above, particularly in holding people accountable together with developing their potential (e.g. challenge and support). Headteachers of 'failing' schools predominantly used the coercive style (more than 66 per cent) whereas headteachers of high achieving schools used more styles (five of Goleman's six styles) and, in particular, used authoritative, affiliative, democratic and coaching styles. Pacesetting styles correlated inversely with school achievement. This echoes exactly Goleman's (2000) research above, which found that authoritative, affiliative and coaching styles, i.e. those emphasizing interpersonal relationships and emotional intelligence, featured most strongly in positive organizational climates, and that coercive and pacesetting styles correlated negatively with organizational climate.

Distributed leadership needs to attend to commitment, motivation and passion as well as simply competence (Lloyd and Trapp, 1999: 333). As these authors remark, competence never makes things happen; commitment and passion create energy and this is the driver of activity. The task of leadership in a self-organizing institution is to foster commitment. Blau (1985) and Lok and Crawford (1999), for example, found that a 'consideration' leadership style exerted a greater influence on commitment than a 'structure' (or task-focused) leadership style.

Lok and Crawford (1999) found significant correlations between commitment and organizational culture, especially job satisfaction: within-job satisfaction (the degree of control that participants possessed in their work) correlated most highly with commitment, followed by praise, the level of interaction with colleagues, the degree of flexibility, the level of acceptance of others, and the degree of professional activity. It is clear, the authors aver, that the higher order levels of Maslow's hierarchy have to be satisfied for commitment to be secure. Further, they found that innovative and supportive subcultures correlated positively with commitment, whilst a bureaucratic subculture had a negative correlation with commitment (see also Brewer, 1994; Kratina, 1990). Commitment, it is clear, is a hugely important element for developing the complex self-organizing institution.

The increase in bureaucratic paperwork reduces commitment because it interrupts much of the 'real business' of teaching and learning. Riley (2000: 42) reports a 90 per cent dissatisfaction rate amongst primary school teachers because of these kinds of demands. If innovation and emergence are to occur, it appears that democratic rather than bureaucratic procedures must predominate in the school.

Significantly, Lok and Crawford (1999) found that organizational subculture (the micro-level of units within a network) exerted a greater effect on organizational commitment than did overall (macro-level) organizational culture. This is an important finding, for it suggests that there is a need for a networked structure rather than an hierarchical structure for the emergent self-organizing school, and that, within a networked organization, the particular unit of the network exerts a more powerful, subcultural, effect on commitment than the whole organization. People need to belong to face-to-face groups (Homans, 1951, 1971).

This takes us back to Chapter 2, where it was suggested that it is important to find the number of groups (formal and informal) that should be formed in the school; small groups are vital for the networked, complex, emergent organization. Innovation and learning, vital elements of the emergent organization, are fostered within small groups and flat, networked, horizontally differentiated structures rather than bureaucratic, hierarchical, vertically differentiated structures. Such groups might be formally established in the school (e.g. Jackson's, 2000 example of trios of school improvement groups), or, indeed they may arise more spontaneously.

Conclusion

This chapter has argued that leadership for self-organization and emergence bears several hallmarks; it:

* moves away from command-and-control styles of leadership, and is democratic;
* is transformational rather than transactional but moves beyond transformational leadership to transcendental, servant leadership and quantum leadership;

- is relational and person-centred;
- is distributed throughout the school and is not the property of a sole individual;
- requires developed emotional intelligence;
- moves away from being coercive and authoritarian and adopts more humanistic principles; it replaces coercion and pacesetting with authoritative, affiliative, democratic and coaching styles;
- creates a safe environment for experimentation and risk taking;
- is concerned to promote the organizational health and climate of the school;
- promotes interdependence, communication, cooperation, diversity and self-organization;
- provides platforms for learning and development;
- is a mixture of push and pull strategies;
- is demanding and supporting;
- is premised on mutual trust and commitment;
- is found in networks, flat management structures and small groups.

The empirical research cited here demonstrates these principles overwhelmingly.

4 Supporting emergence through the learning organization

This chapter suggests that the emergent, self-organizing school has to concern itself with organizational learning, and that elements of the project of the *learning organization* might be useful in this respect. A complex adaptive system has to learn in order to adapt to a changing environment (McCarthy and Tan, 2000). Organizational learning requires the school to possess and develop organizational intelligence and an ability to learn from its internal and external environments. This chapter indicates the role of leadership in this, for example in identifying platforms for self-organization and organizational learning, developing teams and networks as key mechanisms for organizational learning, and supporting risk-taking and experimentation.

Organizational learning, it will be suggested, takes the form of problem-solving and action research, maintenance, adaptive and benchmark learning. These, themselves, are premised on openness, sharing and communication, and a focus on knowledge management. Hence mechanisms should exist within the school for scanning and interpreting the environments in which it is operating, and responding to them. Organizational learning in school takes several forms, operates at several levels, and follows several stages. It also implies changes to working practices if flexibility for emergence and self-organization is to flourish.

At personal and interpersonal levels, complexity theory, in its emphasis on relational development and co-evolution, suggests that positive interpersonal relationships in the school are important, as are the culture of, and the devolution of decision making in, the school, together with the fostering of commitment and enthusiasm.

Organizational learning is the partner to emergence in schools. In this chapter the notion of organizational learning is considered, with particular emphasis being placed on the particular constructs of 'the learning organization'. Though this latter may be a more mechanistic and systems-driven construct than that implied by complexity theory (and indeed Stacey, 2000 argues against systems thinking within complexity thinking), nevertheless, as will be shown in this chapter, it has very many resonances with complexity theory, and offers practical strategies for organizational learning. Indeed the work of Senge (1990), Senge *et al.* (1994) and Senge *et al.* (2000) provides important inroads into organizational learning for schools through the concepts and application of 'the learning organization', which make specific reference to complexity for schools (e.g. Senge *et al.*, 2000: 7).

Schools and organizational learning

Schools are not only places where students learn. If schools are to embody and prepare for emergence then they, in turn, need to become learning organizations, though, as Riley (2000: 48) suggests, many schools are not structured to support this. Russell (1996: 179) suggests that a school as a learning organization needs to present learning as something which applies to everyone, not just to students, and must provide training and development for all its staff.

Senge (1990) and Neil (1995) indicate the paradox, wherein schools are concerned with learning yet, themselves, demonstrate few characteristics of learning organizations, often because of their overemphasis on a paradigm of some people teaching and others being taught. Youngblood (1997: 134–5) suggests that diversity is a key to learning, yet many schools are 'learning impaired' because they teach compliance, resentment, demotivation and repression within hierarchical and bureaucratic structures. However, schools can learn how to learn, they can develop corporate metacognition. Put another way, schools can become intelligent organizations rather than fact warehouses.

The capacity to learn is an indicator of the effectiveness with which the school can embrace change, innovation and adaptation (West-Burnham and O'Sullivan, 1998). Indeed Tan (2000: 33) argues for schools to have a human resource manager. The human resource manager, he argues, should sit alongside other heads of department and senior managers in the school. The tasks of such a person would include:

- planning how the development of teachers (up to 100 hours per year) fits into the overall planning of the learning school;
- sitting on staff selection panels;
- establishing criteria for recruiting staff;
- assessing applicants' openness and willingness to learning;
- assessing interpersonal and communication skills;
- assessing teamworking skills;
- arranging job previews (e.g. presentations by applicants to posts);
- assessing applicants' and teachers' abilities in multi-tasking;
- arranging pre-school oriented placements for students considering becoming teachers;
- developing transparent pay systems in the school, which includes payment for skills and skill development (cf. Lawler *et al.*, 1995).

The reference to incentives and motivation echoes the discussion in Chapter 2. Teachers, argues Tan (2000: 36), should be paid for skills which they have or develop. Beatty *et al.* (1995) sets these skills into five Cs: contribution; competency growth; creativity; collaboration; and commitment, whilst Tan (*op. cit.*) sets them into four main areas: (a) pedagogical knowledge and teaching skills; (b) quality-management abilities (e.g. problem-solving and use of quality management tools); (c) multi-skilling from and membership of different work groups, teams and committees; (d) ability to work in teams.

McMaster (1996: 11) suggests that organizational intelligence can be seen both quantitatively and qualitatively. In the context of a school, this might include the diversity of responses that the school makes, and its ways of thinking, to externally and internally generated input; the amount of information that the school can integrate; or the speed at which the school can generate, process and interpret information. At heart is the capability of the school to reflect on itself and its past and to learn from experience, and to give, receive and act on feedback.

For example, a school may be facing the problem of under-achievement in its higher ability students. The staff meet to generate the greatest possible range of ways of addressing the issue. This takes place on a staff development day, and the subsequent evaluation of proposals and forward planning is completed by the end of the day. Eight lines of approach to the problem are agreed:

1   making greater demands on, and expectations of, students;
2   increasing the amount of higher-order demand in teaching;
3   moving towards increased amounts of authentic and portfolio assessment;
4   increasing the focus in teaching on the development of metacognition;
5   extending differentiation to match tasks to students' multiple intelligences and to raising motivation;
6   increasing the amount of autonomous and project-based learning;
7   providing enrichment activities;
8   developing partnerships with employers and post-school institutions to enhance the breadth and depth of learning.

The school implements these strategies and gathers feedback on their effectiveness from the teachers, students, external partners, examination and assessment performance, as a result of which it makes adjustments to its plans for subsequent addressing of the issue. Here the organizational intelligence of the school is demonstrated in its capacity to identify the problem, to generate diverse solutions, to plan for implementation of several of these simultaneously, to foster partnerships and relationships in the planning and implementation, to gain feedback and to make adjustments in the light of these.

Echoing Hebb's view of learning set out in Chapter 1, McMaster suggests that intelligence is a function of the total number and variety of internal and external connections (see Chapter 7) and also the organization's capability to move between loose and tight coupling, as the occasion demands. Guidance should be sufficiently tight to set a direction but not so tight as to construct autonomy and creativity, i.e. enough to support responsible experimentation but not so much as to allow drift.

McMaster (*ibid*: 130) underlines the importance of flexibility in thinking and organizations if they are to develop their intelligence in terms of, for example:

•   the range of solutions to a single problem or pathways to a single goal (i.e. diversity);

- the number of goals or solutions that can be served by a single action (i.e. economy and efficiency);
- the number of activities or solutions than can be created by individual units in a network (creativity within devolution);
- the speed of adjustment from one action or line of thinking to another, to suit the changing circumstances (responsiveness); and
- the amount of energy required to effect the change (economy).

A learning organization, as Garvin (1993) suggests, is one which is adept at creating, acquiring and distributing knowledge, and using that new knowledge to modify its behaviour and activities. The term 'learning' is significant, for the gerund denotes a process rather than an event, and suggests that sustainability is a key feature – the organization is continually learning rather than reaching a plateau.

In a study of self-managing schools (the embodiment, perhaps, of self-organization), Wong *et al.* (1998: 74) found that flexible approaches to planning, and 'rolling plans' which were capable of constant readjustment to evolving circumstances, were more effective in coping with a turbulent environment than were traditional rational, linear models of planning. Indeed the authors, in a comment close to complexity theory, suggest that interactive models, premised on flexibility, are well suited to responding to the environment (*ibid*: 77).

What is required of the leaders in a school as a learning institution is an identification of which units/teams/groups link most strongly with which other units/teams/groups, and to ensure that those links are enabled in the school (see Chapter 7). In terms of Hebb's principles of associated learning in which close associations are reinforced most strongly, it is being suggested that, though there should be rich links everywhere, there should be different strengths of links between units. Hence one task of the groups and their leaders within the school is to identify with whom they need to link most strongly, how those links can be fostered, and the nature and management of information sharing, communication flow and feedback between these.

Emergent organizations are transformative; they transform themselves. To do this they need to learn how to take their place in a changing world. Hickman (2000) provides a useful introduction to the field in her study of John F. Kennedy High School in Maryland. Here transformation operated at several levels: individual, organizational and societal, by changing significantly the capacity-building capability of the school and, with it, the structures and culture of the school. There were several elements to the 'transformistic framework' of the school, which was in an area of high mobility rates, experiencing poor levels of achievement, low morale, poor reputation, and an inability to attract high-achieving students.

The school ensured that vision statements were turned into practice repeatedly and everywhere and, in this venture, secured the commitment of the parents, students and teachers. The school was led by a principal who combined development programmes and interpersonal relationships with the staff with opportunities for independent and delegated action and decision making. It operated on collaborative and shared leadership between the director and the teachers, and ensured that everybody had the opportunity to take leadership and followership roles (including parents as leaders). This entailed providing opportunities for teams as well as individuals to lead, and leadership and followership roles were based less on position and status and more on interdependence towards achieving common purposes. This led to improved teacher capability for collaborative planning and teaching, and ensured that the students as well as the teachers contributed to the well-being of the school and society.

The staff practised shared values of trust, honesty, service, support and responsibility throughout, and strove to enhance the self-esteem of participants. Indeed the school actively sought to develop interpersonal relationships (parents, teachers, students) and to foster boundaryless relationships; such principles emphasized communication and connectedness, and sought to develop the capability of everyone to learn. Through these interventions, alongside a programme of leadership training, the school prepared its students for meaningful roles as citizens, succeeded in attracting high-achieving students and in revitalizing itself, increased the leadership abilities of all participants, improved its self-image and attracted increased resources (the law of increasing returns). The example provides a useful overview of key elements of schools as learning organizations. Schools, Fullan (2001: 64) argues, must become professional learning communities.

Platforms for organizational learning

Organizational learning in schools concerns attention to school structure, participative decision making based on the goal of empowering teachers, shared commitment and collaborative activity, knowledge and skills, leadership, and the development of systems for feedback and accountability (Marks *et al.*, 1999).

Silins *et al.* (1999) and Watkins and Marsick (1993) suggest that a school's capacity for organizational learning is premised on a collaborative climate, support for risk-taking and initiative, teacher involvement in decision making, and professional development. In particular they suggest that effective leadership for organizational learning takes place in collaborative rather than hierarchical cultures, with teachers seen as partners in, rather than recipients of, decision making. They draw together key features of transformational leadership and distributed leadership discussed in Chapter 3, and they investigated the role that these play in organizational learning. They found three key variables which were important predictors of effective organizational learning: leader ($\rho = 0.30$); active leadership ($\rho = 0.36$) and distributed leadership ($\rho = 0.36$). One can see here the significance of distributed leadership for organizational learning, indeed the researchers found that the total proportion of organizational learning accounted for by distributed leadership was 28 per cent (*ibid*: 10).

Organizational learning in the schools was promoted through open and supportive communication and through the seeking and provision of information to improve teachers' work. Teachers were active participants in decision making, setting the direction of the school, and sharing information with parents and the community. Leaders in such schools, for their part, ensured that systems and structures for support were in place which would also reward initiative and innovation.

To gain some purchase on the issue of organizational learning, specific devices and projects (platforms) can be utilized, for example the project of the school as a learning organization. Pedler *et al.* (1997: 1) define a learning organization as one which not only facilitates the learning of all its participants but, importantly, 'continuously transforms itself'. They suggest several characteristics of a learning organization, for example:

1 *a learning approach to strategy*: experiments and feedback are encouraged and impact on strategy formation;
2 *participative policy making*: all stakeholders contribute to, and participate in, decision making;
3 *informating*: IT is used extensively for wide communication;
4 *internal exchange*: there is wide sharing of expertise and communication is open;
5 *reward flexibility*: a range of rewards is utilized;
6 *enabling structures*: organizational structures are fluid, permeable and mutable to meet the demands of change and innovation;
7 *boundary workers as environmental scanners*: all participants who link with the environment provide feedback from this;
8 *inter-organizational learning*: learning alliances are formed with other organizations;
9 *a learning climate*: learning from experience is fostered (reflective practice);
10 *self-development opportunities*: participants are given opportunities for self-development.

Items 1 and 2 are concerned with strategy; items 3–5 are concerned with 'looking in'; item 6 concerns structures; items 7 and 8 concern 'looking out', whilst items 9 and 10 concern 'learning opportunities'. These five main areas – strategy, looking in, structures, looking out and learning opportunities – resonate powerfully with self-organization and emergence. Further, the list identifies a significant platform for learning, which is electronic communication; this fosters information sharing, the democratization of the workplace, and the linking of distributed knowledge to distributed leadership.

Goh (1998) suggests that there are five 'core strategic building blocks' of the learning organization, which are:

1 mission and vision (which is developed with participants and understood clearly by them all);
2 leadership (which is empowering, supports experimentation and demonstrates commitment);
3 experimentation (which is both supported and rewarded throughout the organization);
4 transfer of knowledge (an ability to learn from knowledge within and outside the organization);

5   teamwork and cooperation (for group problem solving and for supporting innovation).

These five building blocks, he suggests, rest on two foundations: an organizational design which supports learning; and participants' competencies and acquisition of knowledge. With regard to organizational design, Goh's suggestion is that flat, non-hierarchical, decentralized, team-based and organic structures are preferable to hierarchical, formalized structures. Similarly Mohrman and Mohrman Jr. (1995) found that learning organizations tended to have fewer formalized controls on employees and to operate flat structures in which teams were close to decision makers. With regard to participants' competencies, Goh not only underlines the need for training and development, but that this should be team-based (see also Mohrman and Mohrman Jr., 1995).

Marsick (2000: 5–6) identifies five recurrent characteristics of learning organizations:

- continuous learning at the systems level (where individuals learn and share their learning so that the system learns);
- knowledge creation and sharing (where participants think in new ways and dialogue collaboratively);
- systemic thinking capacity (in order to see linkages and feedback loops);
- greater participation and accountability by a larger number of participants (where ideas are encouraged from all participants, without regard to their level in the organization);
- culture and structure of rapid communication and learning (where learning is rewarded and where risk-taking is supported in a blame-free culture).

To address these she suggests a core of practices at the levels of the individual, group and the whole organization (*ibid*: 7–9):

- creating opportunities for continuous learning;
- fostering dialogue and inquiry;
- promoting team learning and collaboration;
- developing systems in order to share learning;
- developing a shared vision through the empowerment of all participants;
- linking the organization with its environment;
- ensuring that leaders promote learning.[1]

The emphasis on sharing of learning is reinforced by Nonaka and Takeuchi (1995); tacit knowledge – a major element of the learning organization – is created through the sharing of ideas and experiences, and is converted into explicit knowledge through dialogue. Such sharing, they suggest, crosses boundaries of departments and levels of seniority, and is internalized throughout the organization and creates new knowledge. One can see that, for them, knowledge is a social matter. This echoes Stacey (2001) and Marsick (2000: 13) in their view that learning comes through sharing of knowledge; hence Marsick advocates collaborative inquiry through action research.

Senge (1990), Senge *et al.* (1994) and Senge *et al.* (2000:7) suggest that platforms for the learning organization can be defined in terms of five disciplines:

- *systems thinking* (seeing relationships to the whole, patterns and interrelationships, which are fostered through feedback and interdependency);
- *personal mastery* (personal vision and commitment to its realization, in which one takes control of one's own life within a realistic assessment of one's situation: 'organizations can learn only if the individuals within the organizations learn'; April *et al.*, 2000: 51);
- *mental models* (examining principles and ways of thinking and their relationships to practice, which have to be studied, disclosed and shared in order for learning to take place, i.e. double-loop learning which requires changes to mental models (Argyris and Schön, 1978); critical reflection and enquiry. In schools where, Senge *et al.* (2000: 7) state, many mental models are 'undiscussable', this involves the capability to talk in a safe and productive environment about dangerous topics);
- *shared vision* (a joint enterprise, rather than an imposed order, which requires communication, the development of positive aspirations and the sharing of personal visions, and how to realize them, by the teachers, administrators and staff in a school in order to foster commitment);
- *team learning* (through dialogue, discussion and collaboration).

The learning organization constructs structures and systems to promote and enhance its learning capability (Dodgson, 1993). For Senge (1990: 63) systems thinking involves seeing relationships rather than finding linear cause-and-effect chains, a view which resonates strongly with complexity theory. Indeed leaders in school, argue Senge *et al.* (2000: 414–8), practise engagement, systems thinking, the leadership of learning and self-awareness. The leader is the lead learner (*ibid*: 425–32). Senge *et al.* (2000: 552–3) pose four challenging issues for 'schools that learn':

1   Does the school have a clear, honest and realistic picture and understanding of its current situation?
2   Is the picture and the understanding shared throughout the school?
3   How does the school utilize this picture and understanding in order to create and share new knowledge?
4   How effectively is this new knowledge realized in action for the desired future of the school?

The emphasis on team learning relates directly to self-organization; team learning, it was suggested in Chapter 2, is dialogical and recognizes the unique contribution of each individual member. Teamwork not only synergizes (April: 1997: 50) but recognizes that some tasks can *only* be achieved by teams. The task of leaders is to identify which tasks *require* teams and which can be achieved by individuals. Forcing unnecessary teamwork, like contrived collegiality, can be unproductive.

If the learning organization is to develop, suggests Senge (1990), then the organization will need to overcome internal micropolitical conflict and create time in which learning can occur. It will need to hold in balance delegation, coordination and control, and enable personal mastery and autonomy to be practised, ensuring that people share and learn from experience. For Senge, the learning organization must continuously adapt to its environment. However, this is not merely a matter of adaptation as a chameleon, which changes itself externally but largely remains the same (Miller, 1997); rather a learning organization must metamorphose; it must become the butterfly from the caterpillar; it must be generative.[2]

Senge *et al.* (2000: 55) suggest that, in schools, this involves:

- learning which is learner-centred rather than teacher-centred;
- encouraging diversity rather than homogeneity – embracing multiple intelligences and a diversity of learning styles;
- understanding interdependency and change rather than the memorization of facts and the striving after 'right answers';
- a continuous exploration of the theories in use by all those involved in education;
- a reintegration of education within webs of social relationships, e.g. linking families, friends and whole communities.

Rolls (1995) takes Senge's work and suggests a range of leadership competencies for each of Senge's five systems and, focusing on the key principle that effective leadership is a function of the willingness of followers to follow (cf. Blank, 1995), suggests followership expectations of the leader (Table 4.1).

One can see in this table an emphasis on the personal attributes and qualities of leadership. Senge (1990: 57–67) sets out several 'laws' for the learning organization, several of which resonate with complexity theory, for example:

- today's problems come from yesterday's solutions (solutions are short-lived, and the present is connected to the past – connectedness is inescapable);
- the harder you push, the harder the system pushes back (don't push change, support it);
- cause and effect are not closely related in time and space (changes are unpredictable, and unitary cause-and-effect models are simplistic);
- small changes can bring big results – but the areas of highest leverage are often the least obvious (it is important to surface blinds areas, e.g. using the Johari Window (Kakabadse *et al.* 1988: 83–6), and to identify levers of change);
- dividing an elephant in half does not produce two small elephants (a system needs to be looked at holistically rather than atomistically).

The suggestion here is that simple cause-and-effect models need to be replaced by looking for relationships and patterns, i.e. by complexity theory.

Though Senge's work sits comfortably with several aspects of complex organizational learning, it is not without its limitations. Stacey (1992: 336), for example, considers it still to be premised on stable equilibrium models, with their emphasis on a shared vision, harmony and consensus. Senge, however, as Stacey makes clear (*ibid.*), does value dialogue and contention, recognizes unpredictability and irregularity, and is against top-down models.

Table 4.1 Leaders' competencies in Senge's five disciplines

Senge's discipline	Leaders' competencies	Followers' expectations
Systems thinking	Expansionist thinking Understanding connectivity Intuition/Perspective/Integration	Understanding the whole

Personal mastery	Compassion
	Acceptance of self
	  and others
	Shared power
	Authenticity
	Nurturance of spirit
	Moral leadership
	Humility
	Mastery
	Orientation to growth
	Risk-taking
	Self-direction
	Tolerance (e.g. of
	  value ambiguity)
	Commitment to learning
	Trust
	Spirituality
	Subordination of the ego
		Encouragement
		Acceptance
		Empowerment
		Trust
		Self-discovery
		Worth following
		Dignity
		Autonomy
		Fulfilled potential
		Growth
		Supported choice
		Independence
		Room to make mistakes
		Support during transitions
		Learning
		Responsibility
		Connecting self and others
		Ownership of results

Mental models	Insight Introspection Challenging assumptions Innovation	Innovation Meaning Challenging assumptions

Shared vision	Principles
	Alignment of personal
	  and organizational values
	Inspiration
	Goals
	Vision
	Vitality
	Mobilize commitment
		Sense of purpose
		Alignment of personal
		  and organizational values
		Motivation
		Clarity
		Collaborative development of vision
		Engagement
		Commitment

Team learning	Cooperation Dialogue Listening Creativity Promotion of harmony Encouragement of relationships	Co-designing Self-expression Contribution Creativity Social unity Relationships

Senge (1990) argues for the need to identify underlying issues rather than superficial manifestations (e.g. symptoms rather than causes), and to focus on deep rather than superficial solutions (e.g. Argyris and Schön's, 1978 double-loop learning). For example, in a secondary school a teacher may complain about the noise in a corridor outside her classroom. The presenting problem is 'noisy students'. However, on closer examination, it is clear that the problem is far more complex: nearly all the students move classrooms to go to the next subject at the end of lessons; there are only two corridors along which students can move, causing congestion and overload at changeover times; the corridors are built from highly resonant materials, so any sound is magnified. Hence, even if the students were completely silent, there would still be noise. If the teacher merely focuses on noisy students she may go out and shout at them to be quiet, but it will have no effect; if the floor is carpeted it may absorb sound, but that is heavier on financial resources. If congestion is to be removed it becomes both a timetabling issue (to accommodate, for example, moving students at different times) and raises the question of whether teachers should move to students or students to teachers. Perhaps the solution is a combination of all of these but, certainly, the solution is not straightforward. The issue here is to look for 'real causes' rather than symptoms, and then to work on these (Senge, 1990: 104; Morrison, 1998: 98).

The task of leverage by leaders is important, identifying those small actions which might bring about larger-scale changes. For example, in schools the rise of portfolio assessment (e.g. Records of Achievement) might be superficially a small, new pedagogical development, involving students in facilitated self-assessment and target setting. However, to conduct portfolio assessment is time consuming, taking time away from other valuable teaching, so it exposes issues of time allowances. Further, it closes the social distance between student and teacher, which some teachers and students may find uncomfortable, so in-service development and preparation are required (e.g. on active listening, and diagnostic and facilitation techniques). In-service development costs money, so budgetary issues are exposed. What began life as a small-scale change raises issues of finance, timetabling, power, and school culture.

Schein (1992, 1993, 1994) and Bennett and O'Brien (1994: 42) suggest that leaders in the learning organization have to create cultures of support for learning, and that this is addressed through the promotion of positive climates and organizational health. Leaders, they argue, have to possess, for example:

- skills in challenging existing practices and assumptions;
- willingness to collaborate and involve others;
- ability to learn quickly, particularly about organizational cultures.

Leaders have to be able to engage other participants in novel ideas and thinking, to transcend their everyday experience. The process of learning in an organization, Schein (1999) avers, regards leaders and the led as collaborative partners in the creation of meanings (see the example of the innovatory secondary school in Chapter 3).

Garvin (1993: 80) argues that the learning organization has the expertise to create, acquire and, in the light of distributed knowledge, importantly, to transfer and share knowledge, changing its behaviour according to the outcome of these (cf. Beeby and Booth, 2000: 7). Indeed distributed, shared, stored and communicated knowledge is vital in an organization which is not to diminish its capacity to learn each time a member leaves (April *et al.*, 2000: 50). Expertise must be shared and stored; it is the school's organizational memory. Knowledge is not only personal but contributes to the autopoiesis of the school – its identity (cf. Coleman, 1999: 36). Garvin (2000: 190–1) makes the important point that sharing knowledge requires attention to the cultivation of the right climate and tone, in which leaders lead discussions sensitively and provide useful, supportive feedback (see also Fisher and Fisher, 1998: 232–3).

Popper and Lipshitz (2000) cite the example of the Israeli Air Force as an instance of sharing knowledge and feedback. After each mission a debriefing takes place, which is frequently longer than the mission itself. The debriefing is characterized by all participants being involved, regardless of rank, and receiving critical and constructive feedback, again regardless of rank – the debriefing is based on democracy and equality (*ibid*: 136). The Air Force has an ability to tolerate and learn from mistakes, and involves itself in close examination of its missions. Such examinations are based on evidence and facts rather than opinion or impressions – the data for evaluation are transparent.

The authors suggest that this debriefing, as a structural requirement of the organization's activities, is an instance of an 'organizational learning mechanism' in which information is systematically collected, analyzed, stored, disseminated and used for future learning. The debriefing separates the personal from the professional, and is used for professional development. It requires substantial investments of time and money. The task of leaders here is to stimulate motivation to participate fully, by devoting time and attention themselves to the activity, by following up the activity with recognition and reward, and by cultivating an atmosphere and situation of trust and psychological safety which minimizes 'defensive routines' by participants (e.g. their willingness to report mistakes) (cf. Grieves, 2000). The sequence, the authors aver, is as follows:

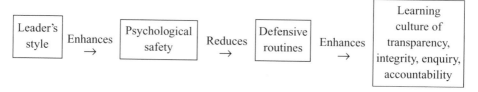

Similarly, Wheatley (1996: 6), referring to the US Army as a learning organization, suggests that after each major piece of action the participants ask themselves: 'What happened?'; 'Why do you think it happened?' and 'What can we learn from it?' (see also Fullan, 2001: 88–9, who discusses the US army's 'After Action' reviews). This is similar to the Plan, Do, Review model of High Scope in schools (Hohmann and Weikart, 1983) and the Do, Review, Learn,

Apply model of planning and training in schools (Dennison and Kirk, 1990) in which the *sharing* of experiences (i.e. communicating and interrelating) is emphasized (*ibid*: 7–10). Indeed Dennison and Kirk (*ibid*: 17) term the pattern of such learning for teachers a virtuous cycle (Figure 4.1).

In education, Fitz-Gibbon (1996: 35–42) makes a powerful case for feedback and the flow of information back into schools in order for them to learn and to emerge into newer forms of self-organization, and her analysis is expressly informed by complexity theory. She argues that increasing the feedback of accurate information to schools on the outcomes of education that they provide is essential for school improvement, as is the reduction of disinformation, misinformation and untried prescriptions (*ibid*: 42). The move, then, is towards evidence-based education and, more recently, towards evidence-informed education (Morrison, 2001b).

Fitz-Gibbon and her colleagues have developed the A-level information system (ALIS), together with other indicator systems at the Curriculum, Evaluation and Management (CEM) Centre at the University of Durham (www.cem.dur.ac.uk), e.g. the Year 11 Information System (YE11IS), the Middle Years Information System (MIDYIS), and Performance Indicators in Primary Schools (PIPS). These are specific projects which are designed to feed back into schools information about their performance on a range of measures, in comparison with the performance of other schools which possess many similar characteristics, i.e. schools with which fair comparisons can be made (in terms of complexity theory, schools learn from the environment/performances of other schools). Data are collected confidentially from schools; the systems and projects utilize a range of performance indicators, including results of public examinations and assessments, questionnaire, purposely devised CEM test material, and other means.

Schools see their own results in comparison with other (anonymous) schools which are in situations similar to their own. This enables one school to compare its 'value-added' performances with those of a similar group of others. The

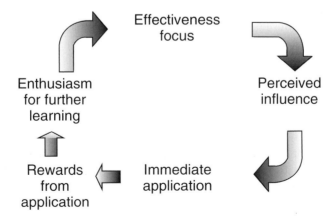

Figure 4.1 The virtuous cycle of learning.

results of each school are confidential to that school, and other schools with whom comparisons are being made are anonymous and unidentifiable. This works positively for the schools, as the 'naming and shaming' regimen of feedback through inspection is avoided, and the results are used formatively, for development purposes. This builds in a sense of commitment by the participating schools – they benefit directly from the feedback of live, meaningful data. The intention of all the CEM Centre work is to provide accurate, rigorous and reliable information – evidence – on which schools can act to improve themselves. Feedback is used by the school for development, improvement and organizational learning.

Strategies for developing organizational learning

A clear model for education here is that of action research which, in many forms, is premised on collaboration (Cohen *et al.*, 2000) and which comprises key elements such as identification of need/problem; analysis of possible interventions to meet the need/problem; implementation of one or more interventions; evaluation of effectiveness of solution; and identification of new need/problem.

Fullan (2001: 125–6) contends that learning in context is an essential feature of organizational learning in schools and brings the greatest 'payoff' because it is the most relevant. He provides an example of school leaders learning (*ibid*: 127–8) through intervisitation, monthly principal support groups, principal peer coaching, study groups, individualized coaching, district institutes (centres) for learning about specific curricular and school matters and on-site visits by supervisors.

Braham (1995) suggests that, in organizational learning, the emphasis is on regarding learning as an integral part and process of everyday activity, and as a cooperative activity which places a premium on relationships. Learning, then, is largely from within, and requires the sharing of knowledge openly (cf. Conley *et al.*, 1988; Southworth, 2000: 281). Leithwood and Steinbach (1995) found that principals of excellent schools made extensive use of other teachers in decision making. Marquardt (1996) summarizes research from the MIT Organizational Learning Center which shows that organizations which learn successfully demonstrate ten major features; these are interpreted in the school context (Table 4.2).

Marquardt (1996) underlines the importance of motivation and incentives in developing these characteristics.

Hong and Kuo (1999) identify three types of learning in the learning organization (pp. 209–10). *Maintenance learning*, they aver, is learning for survival and comprises largely instruction. *Adaptive learning* is benchmark learning (looking to best practice in order to emulate it) and comprises largely sharing. *Creative learning* is designed to take the lead in innovativeness and comprises largely self-study (cf. Miller, 1996).[3] Though these are crude abstractions, nevertheless the authors provide several issues which can be reformulated as questions that schools can ask themselves. These are presented in terms of a self-assessment scale (Table 4.3).

Table 4.2 Ten major features of successful organizational learning

Characteristics of learning organizations	*Characteristics of schools*
1 Scanning imperatives: they constantly scan their environment	1 Examine the pressures on schools and decide which ones require a response; examine how the school can influence the environment
2 Performance gaps: gaps in performance become opportunities for learning	2 Identify areas for improvement in the school, for example in the following areas (cf. Rodger and Richardson, 1985): departmental work; pastoral work; faculty work; whole school curriculum planning work; monitoring and assessment work; age group responsibilities; management work; school improvement work; information technology and knowledge management work; the school climate and health; external relations
3 Concern for measurement: considerable effort is expended in operationalizing key elements of new ventures	3 Identify those aspects of school, teacher and student performance that can and should be measured; identify where measures can be useful, and how this can be done, e.g. measures of added value (e.g. (http://www.cem.dur.ac.uk)
4 Experiment mindsets: the more experimentation takes place, the more the organization can learn	4 Encourage multiple innovations and experimentation in education (with suitable safeguards)
5 Climate of openness: knowledge and communication to be open	5 Ensure that communication is multi-directional and rich, and that information is shared
6 Continuous education: lifelong education becomes an imperative	6 Build in professional development for school development
7 Operational variety: there is a realization that there are several ways of attaining the goals of the organization	7 Encourage diversity of ways of working and approaching problems (e.g. in the areas of 2 in this list)
8 Multiple advocates/champions: everyone in the organization can make suggestions for continuous improvement	8 Operate collegial participation and decision making for improvement projects
9 Involved leadership: leaders articulate the collective vision of the organization	9 Ensure that leaders collect views and synthesize them to an articulated, shared vision (e.g. through Delphi techniques or Nominal Group techniques)
10 Systems perspective: relationships between units of the system are deliberately cultivated	10 Provide opportunities for units to experience genuine (rather than contrived) collaborative work.

Table 4.3 Self-assessment scale for types of learning in a school as a learning organization

1 = not at all	2 = very little	3 = a little	4 = a lot	5 = a very great deal

Kind of learning	Scale				
	1	2	3	4	5
Maintenance learning					
• Do participants understand the ways in which the school works, and do they have adequate preparation and support to work in it?	[ ]	[ ]	[ ]	[ ]	[ ]
• Is documentation available, clear, focused, accurate and utilized?	[ ]	[ ]	[ ]	[ ]	[ ]
• Is adequate induction available for new members of staff?	[ ]	[ ]	[ ]	[ ]	[ ]
• Does the school have protocols and administrative procedures for handling its internal and external relations?	[ ]	[ ]	[ ]	[ ]	[ ]
• Does the school have adequate procedures for responding to requests for information (internally and externally)?	[ ]	[ ]	[ ]	[ ]	[ ]
• Is the school's information system accessible to those who 'need to know' and does it provide different types of required information?	[ ]	[ ]	[ ]	[ ]	[ ]
• Do participants have access to required resources?	[ ]	[ ]	[ ]	[ ]	[ ]
• Do participants have adequate decision-making rights?	[ ]	[ ]	[ ]	[ ]	[ ]
Benchmark learning					
• Is it straightforward for departments to retrieve data from various channels (internal and external)?	[ ]	[ ]	[ ]	[ ]	[ ]
• Is there a method to acquire and sort increasing amounts of data?	[ ]	[ ]	[ ]	[ ]	[ ]
• Do participants know what is happening throughout the school and in similar schools?	[ ]	[ ]	[ ]	[ ]	[ ]
• Are participants willing to share their own working practices with others?	[ ]	[ ]	[ ]	[ ]	[ ]
• Are there feedback mechanisms for decisions taken by departments and groups?	[ ]	[ ]	[ ]	[ ]	[ ]
• Are there multiple channels of communication within the school, and are they used?	[ ]	[ ]	[ ]	[ ]	[ ]
• Does each unit have clear procedures for communication?	[ ]	[ ]	[ ]	[ ]	[ ]
Creative learning					
• Is dated information sorted and stored (e.g. books, documents, computer files)?	[ ]	[ ]	[ ]	[ ]	[ ]
• Are there professional and academic journals available in the school?	[ ]	[ ]	[ ]	[ ]	[ ]
• Does the school provide time and support for free work?	[ ]	[ ]	[ ]	[ ]	[ ]
• Are tools for analysis used in discussions?	[ ]	[ ]	[ ]	[ ]	[ ]
• Are participants used to planning, and are there support structures for this?	[ ]	[ ]	[ ]	[ ]	[ ]
• Are there opportunities for redesigning working practices and procedures?	[ ]	[ ]	[ ]	[ ]	[ ]
• Do participants actively learn from case study material and share ideas and practices?	[ ]	[ ]	[ ]	[ ]	[ ]

Sharing knowledge for organizational learning

The school as a learning organization should be able to access and create new knowledge, using external resources for obtaining knowledge, and integrating new knowledge into the schools and applying it (Huber, 1991). For this the school should provide mechanisms to select, store, access, retrieve and utilize knowledge through a range of media, provide teachers units with incentives to learn, innovate and practise new knowledge, share knowledge and practices between all units in the school, and evaluate knowledge for its potential contribution to developing the school (cf. Tetenbaum, 1998).

Finding a means of incorporating information into an organization's belief or value system turns information into knowledge; information is data that have been classified and interpreted (Devlin, 1991). Data are unused, potential information, and information, once used, potentiates the knowledge-building organization (see Lissack, 1996: 7). Weick and Daft (1984) distinguish between data and knowledge in their notion of 'interpreting information'; they argue that information has to be understood and built into conceptual schemes.

Knowledge is key to the 'business' of schools, and the rate of increase of knowledge doubles every twelve to eighteen months (Fullan, 2001: 22). It is usually created and held by individuals rather than the organization (Grant, 1999: 1). For knowledge to be distributed it has to be both meaningful and organized (Drucker, 1999: 126), perhaps, with established and accepted protocols and languages for sharing it (cf. Probst and Büchel, 1997; Hong, 1999). Indeed Coleman (1999: 39) suggests that knowledge sharing should be part of the incentive and reward system of an organization. Youngblood (1997: 63) suggests replacing the commonly held view of sharing information on a 'need to know' basis, wherein the *holder* decides who needs to know, with the *recipients* deciding what they need to know. He suggests that, if information and knowledge is the lifeblood of organizations, then high quality and 'diverse interactions are the beating heart'; deprived of sharing and interaction an organization suffers cardiac arrest.

Nonaka and Takeuchi (1995) suggest the need for interactive networks of knowledge within the organization. Here Rosenberg (2000) suggests that ICT has a powerful role to play, not only in the sharing of text-based knowledge, but in the potential that multimedia have for visual and image-based sharing – virtually face-to-face communication and rich interaction.

Stacey (2001: 4, 220) suggests that knowledge is not a 'thing', reified and commodified, but an 'active process of relating'. He argues (*ibid*: 5) that it is part of the participatory self-organization of organizations. Knowledge, he avers, is being produced, reproduced and transformed through interaction and relations (*ibid*: 6, 98), and the creation of knowledge is a participatory, communicative activity. Knowledge only becomes knowledge when it is shared and social (cf. Brown and Duguid, 1991, 2000); it resides less in databases than it does in people (Stacey, 2001: 121), as it is the people involved who evaluate its worth. Stacey's views are echoed by Cilliers (2000: 10) in his comment that knowledge, as interpreted data, only becomes meaningful in the process of interaction.

Knowledge is under continuous construction through interaction and relation-ships (*ibid*: 68). Hence the task of 'managing knowledge', if there is such a task (and Stacey 2000: 5 raises this question), and of leadership within this, is to facilitate rela-tionships (e.g. through organizational structures and cultures) so that knowledge construction and sharing are automatic and inbuilt. For Stacey, the organization's capacity for knowledge creation is a function of its capacity to build and sustain rela-tionships. The construction of knowledge is a process of communicative action; Stacey places this so high in importance as to suggest that the future of the organiza-tion is perpetually being constructed, reconstructed and transformed through the 'conversational exchanges' in which its members participate (*ibid*: 181).

Within distributed systems (which complexity theory supports) the issue of sharing knowledge is important (Stewart, 2001: 64), as decisions need to be made on what is shared automatically, or by specific intervention, and on the selectivity needed to avoid communication and information overload. Further, Greengard (1998) and Fullan (2001: 6, 87), reinforcing Stacey, suggest that people will not share their knowledge voluntarily unless they possess sufficient motivation and commitment to do so, i.e. that knowledge exchange and sharing is a social, rela-tional matter. Fullan provides an example (p. 67) of a school in which strong teacher communities worked where collaborative sharing was practised to make breakthroughs in learning. Sharing best practice is a key to school development but it requires a supportive environment for it to occur.

Given the overwhelming information overload which besets most schools, some has to be eliminated, some selected (Hamel and Prahalad, 1994), and the remainder interpreted and, subsequently argues Drucker (1999: 130), has to lead to action. The issue of the management of distributed knowledge in the complex organization has to address several questions:

- Which knowledge will be kept and which eliminated?
- What is the necessary minimum of knowledge that is required for people to work effectively?
- How is knowledge to be selected, stored, accessed, retrieved, processed and used?
- Who holds which knowledge and access to it?
- What information is required to be gained from people and to be given to people, and in what form and time frame?
- What information is necessary for people to work effectively in the organi-zation?

Paraphrasing Drucker (p. 124), people need to ask themselves two main questions: 'What information do I need myself, from whom, when and in what form?' and 'What information do I need to give to others, to whom, when and in what form?' Drucker recognizes the distributed nature of knowledge in his comment (p. 125) that most of the knowledge which executives require does not reside in a central store; it is spread throughout departments and, indeed, outside the organization, hence there is a need for perpetual networking and scanning of the internal environment.

Grant (1996) suggests that knowledge can only be integrated through networking.

In a later paper (1999) he suggests that the coordination of specialized knowledge is particularly difficult for organizations, and that this can be addressed by:

1   rules and directives for coordination;
2   sequencing (identifying the sequence in which specialist knowledge must be sought/used/introduced);
3   routines for coordination (which are worked out through mutual adjustment of specialists); and
4   group problem solving and decision making.

He suggests that 1 to 3 might tend to minimize communication whereas 4 maximizes it. He argues that common knowledge is required for effective coordination; this, he avers, includes language and other symbolic forms of communication; shared specialist knowledge (where there is more than one specialist in an area of knowledge – a feature which is often the case in schools); shared meanings (acquired through extensive formal and informal communication), and recognition of knowledge domains (an awareness of the knowledge that others possess, so that people know who to turn to for different types of knowledge). Grant (1999) stresses that, whilst hierarchies might be useful for *processing* information, they are unhelpful for *integrating* knowledge; this is best addressed through flat structures and team-based approaches.

Stages of organizational learning

An organization which is learning goes through several stages (Jones and Hendry, 1992: 24) (Table 4.4).

Kelly and Allison (1999: 110–12) suggest that organizational learning proceeds – emerges – through five stages:

Recognition of unconscious self-organization
(where command-and-control leadership operates and where self-organization is a 'hidden culture')
↓
Conscious self-organization
(where there are committed and disciplined teams, with open communication and learning, a commitment to 'game plans' and monitoring of performance in the environment)
↓
Guided self-organization
(where committed, disciplined local teams propagate successful lessons and communicate across the wider institution)
↓
Quantitatively guided self-organization
(where statistical models are used to predict)
↓
Consciously competent autopoiesis
(co-evolution within and between environments)

Table 4.4 Stages of organizational learning

Stage	Elements of each stage
Stage One: Foundation	Realizing the need to learn
	Wishing to learn
	Learning how to learn
	Personal development training
	Learning in groups and in teams
	Motivation of teams and groups
Stage Two: Formation	Further skill development
	Support for self-learning
	Individually tailored learning programmes
Stage Three: Continuation	Independent learning
	Career planning
	Sharing responsibility
	Movement in the organization away from hierarchy
	Job enrichment, enlargement and rotation
	Formal assessment schemes
Stage Four: Transformation	Thinking and doing things in a different way
	Changing structures
	Learning how to be different
	Emphasis on leadership
	Development of flat management structures
	Managers as facilitators, enablers and coaches
	Blockages to learning removed
	Willingness to learn from others
	Self-assessment schemes
	Envisioning activities
Stage Five: Transfiguration	Fully developed organization through developed people
	Capability to cope with change
	Learning at all levels
	Devolved responsibility across network
	Formal status replaced by personal expertise

Though Kelly and Allison are looking at industry and commerce rather than education (therefore, perhaps, their reference to statistical prediction may fit uncomfortably with schools), nevertheless their stages from unconscious competence to conscious competence are useful markers of development. Their work matches that of Dubin (1962) who suggests that a progression must take place from unconscious incompetence, through conscious incompetence and conscious competence, to unconscious competence. The process of learning moves from awareness-raising to learning and practice, to reflection and evaluation (see also April *et al.*, 2000: 50). This is akin to the virtuous cycle for schools set out by Dennison and Kirk earlier. It is clear from these stages that learning brings transformation.

Beeby and Booth (2000) indicate different stages of learning, in which levels of learning (individual, team, inter-departmental group and organizational) and formal and informal channels of communication are used between these several levels. Tierney (1999: 121) indicates that communication is essential for promoting learning. Trust is required for the emergence of self-organization to occur (Youngblood, 1997: 120; McNamara, 2001: 3). Trust, suggests Fukayama (1999: 16) is a lubricant to enhance the smooth running of a group or an organization, the opposite of which Youngblood (1997: 123) sees as the degrading annual performance review – surely a message for appraisal and inspection in schools. Procedures for communication and learning might include:

- training and professional development;
- external benchmarking;
- consultants;
- visits to other institutions;
- conferences, workshops, seminars, shows;
- professional journals and papers;
- strategic alliances;
- opportunity to learn from each other.

Within and between each level of organizational learning (individual, team, inter-departmental, organizational, inter-organizational) (Nonaka and Takeuchi, 1995: 57)ʹ, Coghlan (1997) suggests there must be opportunities for experiencing, processing, interpreting and taking action on the information. At the individual level this is a matter of learning content and reflection; at the team level it adds to this the nature of team learning and dialogue; at inter-departmental level it requires attention to different cultural perspectives; at the organizational level and beyond there is a need to integrate the nature of learning at the preceding levels with learning about the environment and the strategy for moving the organization forward. The process is mapped as shown in Table 4.5 (cf. Huber, 1991).

Organizational learning implies the devolution of responsibility, decision making and power across the organization. It 'pushes responsibility down the line' to all elements and individuals in the network, rather than residing within the senior management of the organization.[4]

Table 4.5 Levels of contents of organizational learning

Level	*Process*	*Inputs/outcomes*
• Individual	Acquiring knowledge	Experiences; information;
• Team	Distributing information	conversations and dialogue;
• Inter-departmental	Interpreting information	shared understandings; mutual
• Organizational	Developing the	adjustment and interaction of
• Inter-organizational	organizational memory	systems

Conclusion

Schools which are developing their organizational learning bear several characteristics (Karsten *et al.*, 2000):

- they respond to external pressures;
- they ensure that participants experience success;
- the process of the development of a common vision is more important than the product of a common vision;
- they break the 'harmony model' as this leads to the development of an official culture and rule-following;
- they emphasize feedback and interdependence;
- they have an open culture in which people are free to express ideas;
- they learn from mistakes, and mistakes are tolerated;
- they have decentralized structures, with reduced distinctions made between staff and line managers;
- they move away from traditional notions of teaching towards an emphasis on learning from experience, activity and motivation;
- they have awareness-raising activities of the need for development;
- they employ teamwork;
- they have multiple, diverse objectives and autonomy to use diverse methods.

This latter point is significant, for Karsten *et al.* (2000: 147) suggest that if schools are really to develop as learning organizations then this sits uncomfortably with the pressure of governments to prescribe national curricula and objectives, as these, the authors argue, support bureaucratic and narrowing tendencies. Further, the authors suggest (*ibid*: 154–5) that the most crucial items for schools to address if they are to become learning organizations include improved mechanisms for gaining information from the local environment, together with selecting, processing and distributing that information around the school. The school must have a clear understanding of the wishes of clients and stakeholders, and match these to the school's own strengths. This implies, the authors aver, the use of effective communication within the school and the exchange of ideas.

Clearly, the production of characteristics of organizational learning is an easy task which is not always so simple to enact in schools. Fullan (1998) suggests that there should be a move from an emphasis on *change* to an emphasis on *changing* – the process rather than the idea or the product. As Karsten *et al.* (2000) suggest, it is the interaction of elements rather than simply their denotation that is important.

The emergent, self-organizing school is a *learning organization*, which has high capability for problem solving and problem anticipation. This requires it to possess and develop organizational intelligence. It requires an ability to learn from its internal and external environment. This chapter has suggested that schools should develop their organizational learning capabilities and practices, and that leadership has a critical role to play in nurturing this. This chapter has suggested that this impacts on several fronts. With regard to *leadership*, it has been suggested that leaders should:

- identify platforms for self-organization and organizational learning;
- develop teams and networks as key mechanisms for organizational learning;
- develop vision, commitment and alignment in the school;
- encourage and support risk-taking and experimentation;
- develop strategies – systematic and otherwise – for organizational learning in the school.

With regard to *leadership of learning*, it has been suggested that:

- problem-posing, problem-diagnosis and problem-solving capabilities are key elements of the school as a learning organization;
- capability and capacity for learning need to be amplified;
- openness and sharing are significant qualities of the learning organization, with communication taking place in all directions, within and between all levels;
- information and knowledge sharing, management, use and feedback are critical components of the school as a learning organization;
- mechanisms should exist within the school for interpreting the environments in which it is operating, and responding to them;
- maintenance, adaptive, benchmark, creative and innovative learning should be fostered in the school as a learning organization;
- stages of organizational learning need to be identified, and the location of the school within these should be undertaken;
- the school should develop its own organizational intelligence and flexibility.

With regard to *leading participants* in organizational learning, it has been suggested that:

- positive interpersonal relationships in the school are significant elements of the learning organization;
- the culture of the school is an important seedbed for the learning organization, fostering members' commitment, motivation and experience of success;
- all participants should develop the capacity for organizational metacognition: the ability to review how it is learning and how this can be improved;
- decision making must become decentralized within the school as a learning organization.

This large set of characteristics reflects the fact that the complex, self-organizing school, which is meeting the demands of emergence through developing itself as a learning organization, operates multi-dimensionally. It is complicated as well as complex (Cilliers, 1998). If schools are to become learning organizations then they have to be sensitive and open to their external environment, and it is to this that the next chapter turns.

5 Schools and their environments

Introduction

A primary school in the UK is located in a 'sink' estate; parents play out local enmities in the school playground; many fathers are in prison; many mothers cannot cope; poverty is everywhere. The estate is used by the local authority to place those families who default on home rental payments. Gangs roam the streets, dogs are everywhere and foul the few playing spaces for children, houses are boarded up but have been broken into by thieves looking for scrap metal and by drug users as a venue for their addictions; the physical environment is depressing, with broken furniture, crashed cars and rubbish everywhere.

In school, many children present seriously disturbed behaviour and gross emotional instability. Many children, under the influence of the negative attitudes of their parents and older peers, dislike school and see teachers as authority figures to whom it is, therefore, legitimate to give serious oppositional behaviour, as all the other authority figures with whom they have had contact have given trouble and difficulty to the children and their families. The school struggles to maintain discipline and to provide basic social training in acceptable, non-violent behaviour for its children. For the teachers, the academic National Curriculum of the UK is at a far remove from the presence of difficulties with which they have to cope on a daily basis. The situation is desperate. Children's academic achievement is minimal, nor do they care; many start school unable to speak in a sentence, and many leave the school barely functionally literate or numerate.

The school is over a hundred years old, its red brick building resembling the worst form of institutional workhouse that can be fostered in young minds. The internal fittings are dark, and there are even the green ceramic tiles that used to line the walls of psychiatric hospitals, law courts, government offices and police stations in the UK. Within the school the teachers are, understandably, dispirited; they struggle in their own classroom to keep order and to try to promote a little learning. At lunch breaks they leave the premises, checking their cars each time to make sure that the children or their parents have not burst the tyres or deliberately scratched the bodywork, and spend a few moments of quiet sanity before returning.

The former headteacher retired in despair and ill health, and the new headteacher secured agreement from the local education authority to fund a complete renovation and a building programme to commence within one year of his taking office. Coupled with this, a new nursery department was to be opened in a purpose-built annexe and this would be part of a deliberate strategy of early intervention in the education and socialization of young children. Parents would be encouraged to participate in their children's education in school and at home. A policy of clear, humane, fair and consistent discipline would be established which involved parents, social workers and psychological services and, if necessary, the police.

The headteacher discussed with the staff ways of anticipating the changes which could be made when the new building and renovation were completed, how new pedagogic practices and social development might be promoted in the school and how the internal work practices of the teachers could be developed. The staff agreed a few plans:

- the new building would be maintained in as physically attractive and stimulating a way as possible, with the support of classroom assistants;
- parents would be involved in the classroom on an agreed basis, with a support programme provided to prepare them for this;
- a home-school liaison teacher would be appointed, with non-teaching time provided for home visiting;
- internal communication would be improved;
- joint planning and teaching would be developed;
- an emphasis would be placed on literacy and numeracy;
- raising children's motivation, self-esteem and experience of success would be important areas for focus;
- adult literacy and numeracy programmes would be offered at the school during the day and after hours, in a room specifically prepared for this, which would be a community resource and which would also act as an advice centre, staffed by a local advice bureau.

Within two years the building programme is completed; the transformation is breathtaking. A welcoming and attractive physical environment created, full of light and with stimulating wall displays everywhere. Teachers' morale increases; their sharing of problems, solutions, disappointments, anger, stress and plans increases enormously; their willingness to work together translates into practice, fostering an atmosphere of mutual support. Their awareness of the out-of-school situation of their children increases, so that their ability to work with children becomes more sensitive. Further, the effect on parents, which started as a trickle, develops rapidly (increasing returns). Parents no longer resent the school, and this feeling is passed on to the children; though many parents were poorly educated themselves, nevertheless they take time to do their best to support their children's education at home. The school runs short programmes on effective parenting, and these become popular. There is a perceptible move from hostility to collaboration between home and school, as all parties recognize each other's contribution on behalf of the children.

Of course, this is not to say that there are not immense problems along the way, and the struggle to improve is palpable. The situation reported here actually happened, but is described skeletally. The significance of this description is that the school sensed its external and internal environment; it introduced changes to its internal environment, and this, in turn, brought changes to the external environment.

For a second example, the Thomas Telford City Technology College is a high-profile, multiple-award-winning secondary school in the UK (http://www.ttsonline.net/tts/; Morrison, 1997); it is a 'beacon school' in the UK, i.e. one which has been recognized by the Department for Education and Skills as having outstanding practice and which receives a small amount of funding in order to share that practice with other schools. An outstanding inspection report (http://www.ttsonline.net/tts/ParentInfo/ttsofsted.htm) indicated several features of the school, for example, that it:

- enjoys great popularity with parents, carers and students and has grown in size, with student achievement rising in terms of examination results (increasing returns);
- keeps parents and carers well informed of their children's progress through ten annual reports (i.e. one at the end of each four-week module);
- provides meetings for parents to discuss how they can support their children's education;
- actively encourages feedback from parents, carers, colleagues, and students;
- has extensive links (including overseas work placements) with other schools, locally, nationally and internationally;
- liaises with the local education authority in connection with taking students who have been excluded from other schools;
- provides time for team-based planning (e.g. in subject groups), development, monitoring, assessment and reporting;
- makes extended, high quality use of computers for teaching, learning (e.g. the whole curriculum is on-line), management and administration;
- has increased and relocated its library and independent learning centres into several sites (i.e. a distributed system);
- places great emphasis on developing positive relationships between all members of the student community;
- has an extensive personal tutorial system which is at the heart of much of its success in raising and sustaining student achievement;
- has outstanding leadership at all levels of the school, through the head-teacher, nine deputies and subject heads;
- places emphasis on teamwork and a non-hierarchical structure;
- values everybody's contribution to the school openly;
- celebrates success openly, visually, and verbally throughout the premises;
- encourages parents, teachers, and a range of other outside parties to work together in the school;
- has highly developed internal and external communication, using IT and multimedia extensively;
- has a full-time Director of Careers and Industry Links (a former human resource manager for a large multinational company), who works with a team of staff who have worked in industry;

- has extensive and close contacts with industry;
- has shared space throughout the school (there are no staff rooms) and open-plan spaces where appropriate to facilitate students working with several teachers.

This example is striking in that it embodies several features of complexity theory, viz.: concern to promote increasing returns (Chapter 1); team-based approaches (see Chapter 2); distributed leadership, servant leadership and distributed knowledge (see Chapters 3 and 4); extensive internal and external communication (see Chapter 6); and an emphasis on relationships (see Chapters 2, 3 and 4). Further, as this chapter will discuss, the school is highly sensitive to its internal and external environments and goes to exceptional lengths to cultivate links, relationships and feedback between these two environments: the internal environment is affected by, and affects, the external environment, and the internal environment changes and reorganizes itself in response to the school's changing situation.

The essence of complexity theory states that the organism and its environment interact and shape each other's development and that this is accomplished, to some extent, by each anticipating the other (Waldrop, 1992: 177). Species co-evolve (Stewart, 2001), and the two preceding examples demonstrate this. An open system has permeable boundaries so that such interaction can happen. Connectedness with the wider environment is vital for survival, and relational understanding is as important as cause-and-effect understanding. A complex adaptive system, as Gell-Mann (1994: 17) and Schein (1992: 51) tell us, acquires, evaluates and uses information from its environment.

Southworth (2000: 279) argues that primary schools rely on webs and networks, indeed that webs are a very fitting metaphor for schools because they not only indicate the relationships that exist within schools and between schools and their environments, but also because they challenge the notion that school improvement can be successful simply by rational, linear planning.[1] Fullan (1993: 84) suggests that schools have to be plugged into their local communities if they are to be genuinely learning institutions (cf. Levinthal, 1995; McMaster 1996: 10).

This chapter suggests that leaders in school have several tasks to face in addressing the environment, for example:

- identifying, describing, sensing and scanning the environments in which they operate;
- defining the priorities within these environments;
- deciding their relationships with the environments;
- responding to, and planning for, the environments;
- self-organizing for the environments.

The chapter suggests that, if schools are to cope with the changing environments in which they operate, they need to move towards increasing their networked structures and devolved, team-based organizational structures, with attention being paid to communication and feedback between all parties in the internal and external environments. Further, complex environmental change takes place at several levels of education, and the closing part of the chapter provides examples of this.

Schools managing their internal and external environments

The nature of the relationships between the organism and its environment will change as each emerges, and we cannot consider the one without the other. At different times there will be different relationships between them (Marion, 1999: 84–5, 116–22); they may be competitive, collaborative, symmetrical, asymmetrical, controlling, manipulating, integrated, isolated, dependent, and interdependent at different times and in differing amounts.

The relationship between schools and their environments is neither a one-to-one correspondence (Marion, 1999: 97), nor a one-way causality, neither is it possible to completely define the environment entirety. Relationships are two-way and their outcomes are unpredictable. Schools affect students, who affect families, who affect communities; communities affect families, who affect students, who affect schools. School leadership affects the school, and the school affects the school leadership. Schools and their leadership are, and must be, highly sensitive to their environments. There must be mutual learning from each other, or, to borrow a phrase from environmental education, schools must learn in, about, through, from, and for their environments. Schools must be constantly scanning and sensing their environments and responding to them through their organizational structures (Bradley and Nolan, 1998: 16).

Information, Wheatley (1999: 83) suggests, must be actively sought from everywhere; it must circulate freely, and its consequences for provoking the school to change must be faced. The school changes from being a 'well-defended' organization (*ibid.*), in which information to leaders is only welcomed to the extent that it confirms existing practice, and becomes a dynamic, changing organization based on living with information which may disturb everyday practices (Fullan, 2001). Information is the food of relationships and connections.

Having gained information from the environment, the leaders' task is to develop a view of how to respond to this information, for example, whether to ignore it, disseminate it, act on it, and build it into new developments. For decisions on this to be made it is important for the school to have a protocol for deciding:

- what information must be shared;
- what information should be shared;
- what information need not be shared;
- who needs to receive particular information (and who decides 'who needs').

For example, major pressures and constraints on schools should be matters for all; specific items of subject material might be for certain subject teachers only; general or new approaches to teaching and pedagogy might be for all; items which affect everyone should be discussed with everyone.

One major problem that school leaders face is definitional: deciding exactly what the environments are in which they operate. This operates at several levels. At one level it is cast in terms of participants and stakeholders (Southwest Educational Development Laboratory, 1999), for example:

students;	colleges;	the economy;
teachers;	vocational institutions;	the polity;
parents;	universities;	local education authorities;
families;	employers;	social agencies;
communities;	examining agencies;	businesses;
civic organizations;	volunteer organizations;	society.

At another level the environment can be construed in macro-level terms (Morrison and Ridley, 1988: 32; Hatch, 1997: 68–71; Nolan and Galal, 1998: 313). (Table 5.1).

The relationship is not one-way; schools and environment mutually interact (Figure 5.1).

What characterizes these contexts – participant-centred or macro-environmental – is that there is little likelihood of there ever being any agreement between all these environments. Not only does each change within itself, but it constantly changes the landscapes of the others. Leadership for self-organization then, becomes a matter of swimming in the tide – sometimes with the current, sometimes against it, sometimes outside it (having relative autonomy). It is a matter of white-water rafting rather than controlling the rapids.

The analogy is useful, for it suggests 'bounded instability', which is a hallmark of complexity and chaos theories. Just because it is impossible to model or control a boiling river, that does not preclude the possibility of riding the waves, anticipating

Table 5.1 Macro-environmental contexts of education

Macro-environmental contexts		*Nature of the influence*
Political	$\rightarrow$	Power/control of education and decision making
Ideological	$\rightarrow$	Values and beliefs on education
Economic	$\rightarrow$	Relationships between schools, the economy and employment; priorities for schools
Epistemological	$\rightarrow$	Nature, content and structure of knowledge
Cultural	$\rightarrow$	Cultural production/reproduction through education; cultural values and practices
Sociological	$\rightarrow$	Access, uptake and outcomes of education; education and society
Societal	$\rightarrow$	Service to families and the community
Technological	$\rightarrow$	Effects of information revolution on education and schooling
Psychological	$\rightarrow$	Nature of learning, learning environments and psychological needs
Historical	$\rightarrow$	Causes, antecedents and legacies of educational decision making
Legal	$\rightarrow$	Legal constraints on, and requirements of, education
Physical	$\rightarrow$	Physical and resource constraints on schools; schools and local community
Market	$\rightarrow$	Consumer requirements of schools
Philosophical	$\rightarrow$	Justification and aims of education

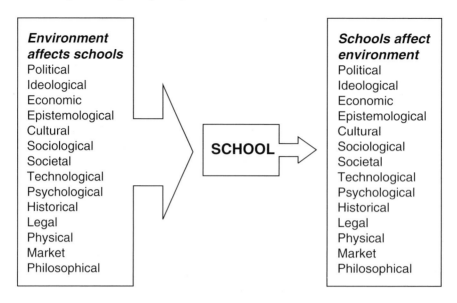

Figure 5.1 Schools affecting and being affected by their environments.

to some extent where one is going (if only in the immediate future) and identifying the major priorities to be faced in navigating a passage – it is the coarse-grained rather than the close-grained picture. In actual terms, this suggests that school leaders constantly need to identify exactly what their major environments are in order to understand the major pressures and constraints from these environments (Beeson and Davis, 2000: 185), for example, the massive intervention of governments in education, frequently to prescribe the contents and assessment arrangements of schools together with the increased bureaucratic machinery of accountability and over-regulation (Karsten *et al.*, 2000). This can be in very specific terms (e.g. pre-scription of curriculum content) or in general terms (e.g. the move to placing schools on a market footing).

Hatch (1997: 75) suggests that distinctions between organizations and environments are comparatively arbitrary. Rather, she argues, we need to define the several environments in which organizations are located. Scott (1992) suggests that those environments themselves will have different degrees and natures of institutionalization. If the environment is highly institutionalized, and the school is one such institution, then the school will need to have its institutional mechanisms and structures formally and strongly arranged (cf. Pfeffer and Salancik, 1978). If the environment is less institutionalized and can make greater demands on schools, then schools have to be more flexible. The argument expressed here is that, for survival, schools and their leaders have to *learn* from their environments, (cf. Hannan and Freeman, 1977), for example through feedback, testing ideas in the environment, discussions with external parties, and responding to demands from the environment.

If schools are to be able to gather intelligence from their environments then, just as in the example of the slime-mould in Chapter 1, they need sensors to catch the messages and communication to transfer the messages. Some sensors will catch coarse-grained, large scale information; others with catch close-grained, fine detail. Further, schools need information systems to process, selectively filter and act on those messages (cf. Kauffman's (1993) suggestion that organizations must learn to ignore some inputs coming into the organization and pressures coming from external sources, as too many data and pressures can act as a brake on developments). This is a two-way matter – just as the school needs to have mechanisms to work with incoming messages, so it needs mechanisms to work with outgoing messages (Figure 5.2).

Cohen and Stewart (1995: 348) suggest that the organism deliberately and proactively seeks out information from the environment in order to learn. They indicate that there are more neural connections *from* the brain to the ear than from the ear *to* the brain, and that some 10 per cent of the fibres in the optic nerve go 'the wrong way'. Sense organs, they argue, do not passively receive information, 'they go fishing for it'. Information, as Bailey (2000: 202) remarks, does not travel from the environment in to the individual, but starts with the individual and moves outwards. Figure 5.2 suggests that leaders will need to develop, for example:

* communication, as it is vital for sensing the environment;
* sensors, as they are necessary for working with the environment;
* internal structures and systems, which have to be capable of giving, receiving, and acting on messages;
* internal co-ordination, which is an important feature for distributing and distributed information at all levels and stages in schools (Swieringa and Wierdsma, 1992).

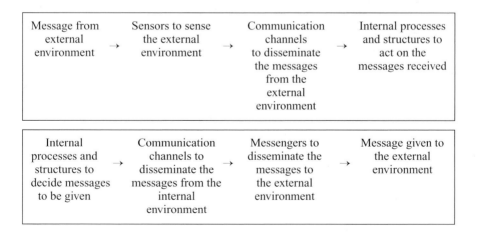

| Message from external environment | → | Sensors to sense the external environment | → | Communication channels to disseminate the messages from the external environment | → | Internal processes and structures to act on the messages received |

| Internal processes and structures to decide messages to be given | → | Communication channels to disseminate the messages from the internal environment | → | Messengers to disseminate the messages to the external environment | → | Message given to the external environment |

Figure 5.2 Schools sensing and responding to their environments.

School leaders will need to address such questions as:

- Who and what are the sensors in the schools?
- What are mechanisms, structures and processes in the school for connecting with the wider environment?
- Who are the parties in the wider environment and how can communications be established with them?
- What are the relationships that should be sought with the wider environment?
- How is information from the wider environment distributed and acted on in the school?
- On what issues should schools be proactive or reactive to the pressures of the wider environment (Coleman, 1999)?
- How can win-win situations with the wider environment be produced (Lewin and Regine, 2000: 67)?

Cohen and Levinthal (1990) suggest that there is a need to increase the 'absorptive capacity' of organizations, i.e. their capability for searching, encoding, decoding, selecting, synthesizing, distributing, interpreting and acting on external information. Such capability building is a key element in leadership for organizational learning (Hong, 1999: 174).

Ashby (1981) and Hatch (1997: 90) suggest a 'law of requisite variety', which states that the variety within the organization or system (e.g. the school) must be at least as great as the variety within the environment. As Pheysey (1993: 28) remarks, a hedgehog's defence system of curling up into a ball is useful for warding off predators but useless in the face of cars! The term she uses is *isomorphism* (*ibid*: 29), the correspondence between the internal and external variety (e.g. a map should correspond well to the landscape being mapped). Indeed, Fullan (2001: 47) argues that organizations reach crisis when they are 'out of synch' with their environments. Capra (1997) points out that the law of requisite variety requires the organization to constantly change and develop, in accordance with the changes in the environment, if it is to survive, i.e. that the organization must learn.

A part of the development of the leaders' ability to respond to signals is the surfacing of key uncertainties (asking difficult questions about the environment). The next stage is: ranking these key questions and uncertainties in terms of priority, scenario building about how to respond to these environments, and providing details of these responses (Clemons and Bradley, 1998: 93). The issue here is for leaders in the school to network with the wider environment, and for this to be co-ordinated, disseminated and shared throughout the school.

Clearly, given the extent of the information which needs to be exchanged between the school and the environment, this cannot be handled through a bureaucratic and hierarchically managed school – it simply becomes unworkable. Hence, leadership in linking with the environment is distributed throughout the school, and is everybody's responsibility (for example, including teachers, students, parents, employers, community groups, colleges and universities). This requires all teachers and adults in the school to open as many channels of communication, working relationships and networks as possible with the wider environment.

Individual teachers and groups of teachers have expert knowledge of the most appropriate links with those aspects of the external environment with which they are involved; leadership is everywhere.

Communication takes place at many levels. For example: governments formally consult with educationists and employers; there are professional associations for teachers; local education authorities consult with parents and teachers; professional development agencies provide links between schools and the wider environment; publishers liaise with schools and teachers; schools bid for categorical funding for sponsored development areas. Further, this has already developed with the numerous forums for vocational education and work placements for secondary school students; these comprise committees made up of representatives from schools, employers, higher and vocational educational institutions, assessment agencies and education authorities. At primary school level this has involved visits to an array of diverse organizations and institutions. At kindergarten level parents and adults are intimately involved in working relationships with teachers. These links are all commonplace in the UK.

The key term here, perhaps, is *partnerships* (Cardona, 2000: 206). There are, however, limits to the notion of partnerships, for it implies discrete roles for the partners, for example the school reaching out into the community and the community reaching into the school. This need not be so. Apple and Beane (1995) provide examples of considerable blurring and overlapping of the roles and tasks of partners in the furtherance of democratic schools. The debate is not new. For example, some parties suggest that parents should be invited into schools to consult with teachers (with asymmetrical relationships present because teachers have expert knowledge), others suggest that parents should be involved in curriculum and policy decision making.

The twin notions of networks (within and outside the schools – K connections and C connections respectively in terms of fitness landscapes, discussed in Chapter 7) and partnerships require attention to:

(a) the qualities required of the participants in order to be effective;
(b) the focus of information exchange and discussion;
(c) the opportunities for information exchange and discussion.

With regard to (a), Kelly and Allison (1999: 171) suggest that the important qualities of such 'eco-technicians' as leaders include: effective interpersonal relations; broad and deep professional knowledge; deserved respect by participants; a grasp of the systems and structures required to implement developments; problem solving; investigative skills; patience and an ability to attend to details. This includes strategies of effective, active listening and communication (see Chapter 6).

With regard to (b) there are several issues for focus. For example, the Department for Education and Skills in the UK suggests several aspects that should be inspected under the umbrella of 'home and community', including:

- business links;
- collective worship;
- community use of school premises;

- relationships with the community and community groups;
- home-school agreements (including the school's aims, values and ethos; the standard of education; discipline; the school's and parents' respective responsibilities for pupil attendance and behaviour, and homework; what the school expects of its pupils; communications and complaints);
- out-of-school activities (including work experience arrangements);
- parent partnerships (e.g. for the education of children with special educational needs);
- parental involvement;
- the prospectus for parents;
- pupil reports.

With regard to (c) there are several opportunities for information exchange (Table 5.2).

In complexity theory terms, the school needs to be prepared to reorganize itself in order to accommodate the implications of information, thus:

The 'law of requisite variety' (Hatch, 1997: 90) suggests here that the greater the degree of complexity in the wider environment, the greater the degree of complexity within the school in order to handle it (see also the discussion of low-C in Chapter 7).

For example, the leader of the science department engages in discussions with (1) scientific associations, (2) universities, (3) colleges and (4) local employers about the need to provide opportunities for more secondary school students to have early positive experiences of science and engineering in society, in order that they opt for these at post-school level. The external environment here is complex, as there are four identified parties as 'players'.

This is matched by increasing complexity in the school. The science leader, recognizing that this will have significant ramifications for timetabling and subject options, brings it firstly to the attention of the other science teachers in her department, and they present a joint paper to the school about the need and the implications of meeting the need. From here, the science teachers meet the School Management Team, the Whole School Curriculum Development Team and the matter is brought to a staff meeting. Arising from the discussions is a recognition of the need to restructure the timetable in order to release students from school to undertake science and engineering experiences for significant blocks of time *in situ*, before having to make subject options. It also suggests the need for increased career advice, the concomitant careers information resources in the school and the timetabling implications of this, so that students have greater opportunities to pursue the issue. Finally, it suggests the need for increasing awareness of the scope of the fields of science and engineering in society and employment.

To accommodate these needs the school timetable is restructured, not only for

Table 5.2 Opportunities for information exchange

Written communication	Home visiting
School prospectus Enrolment and contact pro-formas Notices, letters, newsletters and magazines (multi-lingual) Statutory reporting and assessments Open reports/Records of Achievement/Portfolios Advice on post-school and out-of-school matters Curriculum advice (e.g. shared reading, early literacy and numeracy) Explanations of teaching methods E-mail correspondence about school matters Accessing the school's Web site Invitations to discuss children's progress	To follow up on authorized and non- authorized absence and illness Disciplinary matters Taking a student home (e.g. for security reasons or illness) Suspected non-accidental injury (a matter for social workers) Everyday matters (e.g. the provision of school uniform/appropriate equipment) Academic progress reports

School management	Classroom/school involvement
Governing body of school Parent/teacher associations and councils Curriculum planning committees (e.g. with employers) Homework matters Annual meeting with governors Target setting for the school – school development planning	Cataloguing/working on resources Displaying materials Teaching (a contentious issue) Giving talks (e.g. specialist knowledge and expertise) Transport and assistance on out-of- school activities Running extra-curricular activities Setting out and clearing away materials Hearing children read Attending programmes in schools (as learners)

School visiting	Use of facilities
Parents' evenings or afternoons Open days Parents' interviews Statementing of students with special educational needs Discussion of individual children Admission to school Moving school Leaving school Careers interviewing	Adult education programmes Creche/toddler groups/child care facilities Information centres (with information technology links) Resource centres Onsite facilities (e.g. gymnasia, swimming pools, sports areas, language laboratories, conference suites, technology suites, craft equipment) Vocational education

Events	Advice
Coffee mornings Sales (e.g. clothing sales, fairs) Graduation ceremonies Festivals (e.g. religious) Sports/music/drama events Curriculum events (e.g. environmental education events or a science fair) Photographic displays Careers programmes	Domestic matters Housing and state benefits Legal and social matters Equal opportunities and employment Liaison with formal departments (e.g. social services, education, housing, legal, taxation, immigration, service providers such as electricity and water)

the science teachers, but because of the 'knock-on' effects for major areas of the school, in effect moving from several small periods of study during the day towards two blocks of time during the school day on certain days of the week. Further, it is decided to ensure that several related subjects give heightened coverage of the science and engineering implications of their subjects (e.g. mathematics and languages). For this to happen, the school decides to set up a cross-departmental project group to develop a four-week cross-curriculum project to enhance the awareness of employment and training/education prospects in science and engineering: it will also be an inter-disciplinary consultation group which will be available on a continuing basis for teachers and students alike. At the same time the school recognizes that several of its key staff here have limited knowledge of such employment prospects, so the school: (a) sends two of its staff on very short-term placements with two local employers; (b) brings in advisers on a regular basis from careers services and science and engineering services to discuss careers in these areas with staff and students; (c) consults with local vocational and higher education providers about employment, training and education in these areas.

The example given indicates not only a key issue in the management of change (the fact that innovation in one area has 'knock-on' effects on others), but it recognizes that change brings costs – in support development time, in terms of commitment, in its effects on other teachers, in its budgetary implications. Reorganization in one area frequently leads to reorganization in another area, which involves budgetary reorganization, i.e. it is a leadership matter.

Relations with the environment are two-way. The school is not simply a recipient of externally-derived information; school leaders also need to consider how the school will project itself into the environment, and into which environment it will project different parts of itself. This should be part of the distributed knowledge system, and it raises several questions, for example:

- Does the school have a shared register or details of contact persons and organizations outside and inside the school for different aspects of its work?
- Is such a register universally available?
- Do staff use it?
- Is it clear on what criteria staff should pursue official rather than informal and personal channels of contact?
- How do staff contribute to the register?
- Do staff know how to contribute to the register?
- How is information from the register used and disseminated in the school, and its implications addressed?
- How is the register organized (e.g. within-school contacts and committees/groups; outside-school contacts and organizations; local, regional, national and international links; Web sites; professional associations; feedback from staff development activities; whole-school matters (such as discipline, assessment, reporting and budgeting)?
- How can staff quickly disseminate and discuss information? (e.g. is there a

time provided each day for this? Are staff expected to access internal e-mail each day?)

- Does the school provide time and resources (e.g. information technology) for teachers to scan the environment and act on information from it?
- What arrangements have to be made and procedures observed for staff to leave the premises and for visitors to come into the school in promoting links between the school and the environment?
- Who has responsibility for particular links with external bodies (e.g. funding agencies, assessment agencies, social services, government agencies)?
- How is information prioritized in the school?

More than this, the school leaders need to consider the messages/signals which they wish to give to certain sectors of the outside world, agreement on who should give those messages, and what are the protocols for giving such messages, i.e:

- What should the message be?
- Who should give the message?
- To whom should the message be given?
- How should the message be given?
- When should the message be given?

This is the topic of communication, to which the next chapter turns. It is suggested here that leaders need to ensure that channels of communication within the school and between the school and the external environment are hard-wired into schools' structures and operating procedures, for example in formal committees and advisory panels, and in informal contacts.

Needs analysis

If the school leaders are to act intelligently towards the environment and indeed on information received from the environment, then they will need to undertake some form of 'needs analysis'. This might be undertaken, for example, to:

- identify curricular responses to external factors;
- identify programme provision needs (and gaps in present provision);
- ascertain weaknesses in provision;
- provide information on in-service needs;
- determine where deficits exist so that they can be addressed;
- identify areas for expenditure and educational development.

A need can be defined in several ways (Scriven and Roth, 1978; Lund and McGechan, 1981; Stufflebeam *et al.*, 1985; Rossi and Freeman, 1993; Suarez, 1994). It can be seen as a *discrepancy* or *under-achievement* (a difference between what is and what should be the case); *wants* and *preferences* (e.g. for future planning), reflecting values; *anticipated requirements* for the future; *anticipated problems* for the future; and a *deficit* (where the absence of a feature under review is harmful).

Needs analysis concerns the process of diagnosis for subsequent planning, and both are concerned with gathering information in order to define problems and needs, whether they come from the external or internal environments. There are several components of a needs analysis, for example (Cohen *et al.*, 2000: 391) (Table 5.3).

The intention is to ensure that interventions are appropriately matched to perceived problems or needs, so that the school both meets changing needs in the wider environment and identifies needs for internal change to be able to meet those external needs. The data required for needs analysis and feedback can be derived from several sources, for example:

(a) *quantitative data* from: structured surveys; 'key person' (informants) surveys; structured interviews (Rossi and Freeman, 1993); data from official public sources and documents (e.g. test and examination data, and other surveys); attendance data;

(b) *qualitative data* from: semi-structured interviews with individuals and groups; focus groups; case studies; critical incidents and events; public meetings; nominal group technique and Delphi techniques (Morrison, 1993; 1998).

Table 5.3 Components of a needs analysis

Elements of a needs analysis	Internal and external population	Planned intervention
• The definition of need that is being used	• The target population for an intervention which responds to the needs	• The identification of the exact conditions, problems and needs that the intervention is designed to address
• The nature and type of the problem or need	• The number of people affected or concerned (e.g. the proportion of a total population)	• The appropriateness of the programme intended to address the need
• The indicators of the need or problem	• The location of the need or problem	• The purposes of the proposed intervention
• The size, scope, complexity and range of the problem or need	• The clarification of whose problem it is	• The identification of the target population for an intervention
• The sub-elements of the need or problem	• The density and distribution of the problem	• The present and estimated future size of the target population
• The priorities of aspects of the need	• The incidence of the problem or need	• The feasibility of the proposed intervention
• The severity or intensity of the need or problem	• How widespread is the need	• Responsibility for interventions (who has to take action)
• The causes of the need		
• The consequences if the need is not addressed		
• The consequences of addressing the need		

Rossi and Freeman (1993: 84) suggest that qualitative data are useful for determining the nature of the need, whilst quantitative data are necessary for
determining the extent of the need. The success of needs analysis may depend on
the careful and appropriate sampling and targeting of parties concerned. Suarez
(1994) suggests that needs analysis for the purpose of future planning and development will tend to focus on aims and goals, whilst needs analysis to identify
discrepancies will tend to focus on content, implementation and outcome.

The issue of prioritization of the problems, needs and aspects of the intervention is also critical, particularly because budgetary constraints will affect the
conduct of the needs assessment and its subsequent recommendations. Witkin
(1984) identifies several quantitative methods for identifying priorities (including, for example, ratings, amount of discrepancy between actual and intended
practices or incidence). Lund and McGechan (1981) suggest that the process of
prioritization will need to focus on such issues as:

- the consequences of not meeting the need – as McMaster (1996) says, ignorance is more expensive than education!;
- the number of people affected;
- the meeting of the need by the parties identified (e.g. whether the problem is
  solely a matter for educationists or whether it involves other service sectors);
- the criticality and severity of the needs;
- the sequencing of the need (the order in which the needs must be addressed,
  and whether the addressing of some needs logically and empirically precedes
  the addressing of others);
- the resource implications of meeting the needs (e.g. people, financial and
  budgetary, time, materials and equipment, administrative support);
- the scope of the outcome and the utility of the intervention.

In planning a needs analysis, leaders can take four main steps:

1 decide the purposes of the needs analysis and the definitions of needs that are
   to be used;
2 identify the focus of the needs analysis;
3 decide the methodology, sampling, instrumentation, data collection and
   analysis procedures and criteria to be used to judge the size, scope, extent,
   severity etc. of the need;
4 decide the reporting and dissemination of the results.

Needs analysis enables the school to be informed of the external and internal
environments, so that any internal restructuring of the school can be undertaken
to match the external environment more fittingly.

Complexity theory and education at a macro-level

So far, the discussion of schools and their environments has been at the level of
individual schools and how they relate to their particular environments. However,
complexity theory operates at system-wide levels. Four examples of this are pre-

sented below; the first three report on situations of limited numbers of different providers of education, and the final example indicates the interaction effects of several providers of education.

First, Wallace and Pocklington (1998) report a large scale study of change (emergence), and they indicate how complex change – the wholesale reorganization of around a hundred schools and tens of thousands of children in one local education authority (LEA) in the UK – resonates with several components of complexity theory. Complexity theory here indicates the interactions, principles of self-organization and emergence at several levels, and the complex notion of environments. Interactions within and between levels was a complicated and complex affair, evolving over time, often incrementally.

The LEA, faced with falling rolls and surplus places, had to close schools and reorganize its entire school provision. Such changes required the co-ordinated interaction of several 'players': (1) the existing schools, their governors, head-teachers, teachers, parents and children; (2) the LEA officers; (3) the then Department for Education and Employment (the government office concerned); (4) the local community (e.g. local councillors, parents, local media, local education service providers). Within each level/set of players were many individuals, rendering liaison and co-ordination difficult, as there were different agendas, powers, interests, values, priorities and spheres of influence. The authors (*ibid*: 7–10) identify several characteristics of the complex situation:

- the large number of participants involved in the change (*ibid*: 7); in terms of fitness landscapes discussed in Chapter 7, this demonstrates high-S (high numbers of participants);
- the wide range of groups involved, each of which had their own, differing areas of specialist knowledge and their own, diverse priorities, concerns and briefs (*ibid*: 8);
- the often incompatible interests of members of the different groups, which led to struggles, negotiation, compromise and consequentially, adjustments to the plans for implementation (*ibid*: 8);
- the occasional conflict of interests and allegiances which arose when individuals had to perform dual roles (*ibid*: 9);
- the huge number of management tasks undertaken by the LEA and schools (*ibid*: 9), many of which were a 'continually evolving profile of simultaneous management tasks' (*ibid*: 10), echoing the evolutionary, iterative nature of emergence over time in complexity theory;
- the potential for different interpretations by participants at one level of the actions of participants at other levels (*ibid*: 11), echoing the need for a 'fusion of horizons' in communication, discussed in Chapter 6;
- different degrees of power dispersed throughout the different levels of the system and participants within and between each level (*ibid*: 11);
- the mutual dependence on each other by participants, coupled with limited control over each other (the problems of co-evolution: Stewart, 2001);
- the struggle for consensus through synergy (Wallace and Pocklington, *op. cit*: 11), (see the discussions of 'storming' and 'norming' in Chapter 2);

- the inability of any of the parties or individuals at each level to have complete knowledge of everything that was taking place on the other levels and among participants (*ibid*: 13), despite extensive communication.

To address these, the authors report, required 'a flow of interaction within and between system levels' and extensive 'cross-level communication' (*ibid*: 10); in terms of fitness landscapes (discussed in Chapter 7) this demonstrates high-K (internal connectedness) and high-C (external coupling), and echoes the dynamical, mutually interactive nature of change discussed in complexity theory.

The authors argue that the combination of these factors, interpreted here in terms of complexity theory, led to highly incremental co-evolution (cf. *ibid*: 14), even though the overall parameters were unchanged ('bounded instability': Stacey, 2000). This echoes Stacey's (2000) suggestion that, although long term change can be discussed and boundaries identified, participants must realize that it is open to constant reconfiguration, alteration, and even abandonment.

Wallace and Pocklington suggest that change in complex systems is not fully controllable and that, to understand it fully, it is better to think of the complexity of change as a network (*ibid*: 17), like the neural networks of the brain, with parallel processing and hierarchical levels within the system, with different participants being the nodes in the net, and with extensive inter- and intra-communication being necessary. Indeed, the authors' comments resonate with complexity theory, distributed knowledge, and order without control, for example in their statements that 'the network operates without any single player, representing a node with connections to all other nodes' (*ibid*: 17), and that 'the reorganisation process unfolds without any of the people who make up the parts being able to see the process in its entirety' (*ibid*: 17). Leadership is at all levels and by all participants.

Though the authors suggest that the notion of a network is a useful metaphor, in practice the example they provide indicates that it is more than mere metaphor, it actually happens. This echoes Stacey's (2001) concern to ensure that complexity theory is more than simply a metaphor, and that it is embodied in practice. The authors suggest that coherence rather than control is a more fitting way of describing this large scale change – complexity theory is premised on order without control.

A *second* example can be taken from a group of rural primary schools in the UK, dispersed over some thirty square miles. Some of these were faced with closure for economic reasons, particularly as they were experiencing difficulty in meeting the targets for children's achievements of the government's prescribed national curriculum. The problems lay in two main areas: (1) the staffing required in order to have suitably qualified subject experts in several fields: each school on its own felt unable to provide suitable subject expertise across the full range of the national curriculum; (2) more resources were required to service the full range of the curriculum. Given that each school's budget was limited, as the schools typically were very small – each having between 30 and 120 students – and the budgets were based on a *per capita* basis, the survival of each school seemed impossible.

The headteachers of the schools recognized that it was in everybody's interests to work conjointly. They met together and a solution was proposed: the schools would form a consortium. After a little more than six months in the planning, the new system commenced. Here some of the teachers worked at more than one school, maybe working for two or three days each week in one school, and the remainder in another, or more schools if the subject demanded it (e.g. music tuition). Further, resource packs were prepared for particular subjects (e.g. science, history and geography), which were circulated on a half-termly basis between the schools.

A central reprographics and teachers' resource centre was located at the most accessible school for all the others in the consortium, and material which was not urgent could be prepared there. The centre also housed more expensive equipment in several subjects, which each school itself would not be able to afford, but which could be purchased together and loaned on an agreed rotating basis. In the case of some of the schools whose premises did not include certain facilities (e.g. gymnasia and sports fields), the children themselves would travel from their own school to those other schools, by agreement. Internet links were found to be a vital means of communication. Meetings to plan and review the workings of the consortium were scheduled for a minimum of twice a term, and the consortium employed a part-time secretary to administer its arrangements, transporting materials as required.

What has happened in this example? The internal environment cannot cope with the demands of the external environment without changing its internal structure; the new internal structure of each school demonstrates high inter-connectedness and external coupling (see Chapter 7), a new form of self-organization has evolved in which the 'system' is no longer simply one school, but a group of schools in combination. Relationships and highly developed communication are central to the smooth working of the system, and considerable attention was devoted to these.

A *third* example is of changes to the special educational needs provision in the UK, following from the Education Reform Bill of 1998 (Department of Education and Science, 1988) and the UK government's subsequent *Code of Practice on the Identification and Assessment of Special Educational Needs* (Department for Education, 1994). The example is drawn from the work of Millward and Skidmore (1998). The provision and administration of education for children with special needs had been largely in the hands of the Local Education Authorities (LEAs) until the Reform Act of 1988. Thereafter, schools were able to purchase special needs support themselves, free of the LEA's intervention. LEAs still had a statutory responsibility for providing a formal and legal statement of special educational needs and for providing appropriate education for children from minority groups with special needs, but the management of provision was altered, essentially diminishing the power and control by the LEAs.

The effects of this, argue Millward and Skidmore (57–8), were the promotion of:

- a new relationship between the LEA and the school, wherein the LEA, no longer directing and controlling, was supportive, enabling, nurturing and disseminating good practice, and some limited resource provision, and where the school assumed a much greater degree of control of its handling of special needs;
- LEA strategic leadership was replaced by LEA support for change and development;
- a new collaborative, partnership relationship between LEAs and schools, rather than a directive relationship between the former and the latter;
- school-based and school-specific developments and initiatives rather than the adoption of a single, central, LEA directed model of special education;
- democratic participation, wherein schools (and not just the LEA) would participate in policy formation and decision making;
- a change to the internal structuring of special needs provision by the LEAs.

Millward and Skidmore use the vocabulary of 'emergence', 'emerging governance', 'relationships', 'enabling', 'internal structure', 'restructuring', 'communication', 'community', 'collaboration', 'trust', 'inclusion', all central constructs of complexity theory. Further, the authors quote respondents who report that management is less about telling people and more about spotting 'windows of opportunity' (*ibid*: 64), less about having a 'blueprint' and more about being opportunistic and responsive to unfolding events. Further, they quote a senior LEA official's view of leadership by the LEA as not meaning that the LEA actually has to do everything (*ibid*: 64). The authors comment on the extended dialogue between central and local government about the development of special needs provision (*ibid*: 65), and about the need for central government to lead by creating the conditions in which LEAs and schools are able to improve their special needs provision. All of these ideas resonate with complexity theory. The researchers indicate that, at the time of writing, the future was unclear to all parties, but that it was emerging.

There are several features which indicate complexity theory at work in the example:

- changes to the internal and external activities and environments of the players in the system (e.g. the schools, the LEAs, the central government), and the mutuality of these changes (co-evolution);
- the unpredictability of the evolution of the process and contents of special needs provision;
- the new, emergent self-organization and self-reorganization of the schools and the LEAs that were occasioned by the changes (i.e. each of their fitness landscapes changed in terms of their internal environments (K), their external environments (S), and the nature and extent of their connections with the external environment (C), see Chapter 7);
- the distributed control and leadership amongst all the players in the system, such that the actions of any one affect the actions of the others in the network (high-K, see Chapter 7);

- the significance of feedback, communication, positive relationships and open systems;
- the need for organizational learning (e.g. by the schools and the LEAs);
- the emphasis on inclusion – complexity theory includes all players in interactions for co-evolution.

The schools, placed into a powerful new position, and the LEAs, placed into a less powerful position, changed their internal organization, and hence their fitness landscapes in response to their environments, and, through dialogue (with each other and with central government), also acted to change those environments.

The three examples of macro-level change have tended to be where the system in question is largely monopolistic, or where competitive providers or organizers of education have been largely missing. Complexity theory and fitness landscapes (Chapter 7) also embrace the dynamic co-evolution of competitors, each of which has its own fitness landscape that is affected by the other (e.g. the example of foxes and rabbits in Chapters 1 and 7). An example of this (example *four*) can be seen in the rise of market forces in education, and the rise of local management of schools in the UK, where each school has control over its own budget, and the power of the traditional administrators of education, the local education authorities, is reduced.

In the early 1980s, the government of the UK was seeking to break the 'producer capture' of education by educationists (Adam Smith Institute, 1984), and in Hayekian style, it advocated a freeing-up of the education system in order to make it more responsive to consumer needs. The Education Reform Act of 1988 (Department of Education and Science, 1988) enacted the delegation of financial control of school budgets away from the local education authorities and into the hands of each school's governing body, lifting the restrictions on the maximum numbers of children that schools could take, breaking the notion of school catchment areas, and leading to the establishment of City Technology Colleges and the opportunity for schools to opt out of local authority control (to take on grant-maintained status).

In so doing, it broke the power of the local education authorities to manage schooling (Morrison, 1995), and brought in a raft of measures designed to further the market footing of education (Morrison, 1994: 417–8): competition, consumerism, individualism, choice, diversity, freedom from constraint, privatisation, quality control (through inspection), and information (through compulsory school prospectuses and the publication of 'league tables' of schools' results in national assessments). The intention was to improve the quality of education by the creation of 'magnet' schools (centres of excellence that would grow – 'increasing returns'), and 'sink' schools, which would close. Local education authorities were divested of power in controlling school budgets, in making appointments of teachers, in managing a range of services (e.g. provision of meals, psychological services, special needs support, music instrumental tuition), and they had to reform themselves to become *advisers* on school and budgetary matters, to become school *inspectors* rather than support agencies, and to be involved in competitive tendering for the provision of in-service education and continuing professional development of teachers.

Under the guise of 'freeing up' the system it has been suggested (Ball, 1994) that this was actually the government of the time 'steering at a distance' (wishing to control), with a clearly *dirigiste* agenda (Morrison, 1995), which reproduced, indeed reinforced, the differential cultural capital of the schools, effectively rewarding those with the greatest cultural capital and the greatest opportunity to practise 'possessive individualism and personal initiative' (Bowe *et al.*, 1992: 25), i.e. increasing returns but only for a section of the school population (Morrison, 1994).

Since then, the system has unravelled in ways which were perhaps not expected, for example:

- the number of children excluded from schools has risen dramatically, as schools drive out disruptive children in their press for high examination results;
- several schools are collaborating rather than competing;
- the issues of selective schools and social equality have assumed an increasingly high profile;
- teacher morale has plummeted, with over 50 per cent of teachers leaving in the years 1989–99 (Cosgrove, 2000), mainly due to the working conditions, paperwork, bureaucracy, inspection system, and stress;
- headteachers objected to being placed in the position of 'chief executive' of a budget-driven service rather than being instructional leaders (Grace, 1995);
- teacher recruitment is in crisis, with schools under-staffed, closing for parts of the week, and unable to find subject teachers; the government has had to spend millions of pounds in advertising, with limited results;
- the inspection system, under threat of implosion, has had to reduce its timetables for inspection;
- behaviour problems in school have escalated, and truancy has become a major issue;
- the school curriculum narrowed as minority subjects were too expensive to continue;
- special needs has become a major issue, as children with special needs are seen to be expensive in terms of finite school resources;
- only a tiny number of schools have closed, and successful schools have not expanded in the ways expected, as their success is a function of their limited size;
- the City Technology Colleges project foundered;
- a backlash against the 'reforms' contributed to the ousting of the former government;
- objections were raised about placing education on a market footing; rather, it was a public good (Tang and Morrison, 1998);
- the privatization of music instrument tuition has caused leading musicians to criticize the new system for setting back music education.

It can be seen that there were several parties or players involved, each with its own fitness landscape (i.e. high-S, discussed in Chapter 7): the government had a clear agenda for control and the implementation of a political ideology (Morrison, 1994); the local education authorities changed their powers and functions; the schools gained increasing power and responsibility for the control of their own activities and budgets; a range of ancillary services were devolved and reorganized.

This is not the place to argue the politics of the situation. From the point of view of complexity theory, the example indicates that:

- the fitness landscape of the schools, the local education authorities, the government and the ancillary services change *in relation to each other*; each deforms and reforms the others;
- new forms of self-organization in the parties have emerged (schools have become self-managing; local education authorities have had to learn that they are not all-powerful, the government of the UK has changed, the ancillary services have regrouped);
- the outcomes of the changes could not have been anticipated or predicted in advance; they emerged, often in unintentional ways – the plans of the government were thwarted;
- the internal and external connections of the parties reformed, and new forms of networking, with new powers attached to the parties in the networks, were developed;
- the strategic plans of government were frustrated, not realized in the ways intended, and unpredictable, i.e. the external environment put pressure on other parties in the system (e.g. schools, local authorities), which, in turn, affected the working of the government;
- the government's attempts to exercise a control mentality failed.

Complexity theory signals the futility of long-range planning; such strategic planning simply does not work. Players in the system affect each other in unpredictable ways. Control evaporates.

Conclusion

This chapter has suggested that, if leadership in schools is to be effective in relating schools to their environments, a central feature of complexity theory, then there is a need for leadership to promote schools' abilities to:

- identify, scan and describe the range of environments in which they are located;
- prioritize the demands from their environments and prioritize the nature of their responses to these;
- communicate effectively with their environments;
- gather information from their environments;
- adapt their internal environments to meet the requirements of their environments (the law of requisite variety), i.e. learn from their environments;

- develop networks and partnerships with their environments and communities;
- conduct and act on needs analyses.

Further, this chapter has suggested that 'a system' can be defined at an individual school level or at an entire group level. In terms of fitness landscapes (see Chapter 7), regarding a system as that which embraces more than one school makes for very high-K (internal connectedness of the component parts of the system).

At the heart of the issue of relating schools and their environments lies the notion of communication – with the environment, within the environment and within the school; it is to this that the next chapter turns.

6   Communication

The nature of communication in complexity theory

The example of the Thomas Telford City Technology College in Chapter 5 indicates that communication within the school and between the school and its external environment was extensive, and two-way, using a multiplicity of formal and informal channels. Additionally, outcomes of discussions were shaped during the discussion, rather than being prefigured (the headteacher, for example, listened to the concerns of the students about the provision of facilities for physical education, and acted on this). Feedback was continually being encouraged by leaders, and the school acted on this.

In the networked, connected, knowledge-working, self-organizing school in which interdependence features highly, a premium is placed on effective communication, dialogue and consultation, both within the organization and between the organization and its environment (Popper and Lipshitz, 2000: 143). Emergence and networking require communication and information (Ludlow and Panton, 1992: 5). Co-evolution (of the school and its environment, or of elements within the school) needs effective and rich communication (Stewart, 2001: Chapter 7).

This chapter suggests that communication by leaders and distributed leaders in the complex, self-organizing school bears several hallmarks. For example, it will be dialogical and illocutionary rather than monological and perlocutionary; it will pay considerable and sensitive attention to the contexts of receivers as well as the senders (e.g. their emotions, situations and possible reactions), and this will impact on the register, medium, contents, direction, tone, timing and formality of the messages, keeping 'noise' in the system to a minimum. In this enterprise the reference to Transactional Analysis will argue for the need to avoid 'crossed wires' in communication and the desirability of providing positive feedback. Finally, a self-reporting set of questions is provided to describe the communication within the school, and its fitness for managing complexity, which will inform leaders' actions.

Communicated information is the lifeblood of an organization (Marsick, 2000: 14); rather than managing it (through control), the task of the leader is to disseminate information rather than restrict it, using information as a helpmate rather than adopting 'information chastity belts' (Wheatley, 1999: 97). Information is nourishment rather than simply power; ignorance has to be managed just as knowledge has to be managed (Marsick, 2000: 14). Communication is central to effective complexity leadership (Bryman, 1992: 146; Méndez-Morse, 1999: 15), and the facilitation of change is the facilitation of different forms of discourse, communication, conversation and dialogue (cf. Stacey, 2000: 365). Indeed Stacey (*ibid*: 396, 412) suggests that organizations change when the power relations which are embedded in conversations change or are destroyed, and new ones emerge.

Clampitt and Downs (1993) and Gilsdorf (1998) show a close relationship between productivity and effective communication. Gilsdorf's (1998) empirical study indicates a high correlation ($\rho = 0.0001$) between the clarity, effectiveness of organizational communication and the strength of its organizational culture. She argues that up to 20 per cent of problems in an organization could have been solved by clearer policies on communication.

Kowalski (1998: 36) suggests that communication should be an essential element of preparation for school leadership, and Bennis and Nanus (1985: 33) suggest that effective leadership is inseparable from effective communication. This is, perhaps, commonplace and uncontroversial. Rather, this chapter suggests that particular types of communication are important for the self-organizing school. With the increase in horizontal organization in complexity theory (see Chapter 2), there is a greater need for horizontal communication (Ludlow and Panton,1992: 3). Emergence is a dialogical process (cf. Isaacs, 1993). Communication keeps people informed and involved, both key aspects of self-organization; it fosters positive relationships, greater understanding, and builds ownership (Kanter *et al.*, 1992).

The rise of electronic information sharing can be seen as a move towards rapid, democratizing management in that information is more easily shared, it is transparent and visible, and participants can gain greater confidence, responsiveness and collaboration (Buchanan and McCalman, 1989). This is an important feature of the networked organization. Intranet development can provide the collective yet distributed knowledge and memory of the institution (see April *et al.*, 2000: 50; Gronn, 2000: 323).

April (1997) suggests that technology will increase learning and the empowerment of all participants; not only is it the great equalizer, but it ensures that 'knowledge becomes the core of an organisation's assets' (*ibid*: 51). Further, April *et al.* (2000: 51) suggest that technology can be used to reduce barriers to learning by: (a) flattening the organizational structure and 'shifting the locus of control'; rendering the organization more informed through rapid, easy and timely dissemination of information, and (c) 'making knowledge an accessible resource'. Knowledge, distributed and collective, becomes the primary treasure of the organization.

April (1997; 1999: 232) indicates how, to the ancient Greeks, dialogue lay at the heart of *self*-government (author's italics), underlining the resonance between dialogue and self-organization. Indeed Pondy (1976) and Piccardo (1990) discuss 'leadership through languaging'. For communication even to commence, at least one of the parties has to demonstrate commitment (Guest *et al.*, 1993), and this, too, as Chapter 2 suggested, is at the heart of leading the self-organizing school (cf. April *et al.*, 2000: 69). Commitment occurs through attention to formal and informal communication channels. Ford and Ford (1995: 541, cited in April, 1999) argue that communication and dialogue lie at the heart of change; change is, they say, a communication-based and communication-driven phenomenon.

Dialogue and Socratic questioning, April suggests (*op. cit*: 240), promote inquiry, encourage 'collaboration and team learning, empowerment of people towards a collective vision, and the establishment of systems to capture and share learning' (see also Watkins and Marsick, 1993). Dialogue comprises suspending judgement, identifying assumptions, listening, inquiring and reflection (Gerard and Teurfs, 1997: 16). A learning organization is a social institution which is premised on communication.

At a philosophical level Habermas (1970a; 1970b; 1972; 1979; 1984; 1987) suggests that speech is unavoidably, in principle, oriented towards consensus and every sentence reaffirms the autonomous responsibility for all participants. In language, he avers (1982: 252), are the principles on which a just society is based. His 'ideal speech situation' embodies the characteristics of a just and free society (Morrison, 1996: 2–3) in several terms (Table 6.1).

Table 6.1 Characteristics of the ideal speech situation

- orientation to a common interest;
- freedom to enter a discourse;
- freedom to check questionable claims;
- freedom to evaluate explanations;
- freedom to modify a given conceptual framework;
- freedom to reflect on the nature of knowledge;
- freedom to assess justifications;
- freedom to alter norms;
- freedom to reflect on the nature of political will;
- mutual understanding between participants;
- equal opportunity to employ speech acts;
- recognition of the legitimacy of each subject to participate in the dialogue as an autonomous and equal partner;
- equal opportunity for discussion;
- discussion to be free from domination and distorting influences;
- the consensus resulting from discussion derives from the force of the better argument alone, and not from the positional or political power of the participants;
- all motives except the co-operative search for truth are excluded;
- the speech-act claims of truth, legitimacy, sincerity and comprehensibility are all addressed;
- illocutions replace perlocutions;
- a commitment to generalizable interests.

Table 6.1 is a formidable set of elements by any standards, and it embraces several characteristics of a dialogical relationship, for example (April, 2000: 70–1): listening and speaking without judgement; acknowledgement of each speaker; respect for differences; role and status suspension; balancing inquiry and advocacy; avoidance of cross-talk; a focus on learning; seeking the next level of understanding; releasing the need for specific outcomes; and speaking when 'moved'.

The frequent references to 'freedom' ('freedom from' and 'freedom for'), equal opportunity, absence of domination, and the emphasis on co-operation, commitment, consensus, and higher order thinking skills (cf. Vygotsky, 1978) suggest that in the ideal speech situation are the core elements of effective communication for the networked, self-organizing school. Habermas's principles seems to underline very forcefully the component elements of the self-organizing school which have been set out in preceding chapters.

Dialogue replaces debate in a co-operative search for the best way forward for the organization. April (1999: 234) remarks that dialogue and dialogical relationships, premised on the translation from the Greek to be 'meaning flowing through' (i.e. are dynamic in a dynamical organization), are desirable. April draws attention to Senge's (1995: 19) comment that without a capacity to hold a fruitful conversation 'all that is left is a cacophony of voices battling it out to see who wins and who loses'. Genuine dialogue, argue Senge *et al.* (2000: 75), invites the suspension of everyday assumptions – the willing suspension of disbelief.

The reference to 'illocutions' and 'perlocutions' relates to speech act theory. A speech act (Austin, 1962; Searle, 1969) is 'doing things in saying something'. Utterances, Habermas remarks, 'are never simply sentences' (Habermas, 1970b: 368) which are disembodied from context; rather their meaning derives from the fact that they are set in intersubjective contexts: 'all speech exists in a context of actions and intentions' (*ibid*: 371). Contained in any speech situation is a 'double structure' (Habermas, 1979: 42) of both propositional content (the locutionary aspect or content of communication) and 'performatory' content (its 'illocutionary' aspect or the purpose of the communication) (Morrison: 1995: 94). Communication is both intersubjective and respects the agency, or the freedom, of participants.

In addition to the locutionary and illocutionary aspects of communication, Habermas draws attention to the 'expressive' aspect of speech: the intentions, feelings and wishes of the speaker (Habermas, 1979: 49). This echoes the comments on emotional intelligence in Chapter 3. These three aspects of speech acts (locutionary, illocutionary and expressive) have their own criteria of validity. The locutionary aspects are premised on truth (what we say must be true); the illocutionary aspects are premised on rightness or legitimacy (what we say must be justifiable and acceptable); the expressive aspects are premised on authenticity and sincerity (we must be sincere in what we say), Habermas (1970b). Locutions concern objective content; illocutions concern the intersubjective world; expressives concern the subjective world (Morrison,1995: 97).

The difference between illocutions and perlocutions is this: illocutions are simply 'doing something whilst saying something', whereas perlocutions are 'achieving something by saying something'. In illocutions we do not know what will be the outcome of the communication or dialogue; the agenda is open. In Habermas's words it is 'action oriented to mutual understanding' where 'a moment of unconditionality exists' (Habermas, 1987: 322). Indeed, echoing Senge (1990: 243), this suggests that real dialogue requires the suspension of assumptions by participants, and all participants need to regard each other as colleagues (rather than, for example, combatants). If we wish to avoid the teleological determinism of linear thinking and be genuinely open, then illocutions sit more comfortably than perlocutions in complexity theory (Stacey, 2000).

In school a perlocutionary communication takes places when the teacher tells a child to 'sit down' – the teacher knows in advance what outcome is required. Similarly, the headteacher is acting perlocutionarily in informing teachers of timetable or curriculum changes that will happen. By contrast, a headteacher is acting illocutionarily in asking teachers to meet together to decide what changes are needed in order to improve the ICT support for their teaching (the situation is planned, though the outcome is unknown). Of course, teachers in school are adept at disguising perlocutions as illocutions: the infant school teacher asks the child 'would you like to do a painting?', and even reinforces this with 'I'll help you to put on the overall, so that your clothes don't get dirty'; in fact the infant teacher intends that the child *will* paint, whether she likes it or not!

A further example of an illocution might be an 'expressive' curriculum objective (Eisner, 1985) of a school class visiting a riverside park and discussing what they found of interest there – the situation is set in advance but the outcome is not. An illocution is concerned with understanding and understanding each other. Habermas uses Gadamer's (1975) term 'fusion of horizons' to describe the intention here, which is to understand – hermeneutically, in Habermas's terminology – 'where people are coming from', their backgrounds, biographies and agendas (see also Cilliers, 2000: 10).

By contrast a perlocution is concerned with *achieving* an agenda (a behavioural objective); as Habermas says, it is premised on realizing interests (Habermas, 1982: 237); it concerns strategic, instrumental action towards a preconceived goal. Whereas illocutions concern understanding, perlocutions concern success (Habermas, 1984: 279). In the former, issues of power do not enter the discussion, whereas in the latter they are uppermost. Perlocutions are teleologically determinist. The school subject leader in mathematics acts perlocutionarily in convening a meeting of the mathematics teachers in order to inform staff of new examination requirements from an examining body. She is acting illocutionarily in convening a meeting in order to discuss what can be done to improve children's achievements in problem solving.

A genuinely dialogical communication is open and illocutionary rather than perlocutionary. It does not know its outcomes; they are to be negotiated rather than simply received (see the discussion of Thomas Telford school in Chapter 5). The implication here is that illocutions flourish in open, democratic and collegial management systems whereas perlocutions are the stuff of hierarchical, bureaucratic management styles. From the discussion in earlier chapters one can see that, for leadership in self-organizing, emergent, complex schools, illocutions replace perlocutions, just as distributed leadership replaces hierarchical, command-and-control leadership.

Command-and-control mentalities are perlocutionary; emergent, enabling structures are illocutionary. In modelling the direction of communication, perlocutions are one-way, usually top-down, whereas illocutions are two-way (in a bureaucratic organization) or multi-directional, 360 degrees (in a networked organization). Hence communicative action in complex organizations might be upsetting to the power structures in the organization, just as it might be upsetting to the identities of participants – everyone has to be prepared to change (cf. Stacey, 2001: 182–3). In this sense communication points to double-loop learning (changing mental structures and models, values and principles) rather than single loop learning, which is marked by the absence of such change (Stacey, 2001: 194). Transactional and transformational leaders are essentially perlocutionary, whilst transcendental, servant leaders are illocutionary.

In a vertical organization, perlocutionary communication from the top down is concerned with information in the form of directives, instructions, decisions, policies and commands; communication upwards is concerned with providing information, documentation, reports, opinions and responses. McMaster (1996: 174) suggests that in such a vertical, hierarchical organization the two channels of communication are kept independent of, indeed isolated from, each other, the effects of which are to minimize engagement which, as has been argued throughout, violates a key requisite for self-organization. In a networked organization, illocutionary communication goes in every direction and contains every kind of information for everybody (cf. Robbins and Finley, 1998a: 120).

Communication networks in complexity theory

Law and Glover (2000: 96) and Brown (2000: 118) define five communication networks in schools: the chain; the Y–shape; the star, the circle; and the 'all-channel'.

The chain (Figure 6.1) is a centralized, perlocutionary system of communication with clear lines of communication, though it might not foster rapid or necessarily effectively shared information. It is only as strong as its weakest link, and risks suffering from Chinese whispers as the message is passed along the chain, e.g. as in a cascade model of curriculum innovation (Morrison *et al.*, 1989). The headteacher sends out a message to deputy headteachers that the school budget needs to be adjusted as there is an overspend in mathematics; by the time the message reaches the recently-appointed mathematics teacher, via the faculty head, the mathematics department head, and the other teachers in the department, the new appointee is convinced that her contract is under threat.

The Y–shape model (Figure 6.2) is similar to the perlocutionary chain, though it places the person at the node – the join in the Y – in a powerful position. Those who are close to the node receive the messages more rapidly (and perhaps with less distortion) than those at a greater distance from the node. The model has a

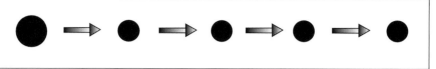

Figure 6.1 The chain of communication.

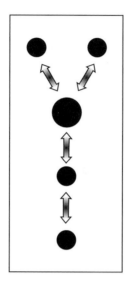

Figure 6.2 The Y-shaped model of communication.

strong hint of centralism and, thus, may not be useful for the networked school. The node may be the informal centre (e.g. the barrack-room lawyer) or may be the formal centre (e.g. a subject head).

The star (Figure 6.3), a strongly centralized system, facilitates centre-periphery perlocutionary communication and *vice versa*. Its success depends on the 'size' of the centre – the centre has to be more powerful or resourceful than the periphery. This is a model which is useful for rapid communication to and from the leaders of a school. On the other hand, all the communication is channelled through the centre, which risks the barriers to communication outlined earlier (e.g. misrouting of information), and centralized control; it is not a model for the networked school. An example of this might be where the headteacher convenes a meeting of the heads of department in order to disseminate her proposals for reform of the reporting system to parents. This is a centrifugal model; a centripetal model in the 'star' system is where the heads of year groups in the school convene a meeting with the headteacher in order to provide feedback to her about the problems of bullying in the school and the need for action.

The circle formation (Figure 6.4) is decentralized, distributed and connected, and in these respects, begins to move towards the networked school. One can notice here that the size of the black circles is the same; there is no circle larger or smaller than

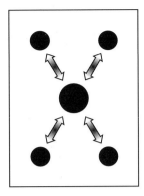

Figure 6.3 The star model of communication.

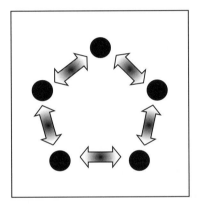

Figure 6.4 The circle of communication.

the others – it is a community of equals. However there are no interstices between the units; communication is only with immediate neighbours (Homans, 1951). However, as the message is passed through the system it can suffer from distortion (Chinese whispers) and the time taken for the message to be fully disseminated can be slow. The headteacher, a *primus inter pares*, sends a written message to the assessment team leader; the assessment team leader adds her own comments, and sends it to the departmental heads and the headteacher; the departmental heads add their own comments and send them to the curriculum development teams and to the assessment team, who send it to the headteacher, who adds her own comments and returns them to the departmental heads and so on.

The 'all-channel' model of communication (Figure 6.5) is illocutionary and most suited to the connected, networked school, with completely distributed knowledge and all channels of communication being shared (Malone, 1998: 267). It suggests democracy and sharing, the free and complete flow of information. On the other hand, it risks information overload, in which case the units need to have their own means of filtering out the significant from the trivial. All leaders in the

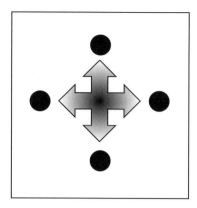

Figure 6.5 The all-channel model of communication.

school share information in every direction and to all other parties, regardless of their level and, as can be seen by the even size of the black spots, all parties are regarded as equals in the communicative process.

Law and Glover (2000: 96) provide a table which indicates how the notion of 'fitness for purpose' can be addressed in the models of communication set out above (to which the Y–shape has been added) and which addresses aspects of the school as an organization (Table 6.2).

One can observe that on key characteristics of the emergent, self-organizing school (flexibility, complexity, morale, organization) the 'all-channel' is the most promising model of communication. It can be seen that the potential feedback is

Table 6.2 Fitness for purpose in communication

Characteristic	*Chain*	*Y–shape*	*Star*	*Circle*	*All-channel*
Speed	Fast for simple tasks	Fast for those closest to node	Fast, but only for simple tasks	Often slow	Flexible
Accuracy	Often good	Often good	Good for simple tasks	Often poor	From poor to excellent
Morale	Low at end of the chain	Varies with distance from node	Can become very low	Can be high	Often very high
Leadership stability	Marked	Marked	Very pronounced	None: can be team focused	Variable
Organization	Emerging stability	Often stable	Often stable	Can be unstable	From flexible to unstable
Flexibility	Low	Low	Low	High	High
Performance	Good for simple tasks	Good for simple tasks; poor for complex ones	Good for simple tasks; poor for complex ones	Good for simple tasks and some complex ones	Very good for complex tasks

strongest in the star and all-channel models; in the star it is centralized whereas in the all-channel model it occurs everywhere. For the information-rich, distributed knowledge and distributed leadership systems it is clear that the all-channel approach is the most fitting.

Formal channels of communication are complemented and mediated by the informal channels of communication which, in many cases, might be more powerful than the formal channels and which emphasize significant elements of the dynamics of organization (and self-organization is a dynamic process) in terms of interests, obligations, influence, status, and strategies. Hoyle's work on micropolitics (1986; 125–49) suggests differences between formal and informal communication as shown below.

Formal Communication	*Informal Communication*
Goals	Interests
Authority	Influence
Departments	Coalitions
Whole institution	Departments and groups
Procedures and protocols	Strategies
Formal power	Informal status
Decisions and delegation	Discussions/resistances/responses
Imposed practice	Bargaining and exchange
Reports, meetings, decisions, notices, proposals, orders	Advice, counselling, informal support

Informal communication, the stuff of informal as well as formal groupings, can exert a potent force in schools, for example to support or resist change, to accept certain leadership proposals, or to subvert, undermine or openly counter them. Doloff (1999) and Gilsdorf (1998) suggest that leaders can engage in social network mapping of communication by posing several issues:

- with whom members of a group communicate;
- the nature of the communication;
- how frequently the communication takes place;
- who initiates the communication;
- to whom teachers and leaders go to find particular kinds of information;
- from whom teachers and leaders seek feedback;
- with whom leaders consult before taking decisions;
- what forms the various communications take;
- whether formal policies exist on communication and how well used they are;
- with whom teachers communicate as part of their everyday work.

This could be a salutary exercise in schools, as it might reveal, for example that:

- headteachers do little initiation, talk to few people, and are only involved in particular kinds of communication;
- seemingly junior or obscure members of the school are approached far more than other teachers/colleagues;

- teachers in unremarkable positions hold considerable sway over members of the school;
- there is silence between certain groups;
- there are unofficial gatekeepers to communication;
- teachers do not always use official channels for communication, information sharing and finding out matters;
- there are significant gaps in communication (the medium, message, sender, receiver);
- there are islands of teachers and senior managers who communicate between themselves but no further.

The informal communication that takes place in a school can be equally powerful, if not more, than the formal communication in the school. Indeed, in the business literature, Ibarra and Andrews (1993) report that the more closely connected employees were to the informal communication network of the organization, the more positively they viewed the climate of the school. Further, Johnson *et al.* (1994: 119) suggest that informal channels of communication tend to be used more than formal channels in conveying messages about the culture of the organization, which as Chapter 4 suggests, lies at the heart of much of the development of organizational learning.

For self-organization and emergence, leaders' communication must be dialogical, illocutionary and comprehensive; it must demonstrate truth, legitimacy, authenticity and sincerity. Communication concerns intentions and purposes and it must strip out of the discussion issues of status and power; the unforced force of the argument alone should hold sway. Communication must be multi-directional.

Modelling communication

Recognizing that communication concerns objective facts, intersubjectivity and subjectivity (Habermas, 1987) sets the scene for familiar modelling exercises of communication, which include characteristics of the sender and receivers of communication that leaders will find useful to consider. Hunt (1980) and Barker and Barker (1993: 11) set out key elements of communication in terms of: the information source, the encoder, the message itself, the channel of communication (and the 'noise' or obstructions to communication: Byers, 1997: 34), the receiver, and the decoder of the message. This can be represented as in Figure 6.6 (adapted from Hunt's and Barker's and Barker's original).

These elements are contained within a context, e.g. structural, organization, cultural, socio-technical, management (Leavitt, 1964). Clearly this is a simplification of the situation, and it omits significant elements (e.g. context, intention, culture, formality of communication channels, status, power, feedback, the quality and quantity of the information). The information source is the sender; the encoder is how the message is encoded (e.g. vocally) (see Kelly (2000: 93); the channel is the medium (e.g. e-mail, lecture, report); the two references to 'message' indicate the potential difference between the message that is communicated

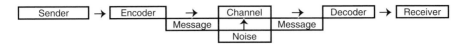

Figure 6.6 Understanding the communication process.

and the message that is received or interpreted; the noise is any barrier to effective communication in the system itself; the decoder is not necessarily the person who needs the message (just as the old-fashioned telegraph officer passed on the received message to the addressee); the receiver is the addressee.

The directional arrows only model the process (like a flow chart) rather than implying that the communication is unidirectional. In the two-way model advocated, the roles of the receiver and sender will be reversed or both parties may adopt both roles. Stacey (2001: 15) cautions against unidirectional models in complexity theory, as they are teleologically determinist. Within this model the several elements can be unpacked a little.

The *sender* will need to consider the content (locutionary) content of the message and the intentions (illocutionary and perlocutionary) in sending the message. Both the sender and receiver of the message will be in a particular position in the organization and have a degree of power, status or influence in it which may affect the contents, purpose, and reception of the message. As Stacey (2001: 149) remarks, power is a constraining force for the inclusion and exclusion of communicative action. Rarely is communication a reciprocal interaction between two equal participants (Kvale, 1996) with symmetrical relations of power; frequently the communication needs of sender and receiver are different (Katz and Kahn, 1966), particularly in a hierarchical organization.

Communication is mediated by status, age, class, race, culture, dress, language, intonation, paralanguage (ancillary aspects of language, e.g. gesture, non-verbal communication) and awareness of 'register' (form of language, e.g. level of formality and informality, degree of colloquialisms used, use of literary quotations, appropriacy of expression for audience and content). Consequently, the content of messages might meet with outright refusal by some participants, regardless of the persuasiveness of those contents. Alternatively, messages of doubtful worth or consequence may be welcomed by particular participants. The issue here is that, as in interviews, messages and communications are not simply cold data, they are located in institutional, personal, and interpersonal contexts. Communication is always located in a *context*; it is situated (Quirke, 1995: 92–5) and relational. As Cohen *et al.* (2000: 278–81) note, communication is a social encounter, not merely information exchange. Communications may contain cognitive content (understanding), emotional and expressive content, and non-verbal action, all of which impact on the message.

It is, perhaps, a natural human reaction first to consider the presenting issues of a communication (e.g. who is saying what and how attractively they are saying it) rather than the contents of the message, just as with disruptive school students we frequently respond to their presenting behaviour rather than its causes or implications, i.e. we tend to respond emotionally before we respond cognitively.

We frequently respond to non-verbal communication before, and more strongly than, verbal communication in a face-to-face meeting. As Van de Ven (1992) and Luke (1998) suggest, non-verbal behaviour (e.g. facial expression and movements – kinesics – and eye contact and gaze – oculesics) can exert a powerful effect on trust, and, as has been argued in previous chapters, trust is a significant component of the complex, self-organizing school. Trust is necessary for open communication and an open school (Tschannen-Moran, 2000: 313). Hence the sender will need to consider not only the intention of the communication but its likely effects on the receiver. As Drucker (1999: 185) states: leaders need to take *responsibility* (his italics) for communication; trust, rather than force, is the hallmark of the new organization (*ibid*: 187).

Senders are also receivers of information and *vice versa*. This suggests that the issue of feedback is crucial for effective communication. Receiving, like sending, is an active process. Indeed, Chapter 2 suggested that feedback is essential for moving people and institutions forward to self-organized criticality, which is the most fruitful state for creativity and imagination, and Chapter 4 emphasized that feedback was an integral feature of organizational learning (Karsten *et al.*, 2000). Feedback in schools can take many forms, for example (Sherman and Schultz, 1998: 163–4):

- conversations;
- correspondence;
- meetings;
- reports (oral, written, by a team or individual);
- performance data;
- external media.

Active listening and responding feature highly in the issue of feedback. Active listeners and receivers are distinguished by their abilities to learn, to listen accurately, to respond, to reflect, to show support, to check, to clarify, to structure, to show interest, to probe, to facilitate. Greenberg and Baron (1997: 319) suggest several elements of active listening:

- understanding the messages sent;
- remembering the message that was sent;
- interpreting (avoiding reading anything into the message that was unintended);
- evaluating (suspending judgement on the message sent);
- responding (replying and indicating that attention is being given to the message);
- hearing (attending carefully to the message).

Ludlow and Panton (1992: 9) suggest that both sender and receiver are at risk from: stereotyping each other, assuming that people behave consistently, being too influenced by first impressions. There is also the 'halo' effect, wherein people respond positively to those who have similar characteristics to themselves and more negatively to those with dissimilar characteristics; they may overlook negative aspects of people, over-accentuate the positive aspects of their make-up, or, indeed, overgeneralize from one or two negative points (e.g. assuming that because a person is not strong on long term curriculum planning they are not strong on short term curriculum planning).

The *medium* of the communication is important. This can take several forms, for example:

- oral: a question, comment, statement, request, meeting;
- non-verbal: a smile, gesture, movement, position;
- verbal: a written message, formal report, informal note, public notice, personal message, newsletter, performance report, survey, briefing paper;
- electronic: e-mail, audio-visual, video-conferencing;
- graphic: notices, pictures, computer-generated images;
- visual: artefacts, symbols, rituals and celebrations (Kouzes and Posner, 1995).

Included here can be what Stacey (2001: 183–5) terms the tools of communication, e.g. the telephone, the letter, the computer, documents and newspapers. In these plans, he includes documents for monitoring and appraisal, databases, and such items as mission statements, policies and vision statements.

Additionally, the issues of *timing* and *the nature of contact* feature in considerations of communication, for example:

- synchronous (simultaneous): telephone, cell phone, video-conferencing, computer discussion programs, face-to-face meetings, audio-conferencing, on-line instantaneous person-to-person discussion or forum discussions;
- diachronous (non-simultaneous): e-mail, voice mail, letter, pager, notice, bulletin boards, fax, non-instantaneous one-to-one and forum discussions;
- face-to-face: meetings, discussion groups, friendship groups, interviews;
- remote: not face-to-face, geographically separated, relying on written and electronic forms, e.g. Internet and Intranet.

Stewart (2001: 60) also suggests the need to consider the potential that person-to-person communication has for interruption. Many oral forms of communication, e.g. telephone calls, video-conferencing, discussions, meetings and group discussions can be interrupted (by accident or design!); many written forms of communication, e.g. e-mails, voice-mail, letters, memoranda and notices have less potential to be interrupted. Some forms of communication (Wallace and Pocklington, 1998: 10) are two-way (e.g. face-to-face discussions, telephone conversations, synchronous communication), whilst others are one-way (e.g. letter, fax, memoranda, diachronous communication).

The timing of the communication is important. Sending a questionnaire on the first or last day of a school term is unlikely to receive a welcome response, or indeed any response at all. Calling a meeting before the school day officially commences is likely to provoke hostility, as is holding a long meeting 'after hours'. The number, quality, and rate of communications are related to their timing: too many, too quickly causes overload, too few, too late causes hostility and loss of impetus.

Nonaka and Takeuchi (1995) advocate the advancement of 'hypertext organizations', where connectedness (through information technology and other means) is high on the list of priorities for the organization, with multiple connections to information. One development with information technology is the construction of e-mails and messages with hypertext links for the furtherance of information exchange and dissemination. Malone (1998) suggests that decentralized decision making is at its most efficient when there is connectedness through communication between the distributed centres of decision making.

The medium, timing and nature of contact on their own are necessary rather than sufficient considerations for effective communication. To complement them attention is required to be given to the match between the sender, receiver and the medium. There are hidden messages contained in formal messages. It is unhelpful to send a message using a channel or medium with which one party is unfamiliar or to which there is limited or no access (though, of course, this is a ploy that is used!). For example, e-mails may be attractive to a sender but a curse to the receiver; a letter or memorandum may frighten or annoy a receiver, regardless of its contents; some people feel uncomfortable using a telephone; others feel uncomfortable or intimidated in a face-to-face meeting.

For example, a headteacher was known for 'management by memo', sitting in the protective environment of his office and issuing edicts. He was comfortable sending explosive directives to senior teachers, couched in formal, venomous and aggressive language, blasted off in moments of personal rage, in barely decipherable handwriting, and requiring an immediate reply. The response of many senior teachers was to do nothing for a few days, then to bombard the headteacher with a plethora of memoranda requiring urgent replies, such that they could not all be responded to in the time available ('upward management'!), and then follow up their messages with face-to-face confrontation, at which the headteacher would back down, apologize and retreat – he couldn't handle the rich setting of face-to-face communication, and hid behind a shield of paper.

Meetings are useful for immediate and rapid dissemination for teams. Face-to-face communication may be a more effective means than written communication for dealing with emotional matters, and a complex message is best communicated through a rich medium like a meeting rather than, say, an e-mail (Lengel and Daft, 1988). The richer the message, the greater is the need for face-to-face communication. The medium must be matched to the message; for example, in a large school a member of staff died from cancer; her death was formally communicated only by e-mail and many of the staff were offended by the insensitivity of this. Further, Larkin and Larkin (1994) suggest that significant information needs to come directly from significant people.

Leonard *et al.* (1998: 290) suggest that face-to-face communication is the richest medium because it uses multiple channels of communication (*ibid*: 292). Using oral, as well as non-verbal (written, visual and hearing) senses, it takes places in real time, it enables immediate feedback to be given and gained, and it is frequently personalized. The writers contrast this with less rich communications, for example faxes, which are single channelled, devoid of social presence, and require communicators to respond to the entire message. They found that people preferred richer media for more complex tasks and less rich media for one-way communication; where communication required a lot of interpersonal participation, then richer media were preferred. Gilsdorf (1998) suggests that leaders wishing to shape employees' behaviour, and employees, conversely, wishing to meet the organization's expectations, were likely to be more successful if they used a considerable variety of channels for communication and the flow of information.

The sender may send the message deliberately or unintentionally in such a way that its main and hidden messages are either heeded or unheeded, interpreted selectively or indeed misinterpreted. Indeed, the language of the message needs attention, for it can convey subtle messages; for example, in a school containing several ethnic groups, sending a written message in one language may ensure that it never reaches the receiver, or else the receiver has to take it to a friend for translation; if the school has ten community languages but the message is only sent in five of those languages then hidden messages about the status of languages and their communities will almost inevitably be imputed.

In Japanese communities people frequently nod and say 'yes' when they mean 'no'; in Mediterranean countries people frequently add an interrogative 'no?' to the end of a sentence in a rising cadence when they are seeking agreement, i.e. when they want participants to say 'yes'! Words are inherently ambiguous; not only do they mean different things to different people but what is innocuous to one party can cause offence to another. The Chinese use of the phrases 'as I mentioned before' and 'of course' are intended innocuously but are offensive to many native English speakers, implying that they didn't listen or learn properly earlier. As before, the implication is that the sender has to consider the possible or likely effects of the message on the receivers.

The issue here is that of 'noise': there are several ways in which the message can be distorted or there may be obstacles to receiving or understanding the message. These might include, for example (Ludlow and Panton, 1992: 12; Robbins and Finley, 1998a: 116–22; 1998b; 119–28; Kelly, 2000: 93–4; Law and Glover, 2000; 89–107):

- selective perception by the receiver (hearing what we want to hear), where receivers respond to their perceptions of the message rather than to its actual message (Beck, 1999: 5) – addressed by checking the clarity of the communication;
- semantic effects, differences in understanding and usage of terms (addressed by ensuring that participants are using the same terms in the same ways, i.e. clarifying meanings);
- failure to understand the contents or intentions of the communication (addressed by attention to meanings and clarity);
- mismatch between the verbal and non-verbal communication, or between the style and content of the written message, or between the contents and the medium of the message (addressed by careful consideration of how to ensure the most appropriate match, by employing multiple channels of

communication, by ensuring honesty in the communication, and by using appropriate non-verbal behaviour);

- insufficient time to digest the communication and respond appropriately (addressed by ensuring that the message is communicated as early, concisely and accessibly as possible, with the minimum of delay, and with realistic response times);
- distractions, e.g. in the surroundings when sending and receiving messages, for example noise, support systems, or by faulty equipment (addressed by avoiding breakdown and interruption, and by seizing the opportunity to communicate);
- differences of status between sender and receiver (addressed by placing the onus of reducing the social or status distance on the shoulders of the higher status holder (Hunt, 1985) and by ensuring that the communication increases the self-esteem of the receiver);
- neglect of the emotional, power and inter-relationship aspects of the communication (addressed by considering these in the eyes of the receiver);
- information overload in the message, so that the trivial is not discernible from the significant (addressed by ensuring that it is rich, useful and prioritized information; ensuring that the right people receive the right information and that everybody is apprised of the minimum necessary information; indeed Conger (1991) suggests that the role of leadership is to prevent overload);
- cultural effects, where cultural norms differ between sender and receiver, e.g. in one culture a day to respond may seem a short time whereas in another culture it may be taken as a long time, or in one culture people will not wish to challenge a proposal (addressed by sensitivity training and intercultural understanding);
- inappropriate routing of the communication, e.g. where communications that are routed through the senior managers are censored or subtly altered, or a particular 'steer' is placed on them (addressed by sending messages to all parties simultaneously);
- inappropriate match between the message and the most appropriate communication medium, e.g. using a lengthy report where a face-to-face meeting might be more suitable (addressed by ensuring that the closest match is achieved);
- insufficient feedback, where one-way communication is quick but risks being inaccurate, whilst two-way communication takes longer but furthers accuracy (addressed by widespread dissemination and widespread feedback through a variety of channels);
- deliberate misinformation, hidden agendas or inadequate information (addressed by openness, honesty, the provision of comprehensive and comprehensible information (Richmond and McCroskey, 1992));
- ambiguity in the message (addressed by ensuring clarity and by selecting the most appropriate medium for the communication);
- insufficient information and information underload (addressed by ensuring that communication of a single piece of information takes place through

multiple channels in combination (Hanson, 1991), differentiated according to the receiver's *modus operandi* and personality), so that people feel less like victims of communication and more like participants in it (Robbins and Finley, 1998a: 123);

- ignoring conflicting information, e.g. the halo effect (addressed by ensuring clarity, comprehensiveness, reflexivity, and the use of multiple channels of communication);
- neglect of the timing and speed of the communication (addressed by careful timing);
- neglect of the venue for the communication (e.g. in whose room/territory the communication takes place, or a neutral territory, or an informal or formal place: Youngblood, 1997: 264);
- neglect of the opportunity for giving and receiving feedback.

Effective communication for leading in the self-organizing institution is not simply a matter of ensuring that the mechanics are correct. Quirke (1995) suggests that disagreement rather than agreement characterizes most communication; this implies that attention needs to be paid to fostering consensus and minimizing offence in communication. He suggests that attention needs to be focused less on the sender of the message and more on its receivers and their needs, wants, emotions, likely responses and make-up. This echoes the point made earlier, that between the sender and the receiver there should be a 'fusion of horizons', each party understanding each other's context.

Communication and Transactional Analysis

In examining the notions of 'noise' and the 'fusion of horizons', work on Transactional Analysis (TA), emanating from counselling, is useful (Berne, 1964). TA is a theory of communication that is based, in part, on a view that people engage in communication in order to meet their need to experience the 'I'm OK; you're OK' feeling (Harris, 1973). Communication here is characterized by issues of power, emotion and relationships. TA identifies three 'ego states' of participants – states of mind or frames of behaviour, as follows:

1 parent (P): critical, setting limits, making and enforcing rules, providing guidance, being the authority;
2 adult (A): logical, recognizing individuals' autonomy;
3 child (C): accepting orders, seeking reward and satisfaction, being driven by feelings, submitting to authority.

We all need positive reinforcement and recognition ('positive strokes' in TA); negative strokes can be very damaging. A 'stroke' is a unit or statement of recognition (Porpiglia, 1997), and the 'transaction' of 'Transactional' Analysis is the exchange of strokes – be they positive or negative. People need strokes, even if they are negative strokes (e.g. the child who constantly seeks the teacher's attention by disruptive behaviour). TA is concerned with diagnosing which of the three ego-states are being implemented in a transaction (a stroke exchange), and where there might be crossed transactions. These can be represented as shown in Figure 6.7.

Here the two parties communicate as adults (A) and communication might be straightforward because horizons are shared. The head of department holds a professional dialogue with a colleague, with no question of differences of power.

In Figure 6.8 relationships are reciprocal, because the parent's (P) actions as a parent are responded to by a person adopting the child's (C) role; both parties are happy with their roles. TA suggests that communication will be smooth as long as the transactions are complementary (i.e. as long as the arrows are parallel). By analogy, the senior member of staff may be the mentor to a junior member of staff, and the mentee is pleased to be placed under the protective wing of her senior.

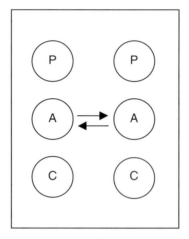

Figure 6.7 Adult to adult communication in Transactional Analysis.

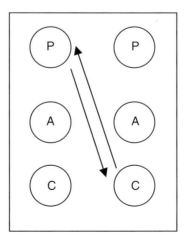

Figure 6.8 Parent and child communication in Transactional Analysis.

In Figure 6.9 the two parties in this communication adopt different and non-complementary roles. One party treats the other as an adult, whilst the other party behaves as a child would to a parent. The novice member of the department wishes to have a degree of directiveness, advice and support from the senior member of staff (C→P), whereas the senior member of staff treats him more as though he is a long-standing and experienced teacher (A→A). The novice becomes anxious, not knowing what to do in certain situations, which then frustrates and angers the senior teacher, who tells the novice to 'grow up' and 'face up to his responsibilities' (when, in fact this was what the novice had been trying to do all along). Relationships fray, the novice reads a range of negative messages into the actions of the senior teacher, and the working situation deteriorates. Communication suffers when a crossed transaction occurs, and it can lead to negative strokes (leading to a situation of 'I'm OK, you're not OK' or 'I'm not OK, you're OK'). A person dominated by the 'I'm not OK' position reads negative meanings into situations which may not exist.

In Figure 6.10 one party treats the other as an adult, whereas the other party wishes to be domineering (parent to child). The headteacher 'talks down' to the head of the humanities faculty (P→C) who, whilst trying to treat the headteacher as an equal (A→A), may be unable to resist reacting by asking the headteacher not to be paternalistic and condescending; this causes the headteacher to become angry, which causes the head of faculty to storm out, and so on; the situation breaks down.

What is clear here is that the concept of 'fusion of horizons' from communication theory can be applied easily to TA. More particularly, leaders as communicators need to be aware of the ego states of participants, the emotional implications of these ego states, the power differentials that these might imply, and the need to ensure that the situation of achieving the 'I'm OK, you're OK' state is achieved as far as possible and through positive strokes in communication.

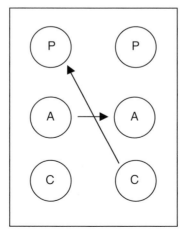

Figure 6.9 Adult and child crossed wires in Transactional Analysis.

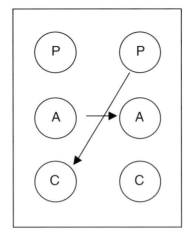

Figure 6.10 Parent and adult crossed wires in Transactional Analysis.

Of course, TA is more complex than this, and it richly repays study, not least because it graphically reflects the phrase 'crossed wires' in communication.

Leadership and communication

Drawing together the preceding discussion it is possible to suggest that leaders need to consider:

- to whom to send the message;
- the purpose of the communication;
- the content of the communication (e.g. facts, opinions, feelings, values);
- the clarity, precision and accuracy of the communication;
- the likely effects of the communication on the receiver;
- the emotions of the participants;
- the context of the communication;
- the possible barriers and facilitators to the communication;
- the timing of the communication;
- the medium and tools of the communication;
- the power statuses of the sender and receiver;
- the language of the communication;
- the feedback from the information and the channels for feedback.

Ludlow and Panton (*op. cit*: 14–16) provide a useful mapping of leadership styles with communication, which can be matched with Hersey and Blanchard's (1993) view of situational leadership (Figure 6.11).

There are several points to observe from this:

1   directing styles register the lowest amounts of communication;
2   consultative and explaining styles register the highest amounts of communication;

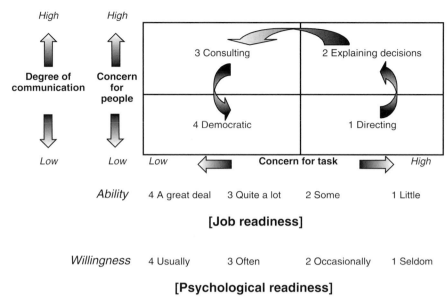

Figure 6.11 Leadership styles and communication.

3   the greater the concern is for people, the greater is the amount of communication;
4   high concern for a task still registers the need for communication;
5   those with high job readiness and those with low job readiness (expertise) register much communication, i.e. communication is pervasive;
6   those with high psychological readiness and those with low job readiness (motivation, willingness, confidence and commitment) register much communication, i.e. communication is pervasive.

Morrison *et al.* (1989) exemplify the model in relation to the development of science teaching in a group of secondary schools. Here, using a 'cascade' model of innovation in a science department, the science teaching moved from a content-driven to a process-driven view of science. To support the changes with teachers, report Morrison *et al.* (*ibid.*), required extensive communication, strong leadership in the early stages of a project (in order to inspire confidence in the leadership and the project, i.e. to be reassured that the leader has a grasp of the situation), and even a degree of autocracy by the leader. As the project unfolded there was a move to a more democratic leadership style, as other participants took hold of the reins of the project. The final result was collaborative and cooperative work, in a style of informed democracy about the project.

Hersey and Blanchard, in contrast to other similar models of leadership (e.g. Blake and McCanse, 1991) suggest that there is no single best leadership style. Which leadership style is chosen varies and is determined by the demands of the particular situation. It is clear from this diagram that, regardless of leadership style, communication is a core element. The attraction of Hersey and Blanchard's model when linked to communication is that it suggests that different kinds of communication will be appropriate for different styles of leadership and different situations. Hence, for those with little readiness (cell one and number one) a more directive style of communication might be most appropriate. For those with greater degrees of readiness (cells two and three and points two and three) a much richer form of communication is required from the leader. For a democratic, devolved style of leadership then one-way, strategic, teleological, perlocutionary communication from the leader reduces as it has passed to the other participants.

Drawing together the issues raised so far, an inclusive model of communication for the self-organizing school can be presented as shown in Figure 6.12.

This model recognizes that the issue of communication is embedded in the social, cultural and contextual contexts of the school and its several systems (e.g. technical, structural, tasks, roles, management, maintenance and development). It recognizes the two-way flow of information, and the ways in which this is interpenetrated by several factors (e.g. power; noise; emotions etc.), i.e. those factors which lie at the centre of the diagram; it also takes into account the important issues of intention and feedback. The model recognizes that communication is ongoing, and is not unidirectional, reflecting the relational and

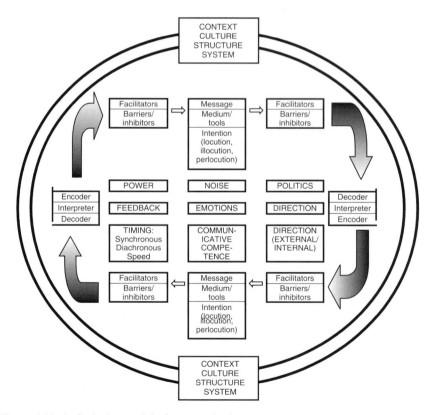

Figure 6.12 An inclusive model of communication.

interactive nature of communication, which is an essential feature of complexity theory – each participant (however defined, e.g. individual, group) influencing, and being influenced by, the other.[1]

Conclusion, implications and evaluation

This chapter has suggested that leadership for the complex, self-organizing school has to embody several features of communication which go to, from and between the distributed and servant leaders in schools. Such communication, it has been argued:

- is dialogical;
- is illocutionary;
- recognizes the social situation of communication and the people who are communicating;
- pays attention to register and context;
- is multi-directional, multi-channelled and multi-media;
- makes full use of formal and informal channels;
- demonstrates truth, legitimacy, authenticity and sincerity;
- seeks the highest possible match between message, people and media;
- reduces the noise in the system to a minimum;
- is differentiated according to the task and people;
- is differentiated according to leadership styles;
- demonstrates fitness for purpose.

These areas can be addressed by posing several questions which school leaders can ask themselves when they are involved in communication. These draw together the substance of this chapter, and underline the centrality of communication in complexity theory:

1   What are the contents of the message in connection with the areas outlined?
2   What are the predominant *kinds* of messages from different sources (e.g. instructions/directions/consultations/information/requests/seeking advice etc.)?
3   Which kinds of messages come from which sources and go to which receivers and target audiences?
4   Which people are included in, and excluded from, different kinds of messages/documentation/reports etc.? Why?
5   What is the source of the message?
6   Who are the senders? Why are they sending the messages?
7   What medium and channel of communication is used (e.g. oral, non-verbal, verbal, electronic, graphic, visual)? Why? How effective are the media of communication for the messages given and received?
8   What register is used? Why? Which is most/least effective, and why?
9   Who are the receivers and the target audiences? Who is included and excluded? Why?

10   What is the purpose of the communication? Why are there these purposes?
11   How effectively are those purposes achieved? How do we know?
12   Are the purposes dialogical/monological?
13   What is the direction of the communication? Why?
14   What are the lines of communication (e.g. a chain, a star, a cascade, a circle, and multi-directional, 360-degree communication)?
15   What are the actual messages that are received? How far do these match the intended messages?
16   Which messages are formal rather than informal? Why? How effective is this?
17   What are the formal and informal channels of communication? Which are used most/least, and for what? Why?
18   What causes 'noise' and breaks in the system of formal and informal communication, with what effects, and why is this? For example:
   •   selective perception by the receiver;
   •   semantic effects, differences in understanding and usage of terms;
   •   failure to understand the contents or intentions of the communication;
   •   mismatch between the verbal and non-verbal communication, or between the style and content of the written message, or between the contents and the medium of the message;
   •   insufficient time to digest the communication and respond appropriately;
   •   distractions;
   •   differences of status between sender and receiver;
   •   information overload;
   •   cultural effects;
   •   inappropriate routing of the communication;
   •   communication medium;
   •   insufficient feedback;
   •   deliberate misinformation, hidden agendas or inadequate information;
   •   ambiguity in the message;
   •   insufficient information and information underload;
   •   ignoring conflicting information.
19   How well apprised are participants of possible noise in the communication system? Why?
20   What is the paralanguage at work in the communication, and with what purposes and effects?
21   How effective are participants at receiving/listening to communication? For example:
   •   understanding the messages sent;
   •   interpreting (avoiding reading anything into the message that was unintended);
   •   evaluating (suspending judgement on the message sent);
   •   responding (replying and indicating that attention is being given to the message);
   •   hearing (attending carefully to the message).

22 What are the outcomes/effects of the communication? Why? Were these what were intended? Why/not?
23 How are the Hawthorne and halo effects of communications addressed?
24 How effective is the timing of, and nature of contact in, the communication?
25 How rapid is the communication system? How effectively does speed of communication match the nature and purpose of the communication?
26 Which communications are synchronous, diachronous, face-to-face, remote? Why? How effective are these? How effective is the match between the message, the channel and the medium? Why/not?
27 What precedes/proceeds from the communications?
28 What is the nature, use and follow-up to feedback from communications? What kind of feedback is sought, and from whom? Why/not?

The chapter has suggested that effective communication in leadership of schools might take from Transactional Analysis the importance of ascertaining the ego states of participants and the need for positive strokes in interpersonal behaviour. Communication, it is clear, is a relational matter, and not merely a matter of data exchange. Given that leadership is distributed, communication between the distributed leaders must be at its optimal level.

7   Fitness landscapes

What is a fitness landscape?

Leaders in schools can use the specific projection technique of constructing fitness landscapes in order to ascertain how well particular groups such as the school/department/subject team, etc. are adapted to the environments in which they find themselves. Fitness is the extent to which the species (e.g. the school, department, subject group, etc.) is adapting to the changing environments in which it finds itself. Fitness, it will be argued, is a function of the degree of connectedness between the number of components *within* a system (e.g. a school), and the number and strength of connections to components *outside* the system. If fitness is to be increased then communication is vital, as different components within and outside the system interact and co-evolve. This chapter indicates how to draw and interpret fitness landscapes. Examples of fitness landscapes of different schools are provided.

A fitness landscape is an interesting tool for schools, departments, faculties, formal and informal groups to use for mapping the territory to be covered in school review and school improvement. Fitness landscapes are premised on connectivity and inter-relatedness – the fitness landscape of one species is affected by other species. In education, for example, in a study of the spatial catchments of schools and their relationships to issues of cultural capital, Byrne and Rogers (1996: 9) use the concept of fitness landscapes to describe and understand the distributions of students who attend different schools according to the socio-economic status of parents. They suggest (*ibid*: 14) that parents can be divided into two species: one species is more predatory, and advantages itself by consumption of educational privileges (e.g. moving into the catchment areas of high-achieving schools) and other parents are 'much more vegetative', simply accepting the schools to which their children have been allocated. The fitness landscape of the former is characterized by high rugged peaks, that of the latter by a few, low, rounded peaks with wide valleys (discussed on page 165). The authors regard secondary schools as 'far from equilibrium' organizations, being 'highly environmentally dependent' (*ibid*: 15). Each species (however defined, e.g. a whole school, or a department within a school, or a faculty) has its own fitness landscape.

A 'fitness landscape' has been discussed by Kauffman (1995), Marion (1999), Stacey (2000) and Stewart (2001). Indeed Lewin (1993: 57) and Cohen and Stewart (1995: 109) refer to 'peaks of adaptiveness' from the biologist Sewall Wright in the 1930s. A fitness landscape characterizes the adaptive evolution of a species, for survival, as a movement across a landscape of fitness points (McCarthy and Tan, 2000), where adaptation to the environment is required. Fitness is the ability to navigate the landscape and survive in it (e.g. by inheriting, copying or developing solutions to problems of adaptation).[1] Species in nature constantly adapt to changing and unpredictable environments without the use of sophisticated techniques for forecasting (McCarthy and Tan, 2000); they self-organize and evolve, constantly modifying their terrain and environment in order to survive.

One has to be careful not to confuse the *concept* of a fitness landscape with a *picture* of a fitness landscape: the fitness landscape is the concept, not the actual landscape. Much discussion usually concerns how it is portrayed as a graphic, i.e. a 3-D map which indicates the ability of a species to survive at optimal conditions in relation to its internal and external environments. A fitness landscape comprises:

(a) *peaks* and *mountains* (each peak represents a component of fitness for survival or adaptability. Peaks on a fitness landscape may be, for example: few, many, high, low, rugged, close, isolated, undulating, angular, widely separated, close, sharply pointed, rounded, smooth, etc.);

(b) *valleys* (which are defined, in relation to the peaks, as spaces between fitness or troughs in the fitness. These may be, for example: few, many, narrow, wide, large, small, long, short, high, low, far apart, close, sheltered, exposed);

(c) *plains* (which are defined as areas of little activity in an organization, and which may be, for example: few, many, high, low);

(d) *roads* and *passes* (i.e. to provide linkages or communication between points in the landscape: some roads and passes will be easy, other will be dangerous; some will be broad and popular, others will be mud tracks that are only for the brave; in some areas there will be no roads, leading to poor communication, and in others the linkages and communications will be plentiful).

An example of this is given in Figure 7.1.

Kauffman (1995), Stacey (2000) and Stewart (2001) remark that moving up a hill marks a move to increasing fitness whilst moving down a hill into a valley indicates decreasing fitness, though sometimes it is necessary to walk down a hill in order to reach the base of another hill (McCarthy and Tan, 2000), i.e. it may be necessary to have a temporary loss of fitness, and greater stability, in order to survive and move towards greater fitness overall (one loses the battle but wins the war). The key to survival is to understand where one fits comfortably. A chamois will have high fitness to survive in its environment if its senses are acute and its legs sure-footed; a leopard will have high fitness to survive in its environment if its speed is explosive, its claws sharp and its camouflage absolute. Each organism evolves its own particular fitness landscape, hence diversity thrives to the 'edge of chaos'. Those which do not evolve and develop their fitness do not survive; they are destroyed by other species. Hence each element or organism must move

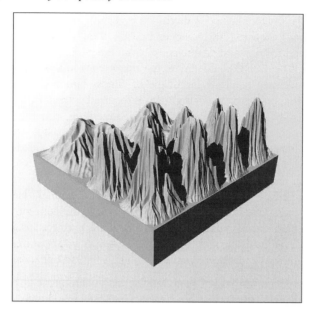

Figure 7.1 Components of a fitness landscape.

towards its own fitness peaks (Stacey *et al.*, 2000: 113), competing with other elements in order to survive.

Fitness is a function of (Kauffman, 1995: 230; Stewart, 2001: Chapter 1):

- N (the number of elements within each species/organism);
- K (the number of connections *within* each species/element – internal connectedness);
- C (the number of connections with other *external* species/elements in the landscape – external coupling);
- S (the number of external species with which each organism interacts).

Indeed the model is frequently termed, from Kauffman, the NK model. When K = 0 then all parts of the system are independent; when K = N – 1 then all parts of the system are internally connected and dependent on each other, and the landscape is rugged. When C = 0 then external coupling is absent; when C = N × S then external coupling is very high.

In a secondary school with ten subject departments, plus an assessment team, a curriculum development team, a senior management team, careers team, and a pastoral team, N = 15. Let us imagine that only three of the subject departments are connected to each other, and the remainder of them work in isolation, and that the assessment, curriculum development, senior management, careers and pastoral team connect with the subject departments, then K = 53 (i.e. {5 cross-school teams × 10 departments} + 3 departmental interconnections). Let us say that the school has external links to six major parties (careers advisers, employers, parents, examinations bodies, social services departments, the local education authority's special needs service), then S = 6, and C (the number of external couplings) minimally might be six, though, if each group in the school has separate links to each of these, then C will rise.

Fitness (F) in a complex environment, is a function of N, K, C and S (Figure 7.2).

In Figure 7.2, for species one, N = 4 (the number of elements within the species), K = 3 (the number of internal connections) and C = 2 (the number of external connections). For species two, N = 2, K = 1, and C = 2. For species three, N = 3, K = 1, C = 0. In the whole diagram, for each species S = 2 (the total number of species minus one, S being the number of species *other than* the one whose fitness landscape is being constructed).

Imagine the scene (cf. Stewart, 2001: 6–12): a fox and a rabbit are competing for survival. A rabbit that is successful in survival may have: (i) fast running power to escape the fox; (ii) good eyesight to see the fox from a distance; (iii) good ability to identify rich grass to grow strong; and (iv) good ability to produce offspring to ensure survival of the species. N = 4, K = 6 (the number of possible interconnections between its four elements) and C = 2. Rabbits without these abilities die from starvation, are prey for foxes, or are unable to propagate offspring, so the species dies. A fox that is successful in survival may have: (i) a good sense of smell; (ii) a good ability to go down rabbit holes; (iii) speed in catching rabbits (N = 3; K = 2; C = 2). Each species has its own fitness landscape; over the course of time each evolves to its peak of fitness so that rabbits do not die out, and neither do foxes. They learn to adapt to each other and evolve and develop for survival. That adaptation constantly requires change: rabbits learn to run faster to evade foxes, and foxes learn to run faster to catch rabbits; everyone runs faster to remain where they are (see the discussion of the Red Queen effect in Chapter 1 (Kauffman, 1995; Stewart, 2001: 7)).

The survival of the rabbit depends, in part, on C – the number of connections with the fox, and *vice versa* (and the adaptiveness of one to the other). McCarthy and Tan (2000) suggest that competition for survival is good, as it forces organizations to learn and adapt – to move towards self-organized criticality – or else

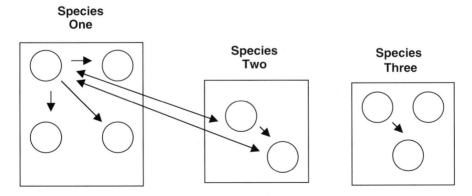

Figure 7.2 A three-species fitness landscape.

face extinction. Enter the human (S_1), bearing a rifle, with dogs (S_2) and ferrets (S_3), who can catch and destroy rabbits and foxes alike, and it is easy to see how the situation becomes more and more complex!

In the example of foxes and rabbits above, the strength of the fitness landscape of the rabbit depends on the quantity of small peaks or N (N = 4) and the height of K (K = 6); the higher and the more rugged the terrain, the greater the fitness. Similarly for the fox: the strength of *its* fitness landscape depends on its number of N connections (N = 3) and the height of K (K = 2). Additionally, the fitness landscape of the rabbit is also influenced by the presence and the fitness landscape of the fox or C (C = 2) and indeed, other species (S). Similarly, the fitness landscape of the fox is also influenced by the fitness landscape of the rabbit or C (C = 2), and indeed, other species (S). The picture is constantly changing: as the rabbit population increases, so might the fox population, which leads to the reduction of the rabbit population, in which case the fox population decreases – they affect each other. They co-evolve. My fitness landscape is affected by your fitness landscape and *vice versa*; they interrelate.

In educational terms imagine that two subjects within the modern languages department of a high school are competing with one another for survival. The teacher of Spanish has traditionally had more status and resources than the teacher of Mandarin, as Spanish is seen as important for (i) western Europe and South America, (ii) trade, (iii) tourism, (iv) music and culture (i.e. N = 4). Mandarin, on the other hand, which until this point was seen as the language of a small minority in the locality, and hence of limited need, now is seen as increasingly important (i) for trade, (ii) for travel and tourism, (iii) for working with communities across the world, (iv) for contacts with China, and (v) for servicing a growing number of Chinese speakers in the region (i.e. N = 5). In the two species here (Spanish and Mandarin), C = 3 (external coupling) – the number of points of contact between them. As resources in the languages department are limited, a decision has to be taken on the future of teaching both languages in the school; the more that Spanish prospers, the less that Mandarin prospers. The fitness level of the Spanish teaching is not as strong as the fitness level of that of Mandarin, and on the same terms (trade, tourism, external contacts), Mandarin is seen to be more powerful (C = 3). The fitness landscape of Mandarin has affected the fitness landscape of Spanish in the school. So should the Spanish teaching wither? In the event, the school decides to become a specialist language centre, so that both languages receive additional support!

Imagine a second example, where school A is competing with School B, in its locality, for children, within a market economy of secondary schools. School A (i) boasts superb resources in all subjects, (ii) has received a very positive inspection report, (iii) has outstanding public examination results in all subjects, (iv) has excellent communication with parents, (v) ensures that its own marketing is well resourced, and (vi) has highly contented students. In terms of fitness this simplistic summary scene can be represented as N = 6 and K = 15 (the number of possible interconnections when N = 5, i.e. 5 + 4 + 3 + 2 + 1). School B, on the other hand, (i) has highly developed community links for employment prospects,

(ii) has above average public examination results in many subjects; (iii) routinely excludes children whose misbehaviour is unacceptable, and so the discipline in the school is strong; (iv) targets its marketing carefully, and thereby spends a limited budget on it and (v) is known for working the students hard. In terms of its fitness this scenario, again over-simplified for clarity, can be represented as $N = 5$ and $K = 10$ ($4 + 3 + 2 + 1$), and between the two schools $C = 2$. On balance it seems as though school A has a stronger fitness landscape than school B, though clearly both landscapes affect each other. If school A increases its marketing and adds further components then it is likely to improve its fitness; if school B improves its student achievement and strengthens its market then it might be fitter than school A. They co-evolve.

The issue here echoes that of Chapter 5, where it was seen as critical for leaders in schools to sense and interact with their environments and participants in those environments. Insensitivity to, and poor connectedness with, the environment (low-C) brings susceptibility to the deformation of the school's fitness landscape by other participants in that external environment (S). Similarly, insensitivity to internal connections (low-K) and an inability to use all the elements within the school (N) in its development can render the school's fitness landscape less than rugged. The key to improving ruggedness is connectivity through communication and interdependence: the higher the K, C, N and S, the greater is the need for communication. As has been argued earlier in this book, these are key matters for leaders at all levels in the school.

The degree and strength of the connectedness of one species with another (C) affects the fitness of each. So, for example, a species which is stranded on the peak of a low hill need not fear being caught there for ever, since the fitness landscape constantly changes as a result of the nature and amount of C (external coupling). The effects of other species will deform/reform the fitness landscape and enable the species to move (cf. Stewart, 2001: 11).

Species with low-K (few intra-connections) have smooth fitness landscapes with maybe only a single rounded hill, like mount Fuji (McCarthy and Tan, 2000); species with high-K (many intra-connections) have rugged landscapes (several small, steep-sided hills, or several foothills for a major peak) cf. Stewart (2001: 9). Small schools may have fewer peaks than large schools. Low-K indicates stability; high-K indicates complexity. Low-K produces a small number of high peaks, i.e. there is a limited number of survival strategies, which may make it easy for competitors to adopt such strategies (Stacey *et al.*, 2000: 114); species in landscapes which are either too rugged or too smooth stand little chance of survival (*ibid*: 114). Networks characterized by low peaks are susceptible to extinction (*ibid*: 114). The greater is the number of peaks, the harder it is to traverse. Survival occurs between too smooth and too high a landscape (Stacey *et al.*, 2000: 151).

Stewart (2001: 33) suggests that, in a fit landscape, K (internal connectedness) must be roughly equal to the product of $C \times S$ (external connectedness multiplied by the number of external species), akin to the law of requisite variety, discussed in Chapter 5. Low-K is relatively unfit if $\{C \times S\}$ is high, as the species is very susceptible to changes in C and S. If C is high then any changes to the organization have significant 'knock-on' effects and hence the organization is unpredictable. If C is too high then the organization is susceptible to any changes and reverberations in the system (*ibid*: 44); if C is too low then the organization's sensitivity to the environment is too low; in the case of the former the organization needs to reduce C; in the case of the latter it needs to increase it.

If K is high and the internal connectedness of the organization is too complex, then, suggests Stewart (*ibid*: 36), the organization becomes too introverted, introspective and bound up in its own operations to be able to address C and S adequately, or to examine the behaviour taking place in the external environment. Hence it needs to trim its internal complexity in order to release its ability to scan the environment and respond to it. An over-intra-connected school is unable to keep its overview of the external environment or to be able to react to it or be proactive in it. Here the law of requisite variety (Chapter 5) must be combined with the caution that too great a degree of internal complexity renders the organization incapable of responding to the external environment and changes in it.

In a school with many departments, each of which can be regarded as external to the other, creating too high a C (external coupling) is dangerous if K (connections *within* each department) is low, as the stability of each department might be reduced. This argues for the dangers of too great a reliance on matrix structures, and suggests that sometimes a hierarchical structure might provide greater stability (Stewart, 2001: 44) and consolidation. Indeed, low-K schools are able to make decisions rapidly.

When $K = \{S \times C\}$ then self-organized criticality has been reached. Where K is low then predictability is high but the organization is in need of constant change. Where K is high then predictability is low, as change in one sub-element impacts on the other sub-elements.

Though the development of a fitness landscape emerges through self-organization, this is not to say that its progress cannot be expedited, and effective leadership might be the catalyst in this situation. For example, in a school which is experiencing drift and underachievement, whose fitness is low (see the example of the failing school later in this chapter), the effect of the appointment of a new headteacher, with a clearly set agenda for reform, devolved onto accountable members of staff, can have the effect of 'turning round' the school.

Several questions can be asked of a fitness landscape, be it for the whole school, the department, formal and informal groups, teams etc., for example:

• How many peaks are there in the school/department/group, etc.?
• What are the elements of N, K, C and S?
• How high are the peaks?
• How rugged is the landscape, and how straightforward or easy to climb (manageable) is the landscape?
• How close to each other are the peaks (how related or integrated are the key activities of the school/department/group, etc.)?
• How rolling is the landscape and how deep are the valleys (how manageable is the school/department/group, etc.)?

- How many major and minor peaks are there, and of what do they comprise?
- Generally, how high or low is the relief of the landscape (how fit is it)?
- How wide or narrow are the bases of the peaks (how stable is the landscape)?
- Where are the peaks located (are they widely distributed or do they cluster together in one area (one faculty or department or the whole school)?
- What lies between the main peaks, e.g. gorges, wide valleys, high plateaux, small peaks (what is the configuration of each landscape)?
- Do people have maps of the peaks, and are the maps clear, used, helpful, sufficiently detailed (do participants know what is happening in the school/department/group, etc.)?
- What are the causes of change in N, K, C, and S?
- How is a journey through the landscape sustained (what resources, maintenance and development support are there in the school/department/group, etc.)?

The notion of a fitness landscape resonates with the work of Hall and Hord (1987: 107–40) on 'innovation configurations' in schools. The intention here is to describe the key features of an innovation, particularly in terms of the perceptions of the participants and stakeholders, so that the degree of match between the perceptions of participants can be exposed. Hall and Hord comment on several components of an innovation in school, for example its relative advantage over existing practice, compatibility with existing practice, complexity, possibility for being trialled, and observability. Additionally, they suggest the need for attention to the value systems and other systems which underpin the innovation and the goals and purposes of the innovation in the school. There is a need, they aver, to examine the critical components of the innovation (those factors which need to be right for success to be assured), the number of innovations within the whole process of change, and the priorities in the innovation in the school.

Hall and Hord (*ibid*: 116), with perhaps unconscious prescience of complexity theory, instance the need for 'mutual adaptation' between external requirements and the internal functioning of the school. They state that the checklist of components or key features of the innovation configuration should be developed by the participants themselves (*ibid*: 123–5), through discussion, interviews and dialogue (self-organization).

Interpreting fitness landscapes

A picture of a fitness landscape, as in topographical maps, might resemble a mountain range, a plain, or a combination of these, see for example Figure 7.3.

In Figure 7.3 the left-hand side contains two rolling peaks whilst the right-hand side indicates a much more rugged terrain with high, sharp peaks which are closely packed. Kauffman (1995) argues that the fittest organizations have the highest peaks, and the best peaks are those which are neither too rugged nor too smooth, and which allow exploration of other peaks (i.e. surveying the environment), a key feature of complexity theory.

Figure 7.3 A rugged and rolling fitness landscape.

If peaks within an organization are too close (closely coupled organizations) then disturbance in one part of an organization will be likely to disrupt another part of the organization (which might be beneficial or, alternatively, could bring collateral damage). If the mathematics department is too closely coupled to the IT department, then changes to the IT department will impact on the mathematics department.

If peaks are widely dispersed (loosely coupled organizations) then their relative isolation might bring the benefits of less collateral damage but the problem of poor communication. If the mathematics department is not closely enough coupled to the IT department then the impact of the IT department on the mathematics department might be inadequate (Figure 7.4).

The ruggedness of peaks is a function of the number of players in the system (K), e.g. individuals, departments, faculties, who directly affect each other. Kauffman (1995) argues that the greater the number of such interdependencies or linkages, the more rugged is the landscape, and where there are fewer interdependencies the peaks will tend to stand out more clearly. Highly complex systems, argues Kauffman, also tend to possess a large number of low fitness peaks and few, indeed if any, highly fit peaks. Hence the fitness of an individual department or unit depends not only on its own situation but also on its situation in relation to the other interdependent parts. For example, in a school the effectiveness of the IT curriculum may depend on the effectiveness of the whole school curriculum development team. A whole school is maximally fit when each of its subsystems is maximally fit.

Therein resides a problem, for a zero-sum model might operate, wherein fitness in one department is bought at the expense of fitness in another (see the

Figure 7.4 Widely dispersed peaks in a fitness landscape.

example of foxes and rabbits earlier in the chapter, though, of course co-evolution is presupposed here). For example, the strength of the mathematics department might be high, but this is because money which might have gone to other departments is diverted into the mathematics department; or the successful teaching methods of the teacher of German might conflict with the teaching methods of the teacher of Russian; or the improvement in music achievement might be because of increased time allowances on the school timetable, which is at the expense of the geography timetable. Thus, the more players and subsystems there are, the greater is the propensity for this to occur – it is very difficult to have a maximally fit organization. On the positive side, it also means that very high peaks will often be surrounded by many intermediate peaks – supporting or staging posts. Though competition and conflict may be inevitable in an adaptive environment, they should not be seen as negating the very powerful need for collaboration.

Closely coupled organizations (e.g. many mountains linked by many roads) are more sensitive to change than loosely coupled organizations, though loosely coupled organizations might enable change to take place rapidly in one area (one part of the landscape, e.g. one school's mathematics department) because it is less impeded by the surrounding terrain (cf. Weick, 1976). Large networks of subsystems may be less affected by change than small networks (the system can absorb change in one subsystem without it disturbing the rest – a single fish in a small pond causes more disturbance than in a large pond). Marion (1999: 162) suggests that a fit landscape is integrated with, and supported by, several resources in the environment, and comprises a network of interdependent systems which, themselves, are fit. Within this, each component part can manage change without it upsetting the overall system, and its size ensures that it can absorb change more easily, and without disturbance, than smaller systems.

Exposed high peaks are buffeted by the weather, whilst those closer to each other and of a similar height are more protected. In a school the mathematics department might be close to the science and IT departments, and they might protect each other, whereas the physical education department has fewer close relations, and might be more exposed to changes in the environment. Different groups reside more comfortably in different parts of the landscape, suggesting the need to match people with roles and tasks in the organization. Some peaks are so sharp that a single step might result in falling off the mountain (i.e. change is highly likely), see Figure 7.5.

Other peaks are more rounded, such that several steps make little difference (a secure system without much change). See Marion (1999: 109), Figure 7.6.

If there are many peaks then there are several departments or subsystems within the organization; fewer peaks indicate a less complex organization. Hence the more rugged the landscape is, the greater is the number of interdependencies within the organization and, by implication, the greater is the need for developed communication linkages. Indeed Kauffman (1993) suggests that an organization might be best divided into 'patches' – smaller units within the network (or 'communities of practice' (Brown and Duguid, 1991)) which interact and constantly communicate with each other (Lissack, 1996: 8). Indeed Lissack (1999: 10) argues that increasing returns require network and community relationships whenever possible. Figure 7.7 indicates three sets of 'patches'.

Fit landscapes have many high peaks but these are not occluded by the presence of too many intermediate peaks (Marion, 1999: 249), though there should be

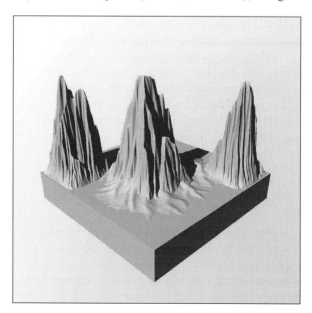

Figure 7.5 Dangerously sharp peaks in a fitness landscape.

Figure 7.6 Rounded peaks in a fitness landscape.

Figure 7.7 A very rugged fitness landscape.

enough intermediate peaks to act as stepping stones onto the higher peaks (*ibid*: 265), see Figure 7.8.

It is important to note that there is no single 'fit' landscape, no blueprint or grand design. At times it is important to consolidate the work of an organization

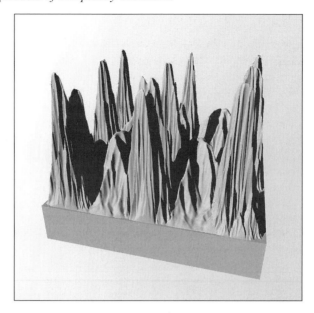

Figure 7.8 Intermediate peaks on a very rugged fitness landscape.

(a rolling landscape); at other times it is important to move the organization forward, overcoming obstacles (a rugged terrain).

Several of the characteristics of a fit landscape emphasize the need for ensuring that organizations operate as networks or networks of networks (Marion, 1999: 247). Coleman (1999: 35) suggests that the connectivity of the peaks is a crucial factor: a few strong ties (roads) produce stable behaviour which is too little for effective learning, whilst many and weak ties produce unstable behaviour in which there is a surfeit of variety for effective learning to occur. Kauffman (1995) argues that flat rather than hierarchical social organizations are more conducive to organizational fitness here, with decentralized decision making. A school which is highly centralized, controlling, bureaucratic and hierarchical might stifle development and have a poor fitness landscape, whilst a school with greater decentralization, distributed leadership and a networked structure might improve its fitness and become more rugged – as Gross (1998: 68) says, the key for leaders is to 'let go' so that fitness and development can flourish. Johnson (1999: 26) suggests that rugged landscapes, although the fittest, also require the greatest investment in skills, resources, flexibility and knowledge.

When fitness is average, innovation and improvement and increasing returns are best addressed by scanning the distant landscape; when fitness is high the fittest elements are closer to home (Kauffman, 1993; Lissack, 1999: 6; McCarthy and Tan, 2000). Similarly, early in the adaptive process fitness might be in the furthest distance, moving closer during the process of becoming fitter (Kauffman, 1996: 5–6).

Constructing a picture of a fitness landscape

A difficulty in portraying a fitness landscape, as conceived by Kauffman and other originators, is the construction of the picture of such a landscape, for there is a high degree of precision in drawing it, based on complex, high level mathematical formulae. Teachers, regardless of mathematical ability, simply do not have the time to devote to this. Moreover, it is unnecessary. A fitness landscape can be drawn freehand by teachers, and, as such, will be a useful heuristic device which is intended to be a spur to development, rather than an exact measurement. It is a projection device. The picture of a fitness landscape can be constructed in seven stages (Table 7.1).

The notion and practice of a fitness landscape is strongly akin to school self-evaluation for school improvement (Rodger and Richardson, 1985). In the

Table 7.1 Stages in the construction of a fitness landscape

Stage	*Task*
Stage One	Identify the purpose for which fitness is being determined
Stage Two	Identify the players and subsystems who are involved in the situation (fitness landscape), i.e. the number of possible peaks. Identify N, K, C and S in the system
Stage Three	Construct the peaks: • the number of actual peaks (fit subsystems of the organization) • the height of the peaks • the contours and shape of the peaks (e.g. sharp, rolling, narrow, wide, leptokurtic – narrow and pointed, platykurtic – wide base and flattened at the tops) • the distance between the peaks (the degree of relatedness between peaks) • the relationship of the intermediate peaks to the main peak (which subsystems are more closely related to which peaks)
Stage Four	Construct the plains: • the area of the plains • the number of subsystems within the plains (unfit subsystems of the organization)
Stage Five	Construct the linkages between the peaks: • the number of communication channels in the organization • where the communication channels operate most effectively (e.g. where the roads are wide or narrow, paved or rough) • whether roads are one-way streets or two-way streets (whether communication is unidirectional or multidirectional) • which roads and passes link which peaks, valleys and plains • where the roads and passes go (e.g. a convoluted route or a direct route)
Stage Six	Review the fitness landscape in order to establish the *causes* of the situation and to *evaluate* the fitness of the organization for survival
Stage Seven	Decide the way forward: • identify what the strengths and the weaknesses are that the fitness landscape has revealed • identify priorities for development • identify how to address these priorities

sequence above, stage one sets the *context*, stages two to five *describe* and portray the landscape, stage six *evaluates* the situation, and stage seven discusses *development planning*. The process resembles closely the process of school development planning, addressing questions such as: 'Where are we now?'; 'Where do we want to be?'; 'How will we get there?'; 'How will we commence?'; 'How will we continue?'; 'How will we know when we have arrived?', (Hargreaves and Hopkins, 1991; Egan 1993).

The process also matches discussions of problem-solving and action research (Chapter 4), where a problem or situation is described, the causes of the situation are identified, proposals to address the situation are considered and a way forward for implementation is planned, leading to subsequent evaluation of the effectiveness of the implementation in addressing the problem or situation.

Creating a picture of a fitness landscape as a projection technique lets participants draw and share their own mental maps of the fitness landscape of the organization, e.g. to look for similarities and differences, and the reasons for these. Once the landscape has been drawn, the most important part of the exercise commences, which is to *use* the information, just as, in school self-evaluation, data act as a springboard into action. The connection between the construction of a picture of a fitness landscape and school self-evaluation echoes the key principle of this chapter: *self*-organization. Further, an important point here is that the exercise is collaborative (Russell, 1996). The construction of a portrayal of a fitness landscape is not a 'once and for all' activity, as schools are dynamical organizations; indeed it would be salutary for schools to undertake the exercise as a 'before and after' activity in a programme of school development to chart what has, in fact, changed.

The fitness landscapes of a successful and a failing school

Two examples of fitness landscapes and their portrayal are discussed below.

Example one: a fit school

School A is a secondary school of 1,200 students in an area of considerable deprivation and unemployment in the UK. It is wishing to develop its IT capability and to become a 'beacon', specialist school in this area. It has several highly motivated and highly qualified staff in this field, and the school has been successful in bidding for considerable external funding to purchase hardware and software and to develop its own intranet. Nearly all the staff are committed to the development, and they have already completed several projects and developments in IT. The project has the support of its senior managers, governing body and parents (who regard it as an opportunity for their children to gain employment). All the staff are involved in the decision making about the move towards this specialism, and several have attended courses of professional development to upgrade and share their expertise. In the course of this development the school has taken a decision that the push for IT will mean that the proposed refurbishment of the science laboratories will be postponed for one year, and the money available for the teaching of mathematics, geography and history will remain at its present level.

As a staff development exercise, each subject department and the senior management team is asked to draw a fitness landscape of the school for the proposed development, leading to several fitness landscapes. One of these is represented below, see Figure 7.9.

The mathematics and geography departments risk being marginalized (they are located at the edge of the fitness landscape and seem to be isolated from many other departments). Many peaks are high and close to each other, suggesting a rugged terrain that supports innovation, and this support is reinforced by the high valleys, intermediate peaks, and extended, plentiful road system. The wide girth of the peaks suggests that they can be scaled and that they already have considerable force – they are substantial peaks rather than needle-like pinnacles. Within the overall landscape of Figure 7.9, Figure 7.10 portrays Area A and describes the mathematics (M) and geography (G) departments, who have little connection with one another and whose fitness for the proposed change may be comparatively slight in that their own developments are being placed 'on hold'.

Within the overall landscape of Figure 7.9, Figure 7.11 portrays Area B and describes the organizational health of the school in terms of: (a) staff expertise (SE); (b) support for the initiative (SI) by the staff and senior managers; (c) communication networks (CN) in the school; (d) time available (TA) to implement the proposal; (e) resources (R) and (f) student achievement (SA). It can be seen that the strongest factors here are staff expertise, support for the initiative, and communication networks.

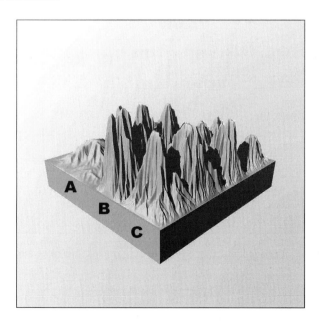

Figure 7.9 The fitness landscape of a fit school.

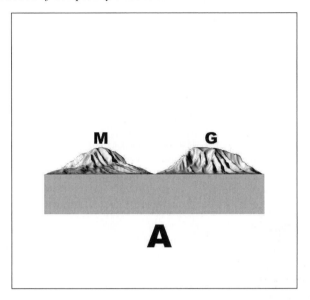

Figure 7.10 Fitness landscape for the mathematics and geography departments.

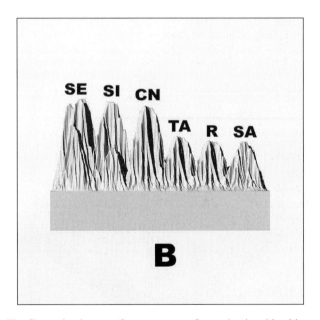

Figure 7.11 The fitness landscape of components of organizational health.

Within the overall framework of Figure 7.9, Figure 7.12 portrays Area C and describes the existing use of IT in the departments of english (E); history (H); modern foreign languages (MFL) and physics (P). Considerable use is in English, history and modern foreign languages, with less in physics.

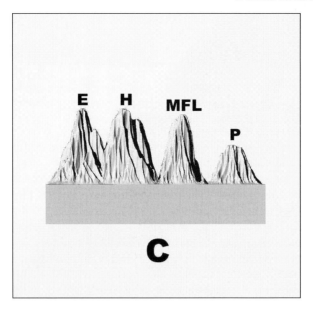

Figure 7.12 The fitness landscape of the use of IT in a school.

The implications for leadership here are, for example:

- the mathematics and geography departments should be drawn into the innovation more fully and communicate with each other more fully;
- the existing communication networks within the school might be utilized more fully and consistently;
- more time is needed to develop the project;
- more consistent use of IT across all departments is required;
- possible staff disaffection needs to be surfaced and addressed;
- there is a risk of innovation overload in having so many peaks, therefore prioritizing of change needs to be undertaken;
- innovators in some departments might co-operate with other less-innovating departments to bring in change;
- sustaining the change might be a focus – the school seems open to, and used to, change, therefore the issue is one of sustaining as well as initiating change.

These are generalized implications and, in practice, the outcomes and discussions will be more detailed because they are contextualized. The portrayal of a fitness landscape as a graphic means of identification and communication of issues is a useful device for stimulating discussion. This is only one of several fitness landscapes, and the intention would be, through sharing landscapes, to arrive at a composite which represented the situation fairly and, by so doing, further the channels of communication and collaboration in the school. Clearly, such a landscape is perception-based, and may suffer from imprecision, subjectivity, bias and unreliability. Nevertheless, much of the work in managing change concerns the management and leadership of perception (Morrison, 1998: 15; Marion, 1999: 221), so it is important to expose these matters in order that participants are aware of the perceptions that exist.

Example two: a 'failing' school

School B, a large primary school of 800 students in the UK, has recently reported poor levels of student achievement, low morale amongst the staff, high and rapid staff turnover, and indiscipline in the student population. The most recent inspection resulted in a very negative report and the threat of being placed into 'special measures' as a 'failing school'. The fitness landscape portrayed here is in terms of student achievement, see Figure 7.13.

Area A portrays students' achievements in two key subjects – mathematics (MA) and science (SC). The scene is of low hills (poor adaptation), quite widely separated, with no visible roads between them – communication between these two areas is undeveloped and they are disconnected and isolated, see Figure 7.14.

Area B is in terms of teacher expectation (TE) and teacher morale (TM). Here teacher expectations, though relatively higher than morale, are still, overall, low. Teacher morale is very low. The distance between expectation and morale is great, as though the two do not inform each other, see Figure 7.15.

Further, the distance between Areas A and B is considerable, indicating their disconnectedness. The lack of roads indicates poor communication. Here the picture is of inertia. There are no peaks to climb, and the number of leaders is low.

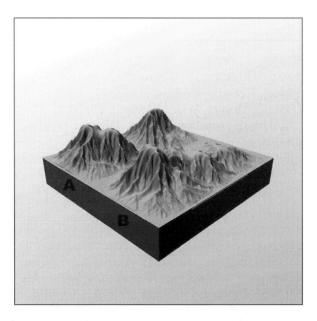

Figure 7.13 The fitness landscape of a failing school.

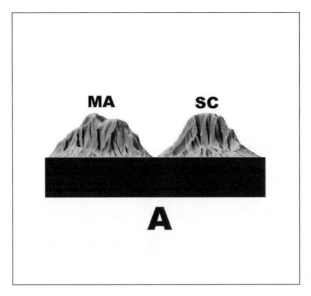

Figure 7.14 The fitness landscape of student achievement in mathematics and science.

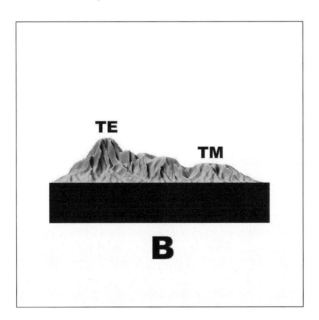

Figure 7.15 The fitness landscape of teacher expectation and teacher morale.

For the most part the teachers are content to graze on the plains. The picture is largely empty of subsystems, indicating an undeveloped school with little possibility for self-organization because too few subsystems exist (Kauffman, 1995). As Lewin and Regine (2000: 56) remark, the greater the diversity of elements and agents, the greater is the possibility for rich emergence. The school seems to be unprepared for innovation, and unfit to address the problem of raising student achievement.

The implications for leadership here are several, for example:

- greater diversity needs to be introduced into the school, for example by age, curricula, experience, expertise, gender, race and culture, if the potential for rich emergence and fitness is to be created;
- more projects and innovations need to be introduced to develop a culture of change and living with emergence/change;
- more accountability needs to be introduced for low levels of achievement and development;
- greater pressure on, and support for, teachers needs to be exerted;
- more demands for change and innovation are to be made of the leaders in the school, with more leaders appointed;
- communication within the school needs to be extended significantly and utilized;
- teachers' expectations of students and of each other need to be increased;
- teacher morale needs to be improved (maybe by involvement in more development activities and greater communication);
- more distributed leadership and leadership development within the school needs to be undertaken;
- generally, more needs to be happening in the school, more projects, more activities; the demand for increasing quantity (i.e. to increase the number of fitness peaks (N) needs to be matched by increasing the quality of activities (to increase the height and ruggedness of the peaks (K));
- more co-operative and collaborative activities need to be undertaken, with shared and devolved responsibility;
- professional development of teachers and leaders needs to be undertaken;
- there is a need for clearer goals, direction and pressure to achieve them.

What we have here are issues concerning the leadership of change and innovation, including: identifying and overcoming resistance and inhibitors to change; facilitation and empowerment of teachers and managers; pressure and support; teamwork and collaboration; organizational culture, ethos and health (which in the school in question seems to be poor), organizational direction, stimulation and the energizing of teachers to change; creating a climate for change by introducing more initiatives and developments, target setting and establishing incentives and rewards for achieving change; and replacing inertia with dynamism (Morrison, 1998).

Developing fitness

In developing fitness it can be seen that several of the issues in the leadership of change present themselves, including, for example:

- vision, goals and mission;
- planning the stages and strategies of change;
- ensuring a rich, diverse landscape which achieves a balance of too little activity with too much;
- matching the participants in change to the changes required;
- leading the change;
- professional development to support the change;
- balancing pressure with support, and concern for task with concern for people (Everard and Morris, 1990);
- developing communication, teamwork and collaboration;
- developing the organizational culture and climate of the school.

In this process leadership plays a critical role, in that leaders are required to move the school forward from a state of inertia to activity by balancing strong leadership with democratic leadership (Morrison *et al.*, 1989). Leaders in schools, the authors suggest, must create a climate for change by initiating several innovations in the school in a telescoped time scale (*ibid.*). In complexity theory terms this can be recast as moving the organization forward to a point of self-organized criticality (maximizing human capital and creativity) but ensuring that this does not become too diffuse and unbounded, i.e. keeping people and organizations at the edge of chaos, in their most productive state (April, 2000: 63).

Leading in a rugged landscape, then, becomes a matter of being cautious about long-range planning, being aware of trends that are taking place, setting the school's sights according to its current fitness level, creating instability (e.g. new initiatives and activities) as necessary in order to disturb a school into action to move up a fitness hill, keeping moving and exploring the landscape for newer peaks, and searching in several places at once (multiple, parallel searching) rather than conducting single searches of the environment (McCarthy and Tan, 2000).

A school whose fitness landscape is strong will possess several features, dependent on the size of the school. The landscape will contain:

- many units and elements rather than being empty;
- many rugged high peaks, many of which are close to each other and all of which are scaleable;
- only a few peaks which are completely exposed;
- very few peaks which are sharp pinnacles;
- many smaller, supporting peaks which lead up to the high peaks but which do not obscure sight of the high peaks;
- roads and links of different sizes between all parts of the landscape;
- inhabitants of the landscape who will be in the most suitable parts for their own make-up placing the right people on the right hill (Lissack, 1999: 6);
- leaders everywhere in the landscape;
- few flat or low-lying areas;
- a combination of rugged and rolling hills.

This is not to say that this will be a blueprint, indeed the preceding discussion argues against blueprints. For leaders of schools this suggests several issues to be faced:

- the role of N, K, C and S in the context of the school;
- how to encourage the development of many peaks (e.g. many projects and many centres of development and innovation);
- how to raise the height of peaks and decide which to consolidate (which projects/departments/units of the network to emphasize and develop);
- how to increase and maximize communication between the peaks (e.g. to ascertain what are the major and minor communication channels, how to ensure that communication is smooth – see Chapter 6);
- how to avoid marginalization of people and departments in the organization;
- how to avoid having too many peaks and too close a distance between the peaks (to decide what are the priorities for development, how to match closeness with autonomy);
- how to ensure that the peaks are scaleable (i.e. that supporting peaks are present, for example in professional development, leadership development, resource adequacy, collaboration);
- how to ensure that people can navigate their way round the landscape (how people access knowledge of the school, its organization and activities, and how they are supported in navigating their way round the organization);
- how to ensure that the most suitable people take on particular tasks and roles (echoing Belbin's (1981) work on roles in teams).

The sequence of using a fitness landscape here, then, is:

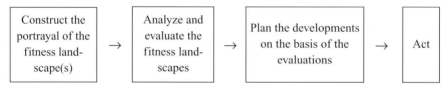

This is, of course, akin to the early stages of action research. The construction and usage of fitness landscapes, like action research, are rooted in collaborative enquiry.

Conclusion

This chapter has argued for the utility of devising and portraying fitness landscapes as techniques for indicating the adaptability of a species to its internal and external environments. Internal and external networking, communication, and co-evolution are hallmarks of the fit school. The construction and portrayal of fitness landscapes strikingly present the situation in a school and bear all the advantages of projection techniques which enable participants to portray and communicate their views and mind sets. Leaders and teachers may find it useful to construct these and to compare their landscapes to look for similarities and differences and the reasons for these. They can become a useful starting point for self-review; they foster communication.

For leaders in school, then, at all levels in all spheres of the school, the implications here reinforce those of other chapters, and extend them, to suggest that leaders should:

- promote the internal connectivity and external coupling of the school through extensive communication and networking throughout the school;
- identify the significant internal and external components with whom connections are needed (N and S respectively), and the nature and strength of connections internally and externally (K and C respectively);
- promote the construction, portrayal, interpretation, evaluation and action arising from fitness landscapes for school development and interpretation (a useful in-service activity, perhaps);
- examine ways of developing the school's/department's/team's, etc. self-organizing and other strategies and ways forward for improving the adaptability of the school/department/team, etc. to its internal and external environments (i.e. to improve the fitness of the group in question, to move towards self-organized criticality, and to examine the criteria for, elements and indicators of, fitness);
- constantly scan and review the external environment to identify changes which will impact on the group within the school, and initiate internal responses to these (i.e. to maintain the group's fitness in an evolving land-scape);
- identify and portray the existing and likely near-future fitness landscapes of other participants within and external to the school, so that the group in question's adaptability and adaptation strategies can be planned;
- identify the people in the school who should be working on developing the several internal and external connections (K and C);
- consider how to promote co-evolution of the groups within the school and external to the school;
- consider how many internal and external connections must, should and could be made, prioritize these and decide strategies to address them;
- consider the existing and the preferred fitness landscape that is desired and how to achieve the preferred landscape, i.e. how to make the 'adaptive walk' (Kauffman, 1995, McCarthy and Tan, 2000) through the landscape;
- identify blockages to improving fitness in the system and ways of addressing these.

This is a large agenda, which reflects the fruitfulness of the concept and practice of constructing and portraying fitness landscapes.

8 Retrospect and prospect

Leadership in schools is at a bifurcation point. With increasing pressures being placed on leaders, coupled with pressures for line management accountability in accordance with putative business practice, the need to discard command-and-control mentalities in schools has long been recognized. At a time when countries all over the world are experiencing profound difficulties in recruiting, retaining, and rewarding teachers and leaders, it is clear that tired models of leadership are simply not working; they are exhausted. In other walks of life leaders are turning to complexity theory to inform their developing practices.

This book has suggested that higher, emergent forms of leadership in schools will need to consider the need for team development, incentives and motivation, human relations, emotional intelligence, servant leadership, and to develop the organizational learning of schools by tapping the creative and interpersonal side of schools. For this to occur, careful attention to developing the emergent self-organization of schools as open systems is needed. This requires attention to sensitive human relationships, trust, the internal and external environments of the school and the micropolitics at work in them, and it also requires extensive and very careful illocutionary communication and feedback within and between these environments. Leadership, it has been suggested, is now distributed through a flat organization and networked, information-rich school, and should concern itself with the organizational climate and health of the school. This newer form of leadership is decidedly not teleological, deterministic, and the stuff of grand plans and blueprints for a certain future. It is much more about the fostering, nurturing and enabling of the emergence of self-organization in an unpredictable and turbulent world. Schools become self-organized rather than organized and controlled, and agendas emerge over time rather than being planned on a grand scale.

This book has been an exposition of key issues in complexity theory. It is suggested that complexity theory unifies several, perhaps disparate, elements of school leadership. What is distinctive about complexity theory is that it draws together all these points, and, like a 'good' theory, gives coherence to disparate elements. It is no coincidence that these several issues have emerged on the educational leadership agenda more or less simultaneously, for they are all facets of the same theory, and an indication of complexity theory at work in schools. Complexity theory has been there all along in schools, operating silently; what is new is that the paradigm shift from modernistic mentalities and modalities of schools and their leadership to complexity-driven mentalities and modalities is emerging into the open. This is important, and it raises several key issues.

1 Complexity theory is not simply a metaphor or an analogy that is convenient for senior managers to use to exhort employees to work or to extort innovations from them. If that is all it is then it is little more than another 'management fad' in high-sounding words (Griffiths, 1997; Micklethwait and Wooldridge, 1997; Stacey *et al.*, 2000) and it should command little attention. No, complexity theory is a reality; it is happening; it is working in practice, whether we like it or not. Though its message is unsettling, for it argues that long-range planning is futile, that control is a chimera, and that the power of bosses is limited, it is *descriptively* accurate. One cannot play Canute and ignore it; it exists. It is a *theory* which explains how and why to practise particular leadership practices.

2 The traditional philosophical position, from Hume, is that one cannot derive an 'ought' from an 'is' without committing a category mistake: simply because I observe complexity theory operating does not mean that I simply ought to accept it. Observing something in action does not provide a moral imperative for furthering it: observing a behaviour does not mean accepting or supporting that behaviour. This suggests the need for further empirical research into the effects of organizing schools on a deliberately complexity theory-driven principle. As Griffiths (1997: 376) suggests, complexity theory may need 'evidence to support its extravagant claims'. This is an adventurous move, though the evidence cited in this book suggests that it shows many signs of being highly beneficial to all participants.

   Complexity theory is a grounded, emergent theory and, hence has explanatory potential. Perhaps it needs further testing, exploration, and investigation; like other sciences, it may require to be tested, refined, modified and extended. What is required is, perhaps, informed scepticism about its sphere and extent of application. Just as total quality management was seen not to live up to its promises in the ways anticipated (Schaffer and Thompson, 1996: 141–8), and indeed many management fads foundered over time (Micklethwait and Wooldridge, 1997), there is a need for rigorous testing of complexity theory for its explanatory potential and its potential to take forward leadership; it is a theory awaiting testing in schools; the claims for its use must be evidence-informed.

3 Complexity theory proscribes simple causality and linear determinism. In that respect it is invidious to suggest that complexity theory is the sole informant of newer forms of leadership. Just as school life is multi-dimensional and to be explained in several ways, so complexity theory needs to take its place alongside other leadership theories that guide and inform practice in schools. What those other theories are, and what is the place of complexity theory alongside them, is a matter for empirical investigation as well as moral debate.

4   This book has advocated several prescriptions for leadership in education, which flow from complexity theory. One has to be cautious here, for in being prescriptive one runs the risk of violating the principle of openness and uncertainty in complexity theory. Complexity theory suggests that the future is unpredictable, hence any absolutist outcomes in prescribing newer forms of leadership will suffer from the same teleological determinism for which command-and-control mentalities were criticized (note that Figure 1.3 ended with a large question mark!). The suggestions in this book for flat management, team-based approaches, servant leadership, distributed leadership, emotional intelligence, organizational learning, micropolitics, communication and so on may not survive, just as certainly as civilizations have to mutate or die. The implications of complexity theory are unpredictable because it espouses uncertainty; pushed to its limits it is an open question whether complexity theory, because of its implied relativism, predicts its own demise. Less gloomy than this, complexity theory is more a theory of *process* than of outcomes. Hence the issues in this book are process issues, suggesting how leaders might act, rather than prescribing fixed outcomes of that action. We must recognize that the prescriptions in this book are pertinent only in the temporal–spatial context in which we currently find ourselves; complexity theory suggests that, when these change, whether the prescriptions change also is an empirical question. Complexity theory theorizes ephemerality.

5   This book has drawn on several research paradigms in presenting evidence to support its central thesis, e.g: quantitative, qualitative, ethnographic, meta-analysis, narrative, action research. The argument for methodological pluralism (democracy in methodology) is important in researching complexity. Even though there exists a strong tradition of numerical approaches to studying complexity (e.g. in several of the seminal texts cited in this book), it is important to note that alternative approaches, particularly narrative and qualitative approaches, are burgeoning and that these, too have been drawn upon in this volume (e.g. Kelly and Allison, 1999; Lewin and Regine, 2000; Stacey, 2000; 2001). Understanding complexity is multi-perspectival, and many of the concepts in this book have stressed the human side of schools; this argues powerfully for interpretive, phenomenological, interactionist and ethnographic approaches to researching complexity theory.

6   Just as there is a strong argument for methodological pluralism, one should complement this with theoretical pluralism (Weick, 1992; Griffiths, 1997), to recognize that complexity theory will be useful for explaining what it is good at explaining, but poor at explaining everything! Certain aspects of schools, leadership and education may be explained and illuminated by complexity theory, but many aspects of these are beyond the scope of complexity theory. Single theory explanations for multiple problems are simply inadequate. As mentioned in Chapter 1, complexity theory is useful for explaining development, evolution, adaptation and survival; its synthetic (contingent rather than analytic) implications have been the topics in this book. A 'good' theory will:

- be logically consistent;
- have considerable explanatory and maybe (though not always) predictive power;
- be parsimonious;
- be fertile in generating research;
- possess internal coherence which it can apply to wider phenomena;
- have its own interrelated constructs, propositions and methodologies;
- set the grounds for its own verification and falsifiability;
- be generalizable;
- be compatible with phenomena;
- be capable of responding to observed anomalies;
- demonstrate precision and universality (Cohen *et al.*, 2000: 1213).

Complexity theory needs to prove itself in several of these areas, though this book has suggested that its potential for success here is considerable.

7 Complexity theory is amoral, yet education is a moral activity. Complexity theory alone cannot provide a sufficient account of education and educational development, for these require moral choices to be made. There are limits to be placed on the potential of complexity theory to guide education and a deliberative, moral enterprise.

8 It can be argued that several of the ideas in this book can stand by themselves without *requiring* complexity theory. Organizational learning, emotional intelligence, flat management, communication, teamwork, organizational climate, networking, knowledge management and the need for environmental sensitivity have all flourished in their own terms without needing specific reference to complexity theory. Is complexity theory redundant then, just another unnecessary consideration in an already overburdened educational world, or only suitable for academics with enough time to eloquently describe its merits? Does one need to learn a theory in order to be an effective practitioner (after all, many governments are driven by pragmatics, rather than principles)? Of course not, but it helps.

However, this book has suggested that an understanding of complexity theory is important and fruitful for leaders, as it explains and justifies *why* particular ideas interrelate and are important. Further, it has suggested ways forward for leadership which flow from principles and justifications. An understanding of complexity theory informs the development of the practice of leadership coherently and richly; it suggests new paths to follow which, in an ever-changing world, is important. The prospect for complexity theory is optimistic; in many ways complexity theory for school leadership is a theory whose time has come.

Notes

1 Complexity theory

1 Whether a survival theory (adapt-or-die) is appropriate for analyzing schools is a moot point (cf. Schultz, 1994). In the competitive, market-oriented view of schools, where unsuccessful schools are supposed to close, this may be appropriate. However, in the real world where most schools do not close, complexity theory becomes less an adapt-or-close issue, and more of an adapt-for-improvement issue.

2 Stacey (2000: 330) suggests that there are limits to the use of the example of Boids, as it is still a teleological example, inasmuch as an external controller, a computer manager, needs only to set the minimal rules and then sit back and watch the system self-organizing itself to his or her predetermined goals (the 'strange attractor' of chaos theory). The goals will only change when the manager – the controller – changes them, i.e. its teleology is cast in the traditional mode of strategic management and a control mentality, whereas complexity theory implies novel and unpredictable goals which generate themselves spontaneously.

3 One can detect in this chapter the use of a theory which does not derive from education but from the natural sciences, economics and mathematics. Though this might be seen as illegitimate, Wheatley (1999: 15) provides a robust defence of such an enterprise, arguing not only for the breaking of traditional disciplinary boundaries, but that it is useful to see where theories might apply in new contexts. Merry (1995; 1998) takes forward this project, suggesting nine major differences between human organizations and the complex adaptive systems of nature:

1 organizations and people have greater cognitive ability than natural complex adaptive systems;

2 humans exert greater free will and intentionality than natural systems;

3 communication and co-operation are stronger and more developed between disparate and diverse human agents than in natural systems;

4 humans adapt individually and socially – they are the adaptive element and develop through synergy and they are more innovative than many non-human organisms;

5 humans are members of several complex adaptive systems, whereas in nature membership is of fewer systems, giving greater creative capacity to humans;

6 organizations are constituted and co-ordinated by socially constructed rules and procedures, whereas in nature these are largely natural laws;

7 humans tend to work in constructed rather than natural environments;

8 organizations co-evolve with artifacts and technology whereas natural systems co-evolve with nature;

9 organizations have to create and export value to participants, whereas natural systems do not.

The first six of these suggest that humans and human organizations have greater evolutionary ability than natural complex adaptive systems, whilst the latter three suggest that a premium is placed on human adaptive abilities. Sustainability becomes a watchword in complexity-driven emergence. There is a powerful message for schools: survival means change. Structures of schools must promote their own demise and replacement. Leading complexity, then, involves leading change.

4 See also Cohen and Stewart (1995: 188) and Ridgway (1998: 8) on the connectedness between lynx and hare populations; and Kauffman (1996: 8) on the relationships between frogs and flies – the frog develops an increasingly sticky tongue and the fly develops increasingly slippery feet.

5 Of course there is, perhaps, a danger of complexity theory being unfairly normative, i.e. of deriving an 'ought' from an 'is' – just because it can be found does not mean that it should be applied, a view against which this book argues.

3 Leadership for self-organization and emergence

1 What is missing from the data reported is any information on the contexts or situations in which the data were acquired, so we are at a loss to know what 'flexibility' turns out to be, or what the 'rewards' in question were, and so on; we are given no insight into how these constructs have been operationalized and data aggregated.

2 This was measured on the Bar-On (1997) Emotional Intelligence Inventory (EQ University, 2000; Abraham, 1999), which covers intrapersonal and interpersonal factors, adaptability, stress management and general mood.

3 Malone suggests that information technology can help to foster trust by making decision makers more informed, by monitoring remote decision makers and by enabling greater communication to take place.

4 Tschannen-Moran (2000: 314) also reports significant relationships between teachers' trust in each other and student achievements.

4 Supporting emergence through the learning organization

1 Marsick (2000: 11–12) reports the Learning Organization Assessment Framework which enables participants to judge their capability and capacity for addressing these several elements. Through sharing learning tacit knowledge becomes active knowledge, critical reflection promotes action research, and communication becomes the vehicle for learning.

2 Youngblood (1997: 149) uses the powerful image of the caterpillar dissolving itself inside its cocoon in order for the 'caterpillar soup' to become a higher form or being – a butterfly – through its hidden, self-organizing, order.

3 Miller (1996) suggests that an organization can learn in six main modes. These are analytical learning, synthetic learning, experimental learning, interactive learning, structural learning and institutional learning.

4 In assessing an organization's readiness or ability to learn, O'Brien (1993) provides the Learning Organization Profile which is devolved into ten categories: strategy and vision; executive practices; managerial practices; organizational structure and job structure; performance goals and feedback; training and education; information; interpersonal behaviour; rewards and recognition, and individual and team development. This has similarities to Kline's and Saunders's (1993) elements for promoting the learning organization: assessment; promoting the positive; safe thinking; risk taking and support; regarding people as resources; learning power; mapping and modelling the organization's vision; systems thinking, and information.

5 Schools and their environments

1 Bormann (1983) and Schultz (1994) regard communication as an essential feature for creating and sharing webs, see Chapter 6.

6 Communication

1 Of course the model misses the dimension of time, the fourth dimension (see also Kauffman's 1995 comments on the limitations of fitness landscapes in indicating their dynamic, time-related evolutionary development, and Stacey, 2001: 94).

7 Fitness landscapes

1 Schein (1992: 51) regards a positive organizational culture as a key to survival. Whether a 'survival' model of organizations is appropriate to describe the situation of schools, or whether it derives from a more fitting model, e.g. symbolic interaction, is raised by Schultz (1994).

Bibliography

AbiSamra, N. (2000) *The Relationship between Emotional Intelligence and Academic Achievement in Eleventh Graders*, Auburn University at Montgomery. http://melting-pot.fortunecity.com/zaire/131/research-intell2.html

Abraham, R. (1999) 'Emotional intelligence in organizations: a conceptualization', *Genetic, Social and General Psychology Monographs*, 125 (2), 209–24.

Adam Smith Institute (1984) *Education Policy (The Omega Report)*, London: Adam Smith Institute.

Allix, N.M. (2000) 'Transformational leadership: democratic or despotic?', *Educational Management and Administration*, 28 (1), 7–20.

Allport, F.H. (1954) 'The structuring of events: outline of a general theory with applications to psychology', *Psychological Review*, 61, 281–303.

Allport, F.H.(1962) 'A theory structuronomic conception of behaviour', *Journal of Abnormal and Social Psychology*, 64, 3–30.

Åm, O. (1994) *Back to Basics. Introduction to Systems Theory and Complexity.* http://www.stud.his.no/~onar/Ess/Back-to-Basics.html

Apple, M. and Beane, J.A. (eds) (1995) *Democratic Schools*, Alexandria, VA: Association for Supervision and Curriculum Development.

April, K.A. (1997) *An Investigation into the Applicability of New Science, Chaos Theory, and Complexity Theory to Leadership, and Development of Guiding Principles for the Modern Leader and Organisation*. Research Report, Cape Town: Graduate School of Business, University of Cape Town.

April, K.A. (1999) 'Leading through communication, conversation and dialogue', *Leadership and Organization Development Journal*, 20 (5), 231–41.

April, K.A. Macdonald, R. and Vriesendorp, S. (2000) *Rethinking Leadership*, Cape Town: University of Cape Town Press.

Argyris, C. and Schön, D. (1978) *Organization Learning: Theory, Method and Practice*, Reading, Mass: Addison-Wesley.

Arthur, B.W. (1990) 'Positive feedbacks in the economy', *Scientific American*, February, 92–9.

Ashby, W.R. (1981) *An Introduction to Cybernetics* (third edition), New York: Harper and Row.

Ashkanasy, N.M., Wilderom, C.P.M. and Peterson, M.F. (eds) *Handbook of Organizational Culture and Climate*, Thousand Oaks, CA: Sage Publications Inc.

Austin, J.L. (1962) *How To Do Things with Words*, Oxford: Oxford University Press.

Bailey, R. (2000) *Education in the Open Society: Karl Popper and Schooling*, Aldershot, UK: Ashgate Publishing Ltd.

Bak, P. and Chen, K. (1991) 'Self-Organized Criticality', *Scientific American*, January, 46–53.

Ball, S. (1994) *Education Reform*, Buckingham: Open University Press.

Banet, A.G. Jr. (1976) 'Yin/Yang: a perspective on theories of group development', cited in K.A. April, R. Macdonald and S. Vriesendorp (2000) *Rethinking Leadership*, Cape Town: University of Cape Town Press.

Barker, L.L. and Barker, D.A. (1993) *Communication* (sixth edition), Englewood Cliffs, NJ: Prentice-Hall.

Barling, J. Slater, F. and Kelloway, E. K. (2000) 'Transformational leadership and emotional intelligence: an exploratory study', *Leadership and Organization Development Journal*, 21 (3), 157–61.

Barnes, L.B. and Kriger, M.P. (1986) 'The hidden side of organizational leadership', *Sloan Management Review*, 28 (1), 15–25.

Bar-On, R. (1997) *Bar-On Emotional Quotient Inventory: Technical Manual*, New York: Multi-Health Systems. http://www.parinc.com/percouns/BarOnEQi9f.html

Bar-Yam, Y. (1997) *Dynamics of Complex Systems*, New York: Perseus Press.

Baskin, K. (1998) *Corporate DNA: Learning from Life*, New York: Butterworth-Heinemann.

Bass, B.M. (1990) 'From transactional to transformational leadership: learning to share the vision', *Organizational Dynamics*, Winter, 19–31.

Bass, B.M. (1998) *Transformational Leadership*, Hillsdale, NJ: Erlbaum.

Bass, B.M. and Avolio, B.J. (1994) *Improving Organizational Effectiveness through Transformational Leadership*. Thousand Oaks, CA: Sage Publications Inc.

Beatty, B.R. (2001) *The Emotions of Educational Leadership*, The Educational Leadership Centre, New Zealand: Waikoto University. http://www.soe.waikato.ac.nz/elc/beatty.html

Beatty, R.W., Dimitroff, N. and O'Neill, D.J. (1995) 'Development pay: aligning employee capabilities with business needs', In H. Risher and C. Fay (eds) *The Performance Imperative: Strategies for Enhancing Workforce Effectiveness*, San Francisco, CA: Jossey-Bass, 323–42.

Beck, C.E. (1999) *Managerial Communication: Bridging Theory and Practice*, Englewood Cliffs, NJ: Prentice-Hall.

Beeby, M. and Booth, C. (2000) 'Networks and inter-organizational learning: a critical review', *The Learning Organization*, 7 (2), 75–88.

Beeson, I. and Davis, C. (2000) 'Emergence and accomplishment in organizational change', *Journal of Organizational Change Management*, 13 (2), 178–89.

Belasco, J. (1990) *Teaching the Elephant to Dance: Empowering Change in Your Organisation*, London: Hutchinson Business Books.

Belbin, R.M. (1981) *Management Teams: Why They Succeed or Fail*, Oxford: Butterworth-Heinemann.

Bell, D. and Ritchie, R. (1999) *Towards Effective Subject Leadership in the Primary School*, Buckingham: Open University Press.

Bennett, J.K. and O'Brien, M.J. (1994) 'The building blocks of the learning organization', *Training*, June, 41–9.

Bennis, W. (1993) *An Invented Life: Reflections on Leadership and Change*, Reading, Mass: Addison-Wesley.

Bennis, W. and Nanus, B. (1985) *Leaders: the Strategies for Taking Charge*, New York: Harper and Row.

Berne, E. (1964) *Games People Play*, London: Andre Deutsch.

Berry, A.J. and Cartwright, S. (2000) 'Leadership: a critical construction', *Leadership and Organization Development Journal*, 21 (7), 342–9.

Bierly, P.M. and Spender, J.C. (1995) 'Culture and high reliability organizations: the case of the nuclear submarine', *Journal of Management*, 21 (4), 639–56.

Blake, R. and McCanse, A.A. (1991) *Leadership Dilemmas: Grid Solution*, Houston, Texas: Gulf Publishing.

Blank, W. (1995) *The Nine Natural Laws of Leadership*, New York: AMACOM.

Blau, G. (1985) 'The measurement and prediction of career commitment', *Journal of Occupational Psychology*, 58, 277–88.

Blau, P.M. (1964) *Exchange and Power in Social Life*, New York: Wiley.

Blau, P.M. and Schoenherr, R.A. (1971) *The Structure of Organizations*, New York: Basic Books.

Bohm, D. (1980) *Wholeness and the Implicate Order*, London: Ark Paperbacks.

Bormann, E.G. (1983) 'Symbolic convergence: organizational communication and culture', in L. Putnam and M.E. Pacanowsky (eds) *Communication and Organizations*, Beverly Hills, CA: Sage Publications Inc, 99–122.

Bottery, M. (1992) *The Ethics of Educational Management*, London: Cassell.

Bourdieu, P. (1976) 'The school as a conservative force', in R. Dale, G. Esland and M. MacDonald (eds) *Schooling and Capitalism*, London: Routledge and Kegan Paul, 110–17.

Bowe, R., Ball, S. J. and Gold, A. (1992) *Reforming Education and Changing Schools*, London: Routledge.

Bradley, S.P. and Nolan, R.L. (1998) 'Capturing value in the network era', in. S.P. Bradley and R.L. Nolan (eds) *Sense and Respond: Capturing Value in the Network Era*, Boston, Mass: Harvard University Business School Press, 3–29.

Braham, B.J. (1995) *Creating a Learning Organization*, CA: Crisp Publications.

Brandon, J. (1992) *Managing Change in Manufacturing Systems*, Olney: Productivity Publications.

Brewer, A. (1994) *Managing for Employee Commitment*, Sydney, Aus: Longman.

Brookshire, M.S. (2001) 'Virtue ethics and servant leadership', *Ethics News & Views*, 9 (3), March/April. www.emory.edu/ETHICS/Newsletter/march2001/brookshire1.htm

Brown, J.S. and Duguid, P. (1991) 'Organizational learning and communities-of-practice: toward a unified view of working, learning, and innovation'. *Organization Science*, 2 (Jan/Feb), 40–57.

Brown, J.S. and Duguid, P. (2000) *The Social Life of Information*, Boston, Mass: Harvard University Business School Press.

Brown, R. (2000) *Group Processes* (second edition), Oxford: Blackwell.

Brown, S.L. and Eisenhardt, K.M. (1997) 'The art of continuous change: linking complexity theory and time-paced evolution in relentlessly shifting organizations', *Administrative Science Quarterly*, 42 (1) 1–34.

Brown, S.L. and Eisenhardt, K.M. (1998) *Competing on the Edge: Strategy as Structured Chaos*, Boston, Mass: Harvard University Business School Press.

Bryman, A. (1992) *Charisma and Leadership in Organizations*, London: Sage publications.

Buchanan, D. and McCalman, J. (1989) *High Performance Work Design: the Digital Experience*, London: Routledge.

Burns, J.M. (1978) *Leadership*, New York: Harper and Row.

Byers, P.Y. (1997) 'The process and perspective of organizational communication', in P.Y. Byers (ed.) *Organizational Communication: Theory and Behaviour*, Boston: Allyn and Bacon, 3–38.

Byrne, D. and Rogers, T. (1996) 'Divided spaces – divided school: an exploration of the spatial relations of social division', *Sociological Research Online*, 1 (2). http://www.socresonline.org.uk/1/2/3.html

Cacioppe, R. (1999) 'Using team – individual reward and recognition strategies to drive organizational success', *Leadership and Organization Development Journal*, 20 (6), 322–31.

Capra, F. (1997) *The Web of Life: a New Understanding of Living Systems*, New York: Doubleday.

Cardona, P. (2000) 'Transcendental leadership', *The Leadership and Organization Development Journal*, 21 (4), 201–6.

Cashman, K. (1998) *Leadership from the Inside Out: Becoming a Leader for Life*, Provo, Utah: Executive Excellence Publishing.

Casti, J. (1997) *Would Be World*, New York: John Wiley and Sons.

Chattel, A. (1998) *Creating Value in the Digital Era*, London: Macmillan.

Chawla, S. and Renesch, J. (eds) *Learning Organizations: Developing Culture for Tomorrow's Workplace*, New York: Productivity Press.

Cilliers, P. (1998) *Complexity and Postmodernism*, London: Routledge.

Cilliers, P. (2000) 'Knowledge, complexity and understanding', *Emergence*, 2 (4), 7–13.

Clampitt, P. G. and Downs, C. W. (1993) 'Employee perceptions of the relationship between communication and productivity: a field study', *The Journal of Business Communication*, 30 (1), 5–28.

Clemons, E.K. and Bradley, S.P. (1998) 'Strategic uncertainty and the future of online consumer interaction', in. S.P. Bradley and R.L. Nolan (eds) *Sense and Respond: Capturing Value in the Network Era*, Boston, Mass: Harvard University Business School Press, 85–105.

Coghlan, D. (1997) 'Organizational learning as a dynamic inter-level process', *Current Topics in Management*, 2, 27–44.

Cohen, J. and Stewart, I. (1995) *The Collapse of Chaos*, Harmondsworth: Penguin.

Cohen, L. Manion, L. and Morrison, K.R.B. (2000) *Research Methods in Education* (fifth edition), London: RoutledgeFalmer.

Cohen, W.M. and Levinthal, D.A. (1990) 'Absorptive capacity: a new perspective on learning and innovation', *Administrative Science Quarterly*, 35, 128–52.

Coleman, H.J. Jr. (1999) 'What enables self-organizing behavior in businesses', *Emergence: a Journal of Complexity Issues in Organizations and Management*, 1 (1), 33–48.

Coleman, M. (1994) 'Leadership in educational management', in T. Bush and J. West-Burnham (eds) *The Principles of Educational Management*, Harlow: Longman.

Collier, J. and Esteban, R. (2000) 'Systemic leadership: ethical and effective', *The Leadership and Organization Development Journal*, 21 (4), 207–15.

Collins, J. (1999) 'The power of catalytic mechanisms', *Harvard Business Review*, July/August, 71–82.

Committee for Children (2000) *Emotional Intelligence*. http://www.cfchildren.org/Puwin96emotint.html

Community Intelligence Labs (1999) *Design Guidelines Inspired by Uri Merry*. http://www.knowledgeecology.com/kenport/guidelines.shtml

Conger, J. (1991) 'Inspiring others, the language of leadership', *Academy of Management Executive*, 5 (1), 31–45.

Conley, S., Schmiddle, T. and Shedd, J. (1988) 'Teacher participation in the management of school systems', *Teachers College Record*, 90, 259–80.

Conner, D.R. (1998) *Leading at the Edge of Chaos: How To Create the Nimble Organization*, New York: John Wiley and Sons Inc.

Cosgrove, J. (2000) *Breakdown: the Facts about Teacher Stress*, London: RoutledgeFalmer.

Coveney, P. and Highfield, R. (1995) *Frontiers of Complexity*, New York: Fawcett Columbine.

Crom, S. and Bertels, T. (1999) 'Change leadership: the virtues of deviance', *Leadership and Organization Development Journal*, 20 (3), 162–7.

Daft, R.L. and Huber, G.P. (1987) 'How organizations learn: a communication framework', *Research in the Sociology of Organizations*, 5, 1–36.

Dalin, P. (1998) *School Development: Theories and Strategies*, London: Cassell.

Dalin, P. and Rolff, H.G. (1993) *Changing the School Culture*, London: Cassell.

Dansereau, F., Graen, G.G. and Haga, W. (1975) 'A vertical dyad linkage approach to leadership in formal organizations', *Organizational Behaviour and Human Performance*, 13, 46–78.

Dennison, W. and Kirk, R. (1990) *Do, Review, Learn, Apply: a Simple Guide to Experiential Learning*, Oxford: Blackwell.

Department for Education (1994) *Code of Practice on the Identification and Assessment of Special Educational Needs*, London: Department for Education.

Department of Education and Science (1988) *The Education Reform Act*, London: Her Majesty's Stationery Office.

De Smet, A.L. (1998) *Understanding Organizations*, Bethesda, MD: NIDA Resource Center for Health Services Research. http://165.112.78.61/HSR/other/DeSmetUnderstanding.htm

Devlin, K. (1991) *Logic and Information*, Cambridge: Cambridge University Press.

Dodgson, M. (1993) 'Organisational learning: a review of some literatures', *Organisational Studies*, 14 (3), 375–93.

Doloff, P.G. (1999) 'Beyond the org. chart', *Across the Board*, February, 43–7.

Drucker, P.F. (1999) *Management Challenges for the 21st Century*, Oxford: Butterworth-Heinemann.

Dubin, P. (1962) *Human Relations in Administration*, NJ: Prentice-Hall.

Duke, D. and Leithwood, K. (1994) *Defining Effective Leadership for Connecticut's Schools*, Monograph for the Connecticut Administrator Appraisal Project, Hartford, Connecticut: University of Connecticut.

Egan, G. (1993) *Adding Value*, San Francisco, CA: Jossey-Bass.

Eisenbach, R., Watson, K. and Pillai, R. (1999) 'Transformational leadership in the context of organizational change', *Journal of Organizational Change*, 12 (2), 80–8.

Eisner, E. (1985) *The Art of Educational Evaluation*, Lewes: Falmer.

EQ University (2000) *Emotional Intelligence*. http://www.equniversity.com/about.htm

Everard, B. and Morris, G. (1990) *Effective School Management* (second edition), London: Paul Chapman Publishing Ltd.

Fairholm, M.R. and Fairholm, G. (2000) 'Leadership amid the constraints of trust', *Leadership and Development Journal*, 21 (2), 102–9.

Finley, M. (1994) 'Meg Wheatley at the Masters Forum', *The Masters Forum*. http://www.mastersforum.com/archives/wheatley.wheatf.htm

Fisher, K. and Fisher, M.D. (1998) *The Distributed Mind: Achieving Higher Performance through the Collective Intelligence of Knowledge Work Teams*, New York: American Management Association.

Fitz-Gibbon, C. T. (1996) *Monitoring Education: Indicators, Quality and Effectiveness*, London: Cassell.

Flannery, T., Hofrichter, D. and Platten, P. (1996) *People, Performance and Pay*, New York: The Free Press.

Ford, J.D. and Ford, L.W. (1995) The role of conversations in producing intentional change in organisations, *Academy of Management Review*, 20 (3), 541–70.

Fukayama, F. (1999) *The Great Disruption: Human Nature and the Reconstitution of the Social Order*, New York: Free Press.

Fullan, M. (1991) *The New Meaning of Educational Change*, London: Cassell.

Fullan, M. (1993) *Change Forces*, London: Falmer.

Fullan, M. (1998) *Change Forces: The Sequel*, London: Paul Chapman Publishing Ltd.

Fullan, M. (2001) *Leading in a Culture of Change*, San Francisco: Jossey-Bass.

Gadamer, H.G. (1975) *Truth and Method*, New York: Polity Press.

Gaines, B.R. (1997) *Knowledge Level Modeling of Agents, Organizations and Teleologies*, http://spuds.cpsc.ucalgary.ca/AIKM97/gaines/KMKL.html

Garrahan, P. and Stewart, P. (1992) *The Nissan Enigma: Flexibility at Work in a Local Economy*, London: Mansell.

Garvin, D. A. (1993) 'Building a learning organization', *Harvard Business Review*, 71, July/August, 78–91.

Garvin, D.A. (2000) *Learning in Action*, Boston, Mass: Harvard University Business School Press.

Gell-Mann, M. (1994) *The Quark and the Jaguar*, New York: Freeman.

Gerard, G. and Teurfs, L (1997) 'Dialogue and transformation', *Executive Intelligence*, 14 (8), 16.

Gibb, C.A. (1954) 'Leadership', in G. Lindzey (ed.) *Handbook of Social Psychology*, 4 (second edition), Reading, Mass: Addison-Wesley, 205–83.

Gibbs, N. (1995) 'The EQ factor', *Time Magazine*, Oct (2), 146 (14). http://www.time.com/time/magazine/archive/1995/951002/951002.cover.html

Gilmer, B. (1966) *Industrial Psychology* (second edition), New York: McGraw-Hill.

Gilsdorf, J.W. (1998) 'Organizational rules on communicating: how employees are – and are not – learning the ropes', *The Journal of Business Communication*, April, 173–201.

Gleick, J. (1987) *Chaos*, London: Abacus.

Goh, S.C. (1998) 'Toward a learning organization: the strategic building blocks', *Advanced Management Journal*, 63 (2), 15–22.

Goldstein, J. (2000) 'Riding the waves of emergence: leadership innovations in complex systems'. http://www.vha.com/edgeplace/think/main_filing2.html

Goleman, D. (1995) *Emotional Intelligence*, New York: Bantam Books.

Goleman, D. (1998a) *Working with Emotional Intelligence*, New York: Bantam Books.

Goleman, D. (1998b) 'What makes a leader?' *Harvard Business Review*, November/December, 93–102.

Goleman, D. (2000) 'Leadership that gets results', *Harvard Business Review*, March/April, 78–90.

Goodwin, B. (2000) 'Out of control into participation', *Emergence*, 2 (4), 40–9.

Grace, G. (1995) *School Leadership: Beyond Educational Management*, London: Falmer.

Grant, R.M. (1996) 'Prospering in dynamically-competitive environments: organizational capability as knowledge integration', *Organization Science*, 7, 375–87.

Grant, R.M. (1999) *Toward a Knowledge-Based Theory of the Firm*, Berkeley, CA: Institute of Industrial Relations, University of California at Berkeley. http://socrates.berkeley.edu/~iir/cohre/grant.html

Greenberg, J. and Baron, R.A. (1997) *Behavior in Organization: Understanding and Managing the Human Side of Work* (sixth edition), Englewood Cliffs, NJ: Prentice-Hall.

Greengard, S. (1998) 'Will your culture support KM?', *Workforce*, October, 93–4.

Greenleaf, R.K. (1995) *Reflections on Leadership: How Robert K. Greenleaf's Theory of Servant Leadership Influenced Today's Top Management Thinkers*, New York: John Wiley and Sons.

Greenleaf, R.K. (1996) *On Becoming a Servant Leader*, San Francisco: Jossey-Bass.

Grieves, J. (2000) 'Navigating change into the new millennium', *The Learning Organization*, 7 (2), 54–74.

Griffiths, D. (1997) 'The case for theoretical pluralism', *Educational Management and Administration*, 25 (4), 371–80.

Gronn, P. (1999) 'Systems of distributed leadership in organizations', paper presented at the Organisation Theory Special Interest Group of the American Educational Research Association, Montreal.

Gronn, P. (2000) 'Distributed properties: a new architecture for leadership', *Educational Management and Administration*, 28 (3), 317–38.

Gross, B. (1998) 'The new math of ownership', *Harvard Business Review*, November/December, 68–74.

Gross, S. (1995) *Compensation for Teams: How to Design and Implement Team-based Reward Programs*, New York: American Management Association.

Guest, D., Peccei, R. and Thomas, A. (1993) 'The impact of employee involvement on organizational commitment and 'them and us' attitudes', *Industrial Relations Journal*, 24 (3), 191–201.

Gupta, N. and Shaw, J.S. (1998) 'Financial incentives *are* effective', *Compensation and Benefits Review*, March/April, 26–32.

Habermas, J. (1970a) 'On systematically distorted communication', *Inquiry*, 13, 205–13.

Habermas, J. (1970b) 'Towards a theory of communicative competence', *Inquiry*, 360–75.

Habermas, J. (1972) *Knowledge and Human Interests* (tr. J. Shapiro), London: Heinemann.

Habermas, J. (1974) *Theory and Practice* (tr. J. Viertel), London: Heinemann.

Habermas, J. (1979) *Communication and the Evolution of Society* (tr. T. McCarthy), London: Heinemann.

Habermas, J. (1982) 'A reply to my critics', in J. Thompson and D. Held (eds) *Habermas: Critical Debates*, London: Macmillan, 219–83.

Habermas, J. (1984) *The Theory of Communicative Action Volume One: Reason and the Rationalization of Society* (tr. T. McCarthy), Boston: Beacon Press.

Habermas, J. (1987) *The Theory of Communicative Action Volume Two: Lifeworld and System* (tr. T. McCarthy), Boston: Beacon Press.

Hall, G.E. and Hord, S.M. (1987) *Change in Schools*, New York: State University of New York Press.

Halpin, W. (1966) *Theory and Research in Administration*, New York: Macmillan.

Hamel, G. and Prahalad, C. (1994) *Competing for the Future*, Harvard: Harvard Business School Press.

Hannan, M.T. and Freeman, J.H. (1977) 'The population ecology of organizations', *American Journal of Sociology*, 82, 929–64.

Hanson, E.M. (1991) *Educational Administration and Organizational Behaviour* (third edition), Boston: Allyn and Bacon.

Hargreaves, A. (1992) 'Time and teachers' work: an analysis of the intensification thesis', *Teachers College Record* 94 (91), 87–108.

Hargreaves, A. (1994) *Changing Teachers, Changing Times*, London: Cassell.

Hargreaves, D. and Hopkins, D. (1991) *The Empowered School*, London: Cassell.

Harris, A. (1998) 'Improving the effective department: strategies for growth and development', *Educational Management and Administration*, 26 (3), 269–78.

Harris, A. (1999) *Effective Subject Leadership*, London: David Fulton.

Harris, A. (2000) 'Effective leadership and departmental improvement', *Westminster Studies in Education*, 23, 81–90.

Harris, T.A. (1973) *I'm OK – You're OK*, London: Pan.

Hartwell, A. (1995) *Scientific Ideas and Education in the 21st Century*, Institute for International Research. http://www.newhorizons.org/ofc_21cliash.html

Hatch, M.J. (1997) *Organization Theory: Modern, Symbolic and Postmodern Perspectives*, Oxford: Oxford University Press.

Hebb, D.O. (1949) *The Organization of Behaviour: A Neuropsychological Theory*, New York: John Wiley and Sons Inc.

Heifetz, R.A. and Lawrie, D.L. (1997) 'The work of leadership', *Harvard Business Review*, January/February, 53–62.

Hersey, P. and Blanchard, K.H. (1993) *Management of Organizational Behaviour: Utilizing Human Resources* (sixth edition), Englewood Cliffs, NJ: Prentice-Hall.

Hertzberg, F. (1987) 'Workers' needs: the same around the world', *Industry Week*, 21 September, 30.

Hickman, G.R. (2000) *Transforming Organizations to Transform Society*, Maryland: Academy of Leadership Press, The James MacGregor Burns Academy of Leadership, University of Maryland. http://www.academy.umd.edu/Scholarship/CASL/klspdocs/ghick_p1.htm

Hinkin, T.R. and Tracey, J.B. (1999) 'The relevance of charisma for transformational leadership in organizations', *Journal of Organizational Change*, 12 (2), 105–19.

Hodgson, G.M. (2000) 'The concept of emergence in social science: its history and importance', *Emergence*, 2 (4), 65–77.

Hohmann, M. and Weikart, D.P. (1983) *Young Children in Action*, Ypsilanti, Michigan: High Scope Press.

Homans, G.C. (1951) *The Human Group*, London: Routledge and Kegan Paul.

Homans, G.C. (1971) *Institutions and Social Exchange*, Indianapolis, Ind: Bobbs-Merrill.

Hong, J. (1999) 'Structuring for organizational learning', *The Learning Organization*, 6 (4), 173–85.

Hong, J.C. and Kuo C.L. (1999) 'Knowledge management in the learning organization', *Leadership and Organization Development Journal*, 20 (4), 207–15.

Hoy, W.K., Tarter, C.J. and Kottkamp, R.B. (1991) *Open Schools, Healthy Schools*, London: Sage Publications Inc.

Hoy, W.K., Tarter, C.J. and Witkoskie, L. (1992) 'Faculty trust in colleagues: linking the principal with school effectiveness', *Journal of Research and Development in Education*, 26 (1), 38–45.

Hoyle, E. (1975) 'The creativity of the school in Britain', in A. Harris, M. Lawn and W. Prescott (eds) *Curriculum Innovation*, London: Croom Helm and the Open University Press, 329–46.

Hoyle, E. (1986) *The Politics of School Management*, Sevenoaks: Hodder and Stoughton.

Huber, G.P. (1991) 'Organizational learning: the contributing process and the literature', *Organizational Science*, 2 (1), 88–155.

Hunt, G.T. (1980) *Communication Skills in the Organization* (first edition), Englewood Cliffs, NJ: Prentice-Hall.

Hunt, G.T. (1985) *Effective Communication*, Englewood Cliffs, NJ: Prentice-Hall.

Iannaccone, L. (1975) *Educational Policy Systems*, Fort Lauderdale, Fl: Nova University Press.

Ibarra, H. and Andrews, S.B. (1993) 'Power, social influence, and sense making: effects of network centrality and proximity on employee perceptions', *Administrative Science Quarterly*, 38, 277–303.

Isaacs, W.N. (1993) 'Taking flight: dialogue, collective thinking and organizational learning', *Organizational Dynamics*, 22 (2), 24–39.

Jacobson, M.J. (2000) *Complexity and Complex Systems: A Brief Overview*. http://emergentdesigns.com/mjjacobson/research/ctcs/Resources/complexity.html

Jackson, D.S. (2000) 'The school improvement journey: perspectives on leadership', *School Leadership and Management*, 20 (1), 61–78.

Jameson, F. (1991) *Postmodernism, or, the Cultural Logic of Late Capitalism*, London: Verso.

Janov, J. (1994) *The Inventive Organization: Hope and Daring at Work*, San Francisco: Jossey-Bass.

Jaques, E. (1990) 'In praise of hierarchy', *Harvard Business Review*, January/February, 127–33.

Johnson, K.B. (1999) *The Development of Progressive and Sustainable Human Complex Adaptive Systems: Institutions, Organizations and Communities.*
http://www.wam.umd.edu/~nafikiri/webcomplex.htm

Johnson, J.D., Donohue, W.A., Atkin, C.K. and Johnson, S. (1994) 'Differences between formal and informal communication channels', *The Journal of Business Communication*, 31 (2), 111–122.

Jones A. and Hendry, C. (1992) *The Learning Organization: A Review of the Literature and Practice*, London: Human Resource Development Partnership.

Kakabadse, A., Ludlow, R. and Vinnicombe, S. (1988) *Working in Organisations*, Harmondsworth: Penguin.

Kanter, R., Stein, B. and Jick, T. (1992) *The Challenge of Organizational Change*, New York: Free Press.

Karr, B. (1995) *Complexity Theory and Rhetorical Invention*. http://english.ttu.edu/courses/5361/papers/paper1_karr_420.html

Karsten, S., Voncken, E. and Voorthuis, M. (2000) 'Dutch primary schools and the concept of the learning organization', *The Learning Organization*, 7 (3), 145–55.

Katz, D. and Kahn, R.L. (1966) *The Social Psychology of Organizations*, New York: John Wiley and Sons.

Katz, D. and Kahn, R.L. (1978) *The Social Psychology of Organizations* (second edition), New York: John Wiley and Sons.

Katz, R. (1997) Higher education and the forces of self-organisation: an interview with Margaret Wheatley, *Cause/Effect*, 20 (1), 18–21.

Katzenbach, J.R. and Smith, D.K. (1993) *The Wisdom of Teams: Creating the High-Performance Organization*, Boston, Mass: Harvard Business School Press.

Kauffman, S.A. (1993) *The Origins of Order*, New York: Oxford University Press.

Kauffman, S.A. (1995) *At Home in the Universe: The Search for the Laws of Self-Organization and Complexity*, Harmondsworth: Penguin.

Kauffman, S.A. (1996) 'Investigations: the nature of autonomous agents and the worlds they mutually create', lecture 1 from the series *Search for a Possible 'Fourth Law' of Thermodynamics for Non-Equilibrium Systems*. http://www.santafe/sfi/People/kauffman/Lecture-1.html

Kelley, R. (1988) 'In Praise of Followers', *Harvard Business Review* 66 (6), 142–148.

Kelloway, E.K., Barling, J. and Helleur, J. (2000) Enhancing transformational leadership: the roles of training and feedback, *Leadership and Organization Development Journal*, 21 (3), 145–9.

Kelly, D. (2000) 'Using vision to improve organisational communication', *Leadership and Organization Development Journal*, 21 (2), 92–101.

Kelly, S. and Allison, M.A. (1999) *The Complexity Advantage: How the Science of Complexity Can Help Your Business Achieve Peak Performance*, New York: McGraw-Hill.

Kiel, L.D. (1994) *Managing Chaos and Complexity in Government*, San Francisco, CA: Jossey-Bass.

Kline, P. and Saunders, B. (1993) *Ten Steps to a Learning Organization*, Arlington, VA: Great Ocean Publishers.

Kohn, A. (1998) 'Challenging behaviourist dogma: myths about money and motivation', *Compensation and Benefits Review*, March/April, 27–37.

Kouzes, J.M. and Posner, B.Z. (1995) *The Leadership Challenge: How to Keep Getting Extraordinary Things Done in Organizations*, San Francisco: Jossey-Bass.

Kowalski, T.J. (1998) 'The role of communication in providing leadership for school restructuring', *Mid-Western Educational Researcher*, 11 (1), 32–40.

Kratina, S. (1990) 'Organizational culture and head nurse leadership: the relationship to nurses' job satisfaction and turnover in hospital settings', unpublished Ph. D. thesis, College of Education, George State University, cited in P. Lok and J. Crawford (1999).

Kvale, S. (1996) *Interviews*. London: Sage Publications Inc.

Lakomski, G. (2000) *Leadership: How To Manage Without It*, paper prepared for the Centre for Educational Leadership, University of Hong Kong, 27 September, http://www.hku.hk/educel/Handout-ProfLakomski.PDF

Larkin, T.J. and Larkin, S. (1994) *Communicating Change: Winning Employee Support for New Business Goals*, New York: McGraw-Hill.

Law, S. and Glover, D. (2000) *Educational Leadership and Learning*, Buckingham: Open University Press.

Lawler, E.E. (1991) *Pay and Organizational Development*, Reading, Mass: Addison-Wesley.

Lawler, E.E., Mohrman, S.A. and Ledford, Jr. G.E. (1995) *Creating High Performance Organisations: Practices and Results of Employee Involvement and Total Quality Management in Fortune 1000 Companies*, San Francisco, CA: Jossey-Bass.

Leavitt, H. J. (1964) *Managerial Psychology*. Chicago: University of Chicago Press.

Leithwood, K. (1994) 'Leadership for school restructuring', *Educational Administration Quarterly*, 20, 498–518.

Leithwood, K. and Steinbach, R. (1995) *Expert Problem Solving: Evidence from Schools and District Leaders*, Albany, New York: State University of New York Press.

Leithwood, K. and Jantzi, D. (2000) 'The effects of transformational leadership on organizational conditions and student engagement with school', *Journal of Educational Administration*, 38 (2), 112–129.

Leithwood, K., Tomlinson, D. and Genge, M. (1996) 'Transformational school leadership', in K. Leithwood, J. Chapman, D. Corson, P. Hallinger and A. Hart (eds) *International Handbook of Educational Leadership and Administration*, Dordrecht, Netherlands: Kluwer, 785–840.

Lengel, R.H. and Daft, R.L. (1988) 'The selection of communication media as an executive skill', *Academy of Management Executive*, 2, 225–32.

Leonard, D.A., Brands, P.A., Edmonson, A. and Fenwick, J. (1998) 'Virtual teams: using communications technology to manage geographically dispersed development groups', in S.P. Bradley and R.L. Nolan (eds) *Sense and Respond: Capturing Value in the Network Era*. Boston, Mass: Harvard University Business School Press, 285–98.

Levinthal, D. A. (1995) 'Organizational adaptation and environmental selection: interrelated processes of change', in M.D. Cohen and L.S. Sproull (eds) *Organizational Learning*, Thousand Oaks, CA: Sage Publications Inc, 195–220.

Levy, S. (1992) *Artificial Life: The Quest for New Creation*, New York: Random House.

Lewin, K. (1935) *A Dynamic Theory of Personality*, New York: McGraw-Hill.

Lewin, K. (1938) *The Conceptual Representation and Measurement of Psychological Forces*, Durham, DC: Duke University Press.

Lewin, K. (1951) *Field Theory and Social Science*, New York: Harper.

Lewin, R. (1993) *Complexity: Life on the Edge*, London: Phoenix.

Lewin, R. and Regine, B. (2000) *The Soul at Work: Listen, Respond, Let Go: Embracing Complexity Science for Business Success*, New York: Simon and Shuster.

Lieberman, A. (ed.) (1990) *Schools as Collaborative Cultures*, London: Falmer.

Lindle, J.C. (1999) 'What can the study of micropolitics contribute to the practice of leadership in reforming schools?', *School Leadership and Management*, 19 (2), 171–8.

Lissack, M.R. (1996) *Chaos and Complexity – What Does That Have to Do with Knowledge Management?* http://www.lissack.com/writings/knowledge.htm

Lissack, M.R. (1999) 'Complexity – the science, its vocabulary, and its relation to organizations', *Emergence: a Journal of Complexity Issues in Organizations and Management* 1 (1) 110–27. http://www.emergence.org/Complexity1.htm

Lissack, M.R. (2000) *Complexity Metaphors and the Management of a Knowledge Based Enterprise: An Exploration of Discovery*. http://lissack.com/writings/proposal.htm

Litwin, G.H. and Stringer, R.A. (1968) *Motivational and Organizational Climate*, Boston, Mass: Harvard University Graduate School of Business Administration.

Lloyd, B. and Trapp, R. (1999) 'Bosses or leaders?', *Leadership and Organization Development Journal*, 20 (6), 332–6.

Loader, D. (1997) *The Inner Principal*. London: Falmer.

Lok, P. and Crawford, J. (1999) 'The relationship between commitment and organizational culture, subculture, leadership style and job satisfaction in organizational change and development', *Leadership and Organization Development Journal*, 20 (7), 365–73.

Lucas, C. (2000) *Self-Organising Systems FAQ*. http://www.magna.com.au/~prfbrown/news97_h.html

Ludlow, R. and Panton, F. (1992) *The Essence of Effective Communication*, Harlow: Prentice-Hall.

Luke, J.S. (1998) *Catalytic Leadership: Strategies for an Interconnected World*, San Francisco, CA: Jossey-Bass.

Lund, B. and McGechan, S. (1981) *CE Programmer's Manual*. Victoria, Aus: Ministry of Education, Continuing Education Division.

Major, D. A. (2000) 'Effective newcomer socialization into high-performance organizational cultures', in N.M. Ashkanasy, C.P.M. Wilderom and M.F. Peterson (eds) *Handbook of Organizational Culture and Climate*, Thousand Oaks, CA: Sage Publications Inc. 355–68.

Malhotra, Y. (1999) *The Role of Information Technology in Managing Organizational Change and Organizational Interdependence*. http://www.it-consultancy.com/background/manorgchange.html

Malone, T.W. (1998) 'Inventing the organizations of the twenty-first century: control, empowerment, and information technology', in S.P. Bradley and R.L.Nolan (eds) *Sense and Respond: Capturing Value in the Network Era*, Boston, Mass: Harvard University Business School Press, 263–83.

Marion, R. (1999) *The Edge of Organization: Chaos and Complexity Theories of Formal Social Systems*, London: Sage Publications Inc.

Marks, H.M., Louis, K.S. and Printy, S.M. (1999) 'The capacity for organizational learning: implications for pedagogical quality and student achievement', cited in H. Silins, S. Zarins and B. Mulford, *Organizational Learning in Australian High Schools: Nature and Practices*, paper presented at the annual AARE-NZARE Conference, Melbourne, November. http://www.aare.edu.au/99pap/sil99461.htm

Marquardt, M.J. (1996) *Building the Learning Organization*, New York: McGraw-Hill.

Marsick, V. (2000) 'Learning Organizations', cited in V. Marsick, J. Bitterman and R. Van Der Veen, *From the Learning Organization to Learning Communities toward a Learning Society*, Information series 382, ERIC Clearinghouse on Adult, Career and Vocational Education, ED-99-CO-0013, Ohio State University, Columbus: Ohio. http://ericacve.org/docs/marsick/marsick3.pdf

Mawhinney, H. B. (1999) 'Reappraisal: the problems and prospects of studying the micropolitics of leadership in reforming schools', *School Leadership and Management*, 19 (2), 159–70.

Mayer, J.D. and Salovey, P. (1993) 'The intelligence of emotional intelligence', *Intelligence*, 17 (4), 433–42.

McCarthy, I.P. and Tan, Y.K. (2000) 'Manufacturing competitiveness and fitness landscape theory', *Journal of Materials Processing Technology*, 107, 1–3, 347–352. http://www.wmg.org.uk/ossu/fitness.html

McDaniel, R.R. (1997) 'Strategic leadership: a view from quantum and chaos theories', *Health Care Management Review*, 22 (1), 321–7.

McLuskey, A. (1997) *Emotional Intelligence in Schools*. http://www.connected.org/learn/school.html

McMaster, M.D. (1996) *The Intelligence Advantage: Organizing for Complexity*, Newton, Massachusetts: Butterworth-Heinemann.

McNamara, J. (2001) *Integral Culture at Work*. http://www.hepmethod.com/INTE-GRAL%20CULTURE%20AT%WORK.html

McPherson, E.D. (1995) 'Chaos in the curriculum', *Journal of Curriculum Studies*, 27 (3), 263–79.

Mendéz-Morse, S. (1999) *Leadership Characteristics that Facilitate Change*, Southwest Educational Development Laboratory. http://ww.sedl.org/change/leadership/history.html

Merry, U. (1995) *Coping with Uncertainty: Insights from the New Sciences of Chaos, Self-Organization, and Complexity*, Westport, Ct: Praeger.

Merry, U. (1998) *Organizational Lifespan LO17822*. http://www.learning-org.com/98.04/0206.html

Michaels, M. (1995) 'The chaos network on-line', *The Chaos Network*, http://www.prairienet.org/business.ptech

Micklethwait, J. and Wooldridge, A. (1997) *The Witch Doctors*, London: Mandarin paperbacks.

Miles, M. (1975) 'Planned change and organizational health', in A. Harris, M. Lawn and W. Prescott (eds) *Curriculum Innovation*, London: Croom Helm and the Open University Press, 192–203.

Miller, D. (1996) 'A preliminary typology of organizational learning: synthesizing the literature', *Journal of Management*, 22 (3), 385–505.

Miller, D. (1997) 'The future organization: a chameleon in all its glory', in F. Hesselbeing, M. Goldsmith and R. Beckhard (eds) *The Organization of the Future*, San Francisco: Jossey-Bass, 119–25.

Millward, A. and Skidmore, D. (1998) 'LEA responses to the management of special education in the light of the code of practice', *Educational Management and Administration*, 26 (1), 57–66.

Mohrman, S. and Mohrman, Jr. A. (1995) 'Organizational change and learning, in. I. Galbraith and E. Lawler (eds) *Organizing for the Future: the New Logic for Managing Complex Organizations*, New York: Jossey-Bass, 87–109.

Morgan, C.L. (1927) *Emergent Evolution* (second edition), London: Williams and Norgate.

Morrison, K.R.B. (1989) 'Curriculum metaphors and control: the old and the new', *Curriculum*, 10 (2), 777–86.

Morrison, K.R.B. (1993) *Planning and Accomplishing School-Centred Evaluation*, Norfolk: Peter Francis Publications.

Morrison, K.R.B. (1994) 'Centralism and the education market: why emulate the United Kingdom?', *European Journal of Education*, 29 (4), 415–424.

Morrison, K.R.B. (1995) 'Habermas and the School Curriculum', unpublished Ph.D thesis, University of Durham.

Morrison, K.R.B. (1996) 'Habermas and critical pedagogy', *Critical Pedagogy Networker*, 9 (2), 1–7.

Morrison, K.R.B. (1997) *Establishing School-Industry Links for Low Achieving Form 4 Students*, Consultation report for the Ministry of Education, Malaysia, School of Education: University of Durham.

Morrison, K.R.B. (1998) *Management Theories for Educational Change*, London: Paul Chapman Publishing.

Morrison, K.R.B. (2001a) 'Simplicity and complexity in contemporary school leadership: a response to Grace', *British Journal of Educational Studies*, 49 (4), 379–85.

Morrison, K.R.B. (2001b) 'Randomised controlled trials for evidence-based education: some problems in judging 'what works', *Evaluation and Research in Education*, 15 (2), 1–15.

Morrison, K.R.B., Gott, R. and Ashman, T. (1989) 'A cascade model of curriculum innovation', *British Journal of In-Service Education*, 15 (3) 159–169.

Morrison, K.R.B. and Ridley, K. (1988) *Curriculum Planning and the Primary Schools*, London: Paul Chapman Publishing.

Neil, J. (1995) 'On schools as learning organizations: a conversation with Peter Senge', *Educational Leadership*, April: 20–3.

Nickse, R.S. (1977) *Teachers as Change Agents*, Washington, DC: National Educational Association.

Nolan, R.L. and Galal, H. (1998) 'Virtual offices: redefining organizational boundaries', In. S.P. Bradley and R.L. Nolan (eds) *Sense and Respond: Capturing Value in the Network Era*, Boston, Mass: Harvard University Business School Press, 299–320.

Nonaka, I. and Takeuchi, K. (1995) *The Knowledge-Creating Company*, New York: Oxford University Press.

O'Brien, M. (1993) *The Learning Organization Profile*, Milford, Ohio: O'Brien Learning Systems.

Palmer, B., Walls, M., Burgess, Z. and Stough, C. (2000) 'Emotional intelligence and effective leadership', *Leadership and Organizational Development Journal*, 22 (1), 5–10.

Peak, D. and Frame, M. (1994) *Chaos Under Control: the Art and Science of Complexity*, New York: W. H. Freeman.

Pedler, M., Burgoyne, J. and Boydell, T. (1997) *The Learning Company: A Strategy for Sustainable Development* (second edition), Maidenhead: McGraw-Hill.

Peters, T. (1989) *Thriving on Chaos*, London: Pan.

Peters, T. and Waterman, R.H. (1982) *In Search of Excellence*, London: Harper and Row.

Peterson, B. (1995) 'La Escuela Fratney: a journey toward democracy', in M. Apple and J. Beane (eds) *Democratic Schools*, Alexandria, VA: Association for Supervision and Curriculum Development, 58–82.

Pettigrew, A. and Whipp, R. (1993) 'Understanding the environment', in. C. Mabey and B. Mayon-White (eds) *Managing Change* (second edition), London: Paul Chapman Publishing Ltd. in association with the Open University Press, 5–19.

Pfeffer, J. (1998) 'Six dangerous myths about pay', *Harvard Business Review*, May/June, 109–19.

Pfeffer, J. and Salancik, G. R. (1978) *The External Control of Organizations: A Resource Dependence Perspective*, New York: Harper and Row.

Pheysey, D.C. (1993) *Organizational Cultures*, London: Routledge.

Piccardo, C. (1990) 'Car makers and marathon runners: in pursuit of culture through the language of leadership', in. P. Gagliardi (ed.) *Symbols and Artifacts*, Berlin: Walter de Gruyter, cited in M.R. Lissack (1999), *op. cit.*

Pondy, L. (1976) 'Leadership is a language game', in M. McCall and M. Lombardo (eds) *Leadership: Where Else Can We Go?* Greensboro, NC: Center for Creative Leadership, 87–99.

Popper, M. and Lipshitz, R. (2000) 'Installing mechanisms and instilling values: the role of leaders of organizational learning', *The Learning Organization*, 7 (93), 135–44.

Porpiglia, T. (1997) 'What is transactional analysis?', *Life Script Counseling Services*. http://www.frontiernet.net/~lscriptc/tal.htm

Prigogine, L. and Stengers, I. (1985) *Order Out of Chaos*, London: Flamingo.

Probst, G. and Büchel, B. (1997) *Organizational Learning: the Competitive Advantage of the Future*, Englewood Cliffs: NJ: Prentice-Hall.

Putnam, L. and Pacanowsky, M.E. (eds) *Communication and Organizations*, Beverly Hills: Sage Publications.

Putnam, R.T. and Borko, H. (2000) 'What do views of knowledge and thinking have to say about research on teacher learning?', *Educational Researcher*, January/February, 29 (1), 4–15.

Quigley, M.E. (1997) 'Quantum organizations', *Executive Intelligence*, 14 (5), 14–15.

Quirke, B. (1995) *Communicating Change*, Maidenhead: McGraw-Hill.

Reynolds, D. (1995) 'The effective school: an inaugural lecture', *Evaluation and Research in Education*, 9 (2), 57–73.

Riches, C. (1993) 'Building teams for change and stability', Unit 4 of E326, Module 1: *Managing Educational Change*, Milton Keynes: Open University Press.

Richmond, V.P. and McCroskey, J.C. (1992) *Organizational Communication for Survival*, Englewood Cliffs, NJ: Prentice-Hall.

Ridgway, J. (1998) *The Modeling of Systems and Macro-Systemic Change: Lessons for Evaluation from Epidemiology and Ecology*, Research Monographs, 8. University of Wisconsin-Madison: National Institute for Science Education.

Riley, K. (2000) 'Leadership, learning and systemic reform', *Journal of Educational Change*, 1 (1), 29–55.

Robbins, H. and Finley, M. (1998a) *Why Change Doesn't Work*, London: Orion Business.

Robbins, H. and Finley, M. (1998b) *Why Teams Don't Work*, London: Orion Business.

Rodger, I. And Richardson, J.A.S. (1985) *Self-Evaluation for Primary Schools*, Sevenoaks: Hodder and Stoughton.

Rolls, J. (1995) 'The transformational leader: the wellspring of the learning organization', in S. Chawla and J. Renesh (eds) *Learning Organizations: Developing Culture for Tomorrow's Workplace*, New York: Productivity Press, 101–8.

Rosenberg, D. (2000) 'Complex information environments: issues in knowledge management and organizational learning', *Emergence*, 2 (4), 136–50.

Rossi, P.H. and Freeman, H.E. (1993) *Evaluation: a Systematic Approach*, London: Sage Publications Inc.

Rost, J.C. (1991) *Leadership for the Twenty-first Century*, New York: Praeger.

Rowden, R.W. (2000) 'The relationship between charismatic leadership behaviors and organizational commitment', *Leadership and Organization Development*, 21 (1), 30–5.

Russell, S. (1996) *Collaborative School Self-Review*, London: Lemos and Crane.

Salovey, P. and Mayer, J.D. (1990) 'Emotional Intelligence', *Imagination, Cognition and Personality*, 9, 195–211.

Santa Fe Center for Emergent Strategies (1999) *Complexity and Business*. http://www.santafe-strategy.com/Emergent_Strategies/complexity_and_business.htm

Santonus, M. (1998) *Simple, Yet Complex*. http://www.cio.com/archive/enterprise/041598_qanda_content.html

Schaffer, R.H. and Thompson, H.A. (1996) 'Successful change programs begin with results', in J. Champy and N. Nohria (eds), *Fast Forward: the Best Ideas on Managing Business Change*, Boston, Mass: Harvard University Business School Publications, 141–56.

Schein, E.H. (1992) *Organizational Culture and Leadership* (second edition), San Francisco: Jossey-Bass.

Schein, E.H. (1993) 'On dialogue, culture and organizational learning', *Organizational Dynamics*, 22 (2), 40–51.

Schein, E.H. (1994) *Organizational and Managerial Culture as a Facilitator or Inhibitor of Organizational Learning*, Massachusetts: MIT Organizational Learning Network Working Paper, 10.004, May 19.

Schein, E.H. (1999) *Organizational Learning: What Is New?* MIT: Society for Organizational Learning. http://learning.mit.edu/res/wp/10012.html

Schön, D. (1983) *The Reflective Practitioner*, San Francisco: Jossey Bass.

Schultz, M. (1994) *On Studying Organizational Cultures*, Berlin: Walter de Gruyter.

Scott, W.R. (1992) *Organizations: Rational, Natural and Open Systems* (third edition), Englewood-Cliffs, NJ: Prentice-Hall.

Scriven, M. and Roth, J. (1978) 'Needs assessment: concept and practice', *New Directs for Program Evaluation*, 1 (1), 1–11.

Searle, J. (1969) *Speech Acts*, London: Cambridge University Press.

Senge, P.M. (1990) *The Fifth Discipline: The Art and Practice of the Learning Organization*, New York: Doubleday.

Senge, P.M. (1995) 'Making a better world', *Executive Intelligence*, 18–19.

Senge, P.M. (1997) 'Communities of leaders and learners', *Harvard Business Review*, 75 (5), 30–2.

Senge, P.M., Kleiner, A., Roberts, C., Ross, R. and Smith, B. (eds) (1994) *The Fifth Discipline Fieldbook: Strategies for Building a Learning Organization*, New York: Doubleday.

Senge, P., Cambron-McCabe, N., Lucas, T., Smith, B., Dutton, J. and Kleiner, A. (2000) *Schools that Learn*, London: Nicholas Brealey Publishing.

Sergiovanni, T.J. (1998) 'Leadership as pedagogy, capital development and school effectiveness', *International Journal of Leadership in Education*, 1 (1), 37–46.

Sherman, H. and Schultz, R. (1998) *Open Boundaries: Creating Business Innovation through Complexity*, New York: Perseus Books.

Silins, H., Zarins, S. and Mulford, B. (1999) *Organizational Learning in Australian High Schools: Nature and Practices*, paper presented at the annual AARE-NZARE Conference, Melbourne, November. http://www.aare.edu.au/99pap/sil99461.htm

Sivanandan, A. (1979) 'Imperialism and disorganic development in the silicon age', *Race and Class*, 21 (2), 111–26.

Slater, R.O. and Doig, J.W. (1988) 'Leadership in education: issues of entrepreneurship', *Education and Urban Society*, 20 (3), 294–301.

Southwest Educational Development Laboratory (1999) *Leadership and Context*. http://www.sedl.org/change/school/leadership.html

Southworth, G. (2000) 'How primary schools learn', *Research Papers in Education*, 15 (3), 275–91.

Spears, L.C. (2001) *Recent Commentary by Larry C. Spears*, Indianapolis: The Greenleaf Center for Servant Leadership. http://www.greenleaf.org/leadership/read-about-it/articles/Recent-Commentary-by-Larry-C-Spears.htm

Spillane, J.P., Halverson, R. and Diamond, J.B. (2000) *Distributed Leadership: Toward a Theory of School Leadership Practice*, Evanston, Ill: School of Education and Social Policy, Northwestern University.

Stacey, R.D. (1992) *Managing the Unknowable*. San Francisco: Jossey-Bass.

Stacey, R.D. (2000) *Strategic Management and Organisational Dynamics* (third edition), Harlow, England: Pearson Education Limited.

Stacey, R.D. (2001) *Complex Responsive Processes in Organizations: Learning and Knowledge Creation*, London: Routledge.

Stacey, R.D., Griffin, D. and Shaw, P. (2000) *Complexity and Management: Fad or Radical Challenge to Systems Thinking?* London: Routledge.

Stein, S. and Book, H. (2000) *The EQ Edge*, Toronto: Stoddart.

Steingard, D.S. and Fitzgibbons, D.E. (1993) 'A postmodern deconstruction of total quality management', *Journal of Organizational Change Management*, 6 (5) 27–37.

Stewart, I. (1990) *Does God Play Dice?* Harmondsworth: Penguin.

Stewart, I. (1995) *Nature's Numbers*, London: Phoenix.

Stewart, M. (2001) *The Co-Evolving Organization*, Rutland, UK: Decomplexity Associates Ltd. http://www.decomplexity.com/Coevolving%20Organization%20VU.pdf

Stewart, V. (1990) *The David Solution: How to Reclaim Power and Liberate Your Organization*, London: Gower.

Stringfield, S. (1997) 'Underlying the chaos: factors explaining elementary schools and their case for high-reliability organizations', in T. Townsend (ed.) *Restructuring and Quality: Issues for Tomorrow's Schools*, London: Routledge, 151–8.

Stufflebeam, D.L., McCormick, C.H., Brinkerhoff, R.O. and Nelson, C.O. (1985) *Conducting Educational Needs Assessment*, Boston, Mass: Kluwer Nijhoff.

Suarez, T.M. (1994) 'Needs assessment', in T. Husen and T.N. Postlethwaite (eds) *The International Encyclopedia of Education*, 7 (second edition), Oxford: Pergamon, 4, 56–60.

Swieringa, J. and Wierdsma, A.F.M. (1992) *Becoming a Learning Organization: Beyond the Learning Curve*, Wokingham: Addison-Wesley.

Tagiuri, R. (1968) 'The concept of organizational climate, in R. Tagiuri and G.W. Litwin (eds) *Organizational Climate: Exploration of a Concept*, Boston: Mass: Harvard University Graduate School of Business Administration, 11–32.

Tam, W.M. and Cheng, Y.C. (1996) 'A typology of primary school environments', *Educational Management and Administration*, 24 (3), 237–52.

Tan, C.H. (2000) 'High-performance human resource strategies in learning schools', *The Learning Organization*, 7 (1), 32–9.

Tang, F.H. and Morrison, K.R.B. (1998) 'When marketisation does not improve schooling: the case of Macau', *Compare*, 28 (3), 245–62.

Teacher Training Agency (1998) *National Standards for Subject Leaders*, London: Teacher Training Agency.

Teacher Training Agency (2000) *National Standards for Headteachers*, London: Teacher Training Agency.

Tetenbaum, T.J. (1998) Shifting paradigms: from Newton to Chaos. *Organizational Dynamics*, Spring, 21–32.

Tichy, N.M. and Devanna, M.A. (1986) 'The transformational leader', New York: Wiley. Quoted in K.A. April, R. Macdonald and S. Vriesendorp (2000) *Rethinking Leadership*, Cape Town: University of Cape Town Press.

Tierney, P. (1999) 'Work relations as a precursor to a psychological climate for change', *Journal of Organizational Change Management*, 12 (2), 120–33.

Tjosvold, D. and Wong, A.S.H. (2000) 'The leader relationship: building teamwork with and among employees', *Leadership and Organization Development Journal*, 21 (7), 350–4.

Tolle, E. (1999) *The Power of Now*, Novato, CA: New World Library.

Tran, V. (1998) 'The role of emotional climate in learning organisations', *The Learning Organization*, 5 (2), 99–103.

Tschannen-Moran, M. (2000) 'Collaboration and the need for trust', *Journal of Educational Administration*, 39 (4), 308–31.

Tuckman, B.W. (1965) 'Development sequence in small groups', *Psychological Bulletin*, 63, 384–99.

Tuckman, B.W. and Jensen, M.A.C. (1977) 'Stages of small-group development revisited', *Group and Organization Studies*, 2, 419–42.

University of Miami Department of Educational Leadership (2001) *EDL Principles*. http://www.muohio.edu/edl/general/principles.html

Van de Ven, A. (1992) 'Suggestions for studying the strategy process: a research note', *Strategic Management Journal*, 13, 169–88.

Von Bertalanffy, L. (1968) *General Systems Theory*, New York: George Braziller.

Vygotsky, L. (1978) *Mind in Society: the Development of Higher Psychological Processes* (ed. M. Cole), Cambridge, Mass: Harvard University Press.

Waldrop, M.M. (1992) *Complexity: the Emerging Science at the Edge of Order and Chaos*, Harmondsworth: Penguin.

Wallace, M. (1996) 'Policy interaction and policy administration', *Educational Management and Administration*, 24 (3), 263–75.

Wallace, M. and Pocklington, F. (1998) *Managing Complex Change: Large Scale Reorganisation of Schools*, paper presented at the annual meeting of the American Educational Research Association, San Diego. April 13–17, ERIC no: ED423607.

Watkin, C. (2000) 'The leadership program for serving headteachers: probably the world's largest leadership development initiative', *Leadership and Organization Development Journal*, 21 (1), 13–19.

Watkins, K.E. and Marsick, V.J. (1993) *Sculpting the Learning Organization: Lessons in the Art and Science of Systemic Change*. San Francisco: Jossey-Bass.

Weick, K.E. (1976) 'Educational organizations as loosely coupled systems', *Administrative Science Quarterly*, 21, 1–19.

Weick, K.E. (1992) 'Agenda setting in organizational behavior: an allegory of organizational studies', *Administrative Science Quarterly*. 41 (2), 310–13.

Weick, K.E. and Daft, R. (1984) 'The effectiveness of interpretation systems', in K.S. Cameron and D.A. Whetten (eds) *Organizational Effectiveness: a Comparison of Multiple Models*. Orlando, Fl: Academic Press, 70–93.

West, M. (1999) 'Micropolitics, leadership and all that … The need to increase the micropolitical awareness and skills of school leaders', *School Leadership and Management*, 19 (2) 189–95.

West-Burnham, J. and Davies, B. (eds) (1996) *Reengineering and Total Quality in Schools: How to Reform and Restructure Your School to Meet the Challenge of the Future*, London: Pearson Education.

West-Burnham, J. and O'Sullivan, F. (1998) *Leadership and Professional Development in Schools*, London: Pitman.

Wheatley, M. (1996) 'The new science of leadership: an interview with Meg Wheatley', *Insight and Outlook: an Interview with Meg Wheatley*. http://www.scottlondon. com/insights.scripts/wheatley.html

Wheatley, M. (1999) *Leadership and the New Science: Discovering Order in a Chaotic World* (second edition), San Francisco: Berrett-Koehler Publishers.

Wickens, P. (1987) *The Road to Nissan: Flexibility, Quality, Teamwork*, Houndmills: Macmillan.

Wickens, P. (1995) *The Ascendant Organization*, Basingstoke: Macmillan.

Witkin, B.R. (1984) *Assessing Needs in Educational and Social Programs*, San Francisco: Jossey-Bass.

Wong, K.P., Edwin, Sharpe, F.G. and McCormick, J. (1998) 'Factors affecting the perceived effectiveness of planning in Hong Kong self-managing schools', *Educational Management and Administration*, 26 (1), 67–81.

Yeats, W.B. (1962) 'The second coming', in A.N. Jeffares (ed.) *Yeats: Selected Poetry*, London: Macmillan.

Young, C.A. (1996) *Validity Issues in Measuring Psychological Constructs: The Case of Emotional Intelligence*. http://tropchim.human.cornell.edu/tutorial/young/eiweb2.htm

Youngblood, M. (1997) *Life at the Edge of Chaos*, Dallas, Texas: Perceval Publishing.

Youngblood, M (1998) 'Leadership at the edge of chaos', *Paradigm Shift International*. http://www.parshift.com/Speakers/Speak006.htm

Zohar, D. (1990) *The Quantum Self: Human Nature and Consciousness Defined by the New Physics*, New York: William Morrow.

Index

action research 91, 97, 101, 104, 178, 186
adaptation 6, 167–9, 192
'adaptive walk' 187
autocatalysis 15
autopoiesis 15, 102, 109

bifurcation 6, 14, 24, 188
boids 10, 40, 58, 192
bounded instability 119, 131
bureaucracy 18, 20, 37, 83–4, 87, 89, 135
'buttercup effect' 38
'butterfly effect' 26

cause and effect 8, 61, 98, 189
cell assembly 73
change 75–6, 80–1
chaordic systems 23
chaos theory 7, 14, 23, 26, 38, 72, 119, 192
City Technology Colleges 12, 116–17, 134, 138, 142
closed systems 15
coercion 57, 90
co-evolution 26, 91, 130–1, 133–4, 138, 173, 186–7
collaboration, *see* cooperation
command and control 11, 16, 19, 23–4, 32, 37–8, 47, 56–63, 69, 85, 89, 109, 143, 188, 190
communication 20, 30, 67, 80, 95, 111, 117, 121, 126, 131, 133, 137, 138–63, 184–5, 194; barriers to 153–5; direction of 143–9, 160–2; elements of 158, 160–1; informal 148; medium of 147–9, 151–2; model of 146–61; nature of 138–43; noise in 153–5, 161–2; timing of 151–2; *see also* feedback
community 66, 69, 70, 72–4, 76–7, 96, 115, 119, 122–4, 130, 140, 153, 168, 174
competition 11, 12, 21, 25, 28, 37, 43, 134, 167, 173
complex adaptive systems 8, 9, 11–12, 14, 18, 23, 26–8, 192, 193
complexity theory
    defined 5–26, 117; elements of 8; macro-level 10, 129–36; nature of 6–26, 133–4
'complex responsive processes' 12, 27
compliance 24, 50–1, 57, 60, 69, 73, 78, 92; *see also* command and control
connectedness 6, 8, 17–19, 20–1, 24, 28, 30–1, 35, 77, 93, 95, 99, 117, 121, 131–2, 136–7, 152, 167–70, 182, 193; *see also* fitness landscapes
control 8, 10, 14, 19, 20, 38, 48, 58, 60, 69, 83, 87, 89, 130, 131, 133, 189; *see also* command and control
cooperation 25, 41, 47, 60, 87, 90, 95, 107–9, 123, 140; *see also* teams
cultural capital thesis 26, 135, 164

democracy 6, 19, 60, 69–70, 80, 102, 139–42, 145, 159, 161, 190
dialogue 46, 80, 97–8, 100, 111, 133, 138–42, 148
differentiation 37–8, 89
dissipative structures 14
distributed knowledge 19, 102, 117, 144
distributed leadership, *see* leadership
distributed systems 10, 23, 108
double loop learning 98, 101, 143

edge of chaos 7, 23–4, 38, 62, 165, 185
emergence 7–9, 21–6, 29, 61, 67, 71, 81–8, 94, 133, 148, 170, 188
emotional intelligence 57, 77–82, 87–8, 90, 141, 193

empowerment 11, 21, 47, 59, 60, 67, 97, 139, 140, 184
entropy 13, 18
environment 14–15, 28–9, 114–37
evidence-based education 103–4
exchange theory 64–5
expectancy theory 64–5

feedback 17–19, 25, 30, 63, 102–4, 112, 118, 120–1, 124–5, 138, 148, 150
fitness landscapes 20–5, 30, 123, 131, 133–4, 136, 164–91, 193–4; components of 165–6, 185; construction of 177–8; developing 184–6; interpretation of 171–6; portrayal of 166–83; *see also* connectedness
flexibility 18, 20, 29, 38, 64, 71, 79–80, 87, 89, 91, 93–4, 113, 146, 176
fractals 38
'fusion of horizons' 142, 155

generalists 53–4

Habermas 140–2
hierarchy 37–8, 57–63, 71, 72, 89, 110
high reliability schools 39, 62
holarchies 57

'ideal speech situation' 140–1
identity 15, 28, 43–4, 47, 64, 102
illocutions 138, 141–3, 145, 149, 161
incentives 21, 35, 47–50, 52, 55, 65, 104, 107, 184, 188; *see also* motivation
increasing returns 17, 25–6, 67, 95, 115–7, 134, 135, 174, 176
information, 30, 118, 124–5, 138, 199; *see also* feedback, knowledge
intensification thesis 24, 30

knowledge 19, 74–5, 102, 107–9, 117, 139

'law of requisite variety' 122, 124, 136, 169, 170
leadership
    and emotional intelligence, *see* emotional intelligence; and motivation, *see* motivation; command and control, *see* command and control; development 74–7, 122; distributed 23, 59, 71–7, 88–9, 117; of learning organizations 92–3, 98–101, 113; of teams 45–55, *see also* teams; role 59, 61–2, 71, 126,

136–7, 181, 185; servant 23, 69–70, 117; style 79–82, 88, 161; systemic 73; transactional 57, 64–9, 81, 89–90, 143; transcendental 69–70; transformational 57, 64–9, 81, 89–90, 143; quantum 30–1
learning 104–5
learning organization 27, 74, 91–113, 140, 193; *see also* organizational learning
'loosely coupled organizations' 19, 20–1, 54, 60, 172, 173

marketization 12, 119, 120, 134–5, 168–9, 192
Maslow 50, 89
memory 18, 19, 30, 102, 112, 139
micropolitics 35–7, 44, 54–5, 83, 98–9, 188
mission statements 58–9, 94–5, 151
modernism 16, 27, 189
motivation 35, 47–50, 52, 55, 65, 71, 74, 76–8, 81, 88, 92, 102, 159, 188

needs analysis 127–9
negentropy 13
networks 14, 19, 20, 30–1, 41–7, 72, 89, 123, 131, 138, 140, 143; *see also* environment, connectedness
nonlinear systems 7, 8, 9, 13, 16, 24, 26, 46, 54, 57, 69

open systems, 7, 8, 15, 82, 134, 188
Open Systems Theory 6–7
order 8, 9, 14, 57, 58, 71, 83, 131
organizational climate 79, 81–9, 95, 188
organizational health 61, 81–9, 179, 180
organizational intelligence 93, 112
organizational learning, 21, 65, 68, 74, 91–113, 121, 150, 188, 193; components of 17, 95–105; kinds of 104–5, 193; platforms for 95–105; stages of 109–11; *see also* learning organization

perlocutions 138, 141–4, 149
postmodernism 5, 16
predictability 7, 23–5
punctuated equilibrium 46–7

quantum leadership, *see* leadership

Red Queen effect 24–5, 167
re-engineering 27

relationships 19, 30–1, 67, 70–1, 76, 107–9, 117–8, 126–7, 132–3
relative autonomy 27

Santa Fe Institute 7, 31
self-organization 10, 13–21, 22, 25, 28, 35–55, 57, 61, 94, 98, 117, 139, 148, 170
self-organized criticality 23–4, 30, 62–3, 150, 167, 170
sensing 117, 121–2, 187
servant leadership, *see* leadership
specialists 53–4, 74–7
speech acts 141–4
synergy 23, 60, 85, 130

teams 23, 38, 41–53, 94, 98, 112, 116–7, 140
'tightly coupled organizations' 19, 20, 54
Transactional Analysis 155–8, 163
transactional leadership, *see* leadership
transcendental leadership, *see* leadership
transformational leadership, *see* leadership
trust 19, 40, 44–5, 51, 52, 57, 61, 65, 68, 80, 85–7, 90, 95, 100, 102, 111, 133, 150, 188, 193

vision statements 58–9, 94–5, 151